Coaching Volleyball

Building a Winning Team

Carl McGown
Brigham Young University

Hilda Fronske
Utah State University

Launa Moser
Preston High School

Allyn and Bacon

Boston ▪ London ▪ Toronto ▪ Sydney ▪ Tokyo ▪ Singapore

Publisher: Joseph E. Burns
Vice President and Editor-in-Chief: Paul A. Smith
Series Editorial Assistant: Annemarie Kennedy
Executive Marketing Manager: Rick Muhr
Production Administrator: Deborah Brown
Editorial-Production Service: Omegatype Typography, Inc.
Composition and Prepress Buyer: Linda Cox
Manufacturing Buyer: Julie McNeill
Cover Administrator: Brian Gogolin
Electronic Composition: Omegatype Typography, Inc.

Between the time Website information is gathered and published, some sites may have closed. Also, the transcription of URLs can result in typographical errors. The publishers would appreciate notification where these occur so that they may be corrected in subsequent editions.

Many of the designations used by manufacturers and sellers to distinguish their products are claimed as trademarks. Where those designations appear in this book, and Allyn & Bacon was aware of a trademark claim, the designations have been printed in initial or all caps.

Library of Congress Cataloging-in-Publication Data

McGown, Carl
    Coaching volleyball: building a winning team/Carl McGown, Hilda Fronske, Launa Moser,
        p. cm.
    Includes bibliographical references.
    ISBN 0-205-30958-5 (alk. paper)
        1. Volleyball–Coaching.   I. Fronske, Hilda Ann.   II. Moser, Launa.   III. Title.

GV1015.5.C63 M34 2001
796.325–dc21   00-032296

Printed in the United States of America

10 9 8 7 6 5   05 04

For the Long Beach First Ward All Church Volleyball
Championship Teams…where it all began
—Carl McGown

To our future teachers and coaches here
at Utah State University
—Hilda Fronske

To my husband Stephen and children Jaaron, Stefan, Courtney, and Ty,
who have suffered every volleyball
season with me

Thanks to all my 'girls' who allowed me to meddle in their lives during
volleyball season, and who made it all worthwhile

To my mother, who taught me to always do my best
and to be a finisher
—Launa Moser

Contents

Preface

If you are just beginning a coaching career or have been looking to begin one, *Coaching Volleyball: Building a Winning Team* will answer many of your questions. If you are already a coach and want your players to leave school with something more lasting than a championship, or if you want to find ways to instill motivation into your teams as well as stimulate your own approach, this textbook will provide guidance and direction.

In this text, Carl McGown, an NCAA men's champion, who many consider the guru of volleyball; Hilda Fronske, an author of two coaching texts; and Launa Moser, a 23-year high school volleyball coach who has won multiple state championships, have pooled their talents and strategies.

In one of the most complete books on coaching volleyball on the market, this book covers every aspect of winning volleyball from the beginning basic skills to assistance in guiding talented athletes. It will help you with tryouts, putting a team and practices together, setting up offense and defense, coaching games, and, in addition, provide strategies for dealing with parents and administrators.

In addition to cues and drills, the book contains photographs and diagrams to illustrate individual and team play. In the appendix are sets of coach's masters (stats charts, practice schedule, etc.) to copy, which will simplify a coach's job.

Coaching Volleyball contains the keys to a winning program from the elementary to the collegiate level.

ACKNOWLEDGMENTS

Carl McGown

I would like to thank Hilda and Launa for their dedication and persistence.

Hilda Fronske

I would like to thank Kelli Parsons, a student at Utah State University, for her time, hard work, and dedication to helping us meet the deadline. Thanks for the great illustrations, drill diagrams, typing, and editing. I am grateful to Grayson DuBose for his shared expertise and to Coach Al Brown, Assistant Basketball Coach for the Lady Vols Team at the University of Tennessee, for his support and encouragement with the challenge chapter.

I also thank my good friend Patsy Bradfield.

Launa Moser

I wish to thank my administrators, Al Koch and Reid Carlson, for their patience in teaching me how to work with administrators. I am indebted to my assistant volley-ball coaches, Jill Hobbs, Jillanne Forsyth, and Jeri O'Brien, and our junior high coach, Shaunna Fuhriman, for their suggestions, edits, and assistance in the coaching journey.

We would like to thank Allyn and Bacon, including our editor, Joe Burns, for his insight and the opportunity to publish with Allyn and Bacon; and Tanja Eise, for her time and patience with all our questions.

CHAPTER 1

Is Coaching for You?

Is coaching for you? Do you have what it takes to be a good coach? What is a good coach? Does winning determine whether you are a success? These are questions that are best addressed before you start to coach. The answers will decide your direction as a coach, your style, and your goals. Only you can really answer these questions.

The first thing to answer is: Why are you coaching or even considering coaching? Love the sport? Driven to be successful? Enjoy working with kids? Like teaching? Forced into it? In it for the money? For the fame? The basic reasons you are coaching are very important. They will be the base or support from which your most important decisions in coaching are made.

If your reasons for coaching are for fame, glory, or money, your choices will be directed for your own good. However, if your basic reasons are for the love of the sport and the love of athletes or for the love of teaching, your choices will be for your players' best interests. John Wooden (1988), the legendary former men's basketball coach at UCLA, states:

> You must love your boys to get the most out of them and do the most for them. I have worked with boys whom I haven't admired, but I have loved them just the same…I feel that my love for young people is the main reason I have stayed in coaching and have refused positions that would have been more lucrative. (p. 60)

Before you say yes to coaching, think about the impact your decision will have on you and on others.

COACHING TAKES MANY HOURS

Coaching takes many hours, not just during the season but also during the off-season, with camps, conditioning, weight lifting, spring practices, and players' and coaches' clinics. These off-season hours are not usually compensated. Depending on your level, coaching can also entail helping players with scholarships or recruitment. Good coaches invest their whole lives, it seems, in coaching. Odom (1998) tells us what it takes to be successful:

> A passion for the game and a passion for the people are the two most important traits for a coach—not necessarily in that order. I think those two things are all encompassing. The passion is the basis of good teaching, because if you have a passion you want to share it. A passion indicates that you want to share with somebody whether it is love or talent. So a coach with passion has a head start. (p. 42)

WHAT EFFECTS DO COACHES HAVE ON PLAYERS?

It depends on where you, the coach, have your focus. Do you have the players' complete well-being in mind, or just the part that could win you games? Are the players important to you as people or just as athletes? Do you realize what impact your coaching can have on the rest of their lives? Do you want your players to love the sport long after their playing careers with you are over, or is winning the only thing that is important to you? Playing on a team with a coach who has the right goals can teach the following life principles:

Responsibility	Communication
Commitment	Conflict resolution
Work ethic	How to win and lose graciously
Setting goals	How to learn and grow from mistakes
Teamwork	Control of emotions
Sportsmanship	Focus

WHAT DO YOU WANT TO ACHIEVE?

As a coach, are you most interested in the momentary pleasure of a win, or the lifelong contribution to a person's quality of life? Six-time national champion coach Pat Summitt of the Tennessee Volunteer women's basketball team asserts that "really when I teach basketball, I am trying to teach our players about life" (1998, p. 212).

Winning is a tangible thing you can feel, see, and taste. Your peers will laud you and your ego will soar. Winning the right way, without sacrificing your players on the altar of your ego, can be of enduring value. Can you both win *and* be a positive influence in your players' lives? Yes, if what is most important to you is players first and winning second. Your foremost focus needs to be on helping the players.

Something we continually teach our players is that if they help their teammates to be the best they can be (e.g., "go" calling, telling them where to hit or how many are up on the block), we all win. Their teammates will likely return the favor, and all of the team members' minds will be focused on the game.

The same principle applies to coaches. Work for the well-being of your players, and you will be the winner also. That is, if you coach with the right focus in mind, you win even if you don't win the game. According to LaVell Edwards, coach of the successful Brigham Young University football program (1995):

> Much more important than these other side benefits of coaching are the relationships you're able to generate and maintain. The longer you coach the more of these relationships you're able to have. Coaching puts you in a position where you can touch many lives and where you can be touched by many lives. (p. 182)

I can hear some of you saying, "Well, sounds great, but the administration won't keep me in the program long if I don't produce." If you put your players first, you will produce. Players coached with their best interests at heart are happier, work harder, and are more loyal to their coaches and the program. Parents and administrators are supportive. It is a win-win situation.

HOW IMPORTANT SHOULD YOUR PLAYERS BE TO YOU?

Again, Wooden tells it as it should be: "You follow a good many of them the rest of your life, and their joys and disappointments become your joys and disappointments. You love to see them excel in whatever profession they pursue" (Wooden, 1988, p. 66).

SUMMARY

So, you need to look long and deep inside yourself and decide what is most important to you—wins and trophies? Or a legacy of personal building blocks that you have ingrained in every player you will coach? And it doesn't stop with just the players you coach, because they will pass on the skills they have learned from you to everyone they come in contact with. It's your call. What will it be?

CHAPTER 2

Best of the Best Coaching Philosophies

There are many philosophies of coaching that will lead to success. In our search to excel we have found that if you want to be the best, learn from the best. Besides our own philosophies that we have honed and polished through years of coaching, we will present supporting philosophies from some of the most successful coaches in a variety of athletic disciplines from whom we have learned. Why try to reinvent the wheel? If you want to be successful, emulate the coaches who already have been successful.

How important is a philosophy to your success as a coach? Many coaches believe that it is essential to formulate a sound coaching philosophy in order to develop a successful program. Lou Holtz, who is one of the most successful college football coaches and who has won a national championship and national Coach of the Year honors, gives the following advice:

> As a leader your attitude has a powerful effect on others.... You have an obligation to develop a positive attitude, one that inspires the people around you to achieve the impossible. Great leaders also possess a passion for their causes.... If you want to lead, that is the responsibility you must accept. And it starts with your own fervor. You can't fake it. If you don't have a genuine hunger to accomplish something, you won't be able to lead anyone effectively. But if you have passion, you'll find it's an infectious thing. You'll transmit it to others who will pledge heart and soul to your principle. (1998, pp. 4–5)

Holtz lists some key elements for any coach to develop who wants to be the best: positive attitude, passion, fervor, and a hunger to accomplish something. But a coach can't get out there in the thick of things and make it happen, no matter how hungry he or she is. A coach is essentially a backstage prompter. A coach's days of being the "go-to" person (if there ever were such days) don't matter now. So how do coaches take passion, fervor, and positive attitude and infuse them in their charges? Adhering to the following strategies will not only help you do just that, but will also provide you with personal satisfaction.

BE A TEACHER FIRST

Before you can be a coach, you must be a teacher. You must motivate, educate, discipline, and care for your athletes. The very best teachers teach best by example. Your players will learn far more from your actions than from your words.

What do you do in a tight situation? How much composure do you exhibit? Can you keep your mind focused on the game? How important are your players compared to the win?

Coaches don't start out their first year being great. Yes, they might win, but wins by themselves do not define a great coach. Great coaches are developed by their experiences and the knowledge they gain from them, which leads us into the next element.

BE WILLING TO CHANGE

Every year, learn something new and add it to your program. Go to clinics, read books, study videos, watch the best teams warm up and practice, and so on. If you are not rowing upstream you'll be drifting down. Continuing to learn will keep the game alive and exciting for you, too. As Mike Schlappi, a two-time gold medalist in wheelchair basketball and the only player in the nation to be a member of the past three Olympic teams, notes: "If we resist change, we'll fail; if we accept change, we'll survive; and if we create change, we'll succeed" (1998, p. 61).

Volleyball is not static—it changes constantly. What worked twenty years ago will not work as well now. Don't resist change; instead, embrace it. Mike Wolf, whose book *The Packer Way* chronicled the Green Bay football program's phenomenal success, observed this about coaching: "To stay on top, you have to raise your standards" (1998, p. 252). Be the first to raise your standards, be the one others will follow.

You want to challenge your players and yourself every year. That is what coaching clinics are for. Take the opportunity every time you can to go listen to other coaches talk about what works for them and about new techniques and ideas. If you come away with just one new idea or method that will work for your team or for just one player, it will be worth it. You never can learn or know enough. Wolf concurs: "Constantly ask questions and don't be afraid of the answers. The only way to obtain the information you need to allow you to make proper decisions is to keep an open mind and maintain a relentless curiosity. Never adopt the attitude that because you have reached a certain professional status, you now have all the answers" (1998, p. 39).

Learning isn't just for the beginners, as Rick Pitino, head coach of the Boston Celtics and a former NCAA champion coach, illustrates. Even after all he has accomplished, here is what he says about John Wooden: "John Wooden never embraces success. He stayed prepared, hungry and driven no matter how many championship banners they hung in Pauley Pavilion.... He worked harder and harder every year.... Commit yourself to constant improvement. Never rest on success" (1997, pp. 254–255).

BE POSITIVE

Catch your players doing it right and praise them. Players who are coached by a person who uses praise to motivate instead of fear are more willing to try new things and to go beyond their comfort zone with confidence. They perform better under pressure and are able to keep their minds focused on the game instead of on their coach's reactions (see Figure 2.1). By being positive you empower them to rely on themselves, to trust their own instincts and intelligence, and in reality, to grow. As Mark Twain said, "Most of us can run pretty well all day long on one compliment."

ESTABLISH PRIORITIES

Remember, it is just a game, and there *are* more important things in life. Keep things in perspective. Your family and your players' families should be top priorities. Education should also come before volleyball. Rick Majerus, basketball coach at the University of Utah, who has an outstanding winning percentage of .736, says: "I tell recruits and their parents...the most important thing is education" (1999, p. 58). We should encourage our players to work hard and give all they've got, in the right time and place, but after all is said and done, there is more to life than volleyball.

EMPHASIZE WORK ETHIC

Work hard. If you read any successful coaches' books, you will see that a recurring theme in them all is hard work. University of Tennessee women's basketball coach Pat Summitt tells opponents: "Here's how I'm going to beat you. I'm going to outwork you" (1998, p. 117).

Winning isn't everything, but making the effort is. When the players have invested lots of their time and effort in a sport, they hate to lose, which creates commitment. Summitt goes on to say: "If there is one thing I cannot abide, it's lack of effort.... But I can tell you this: The harder you work, the harder it is to surrender. Tennessee wins because, in the end, our players feel they have worked too hard not to" (1998, p. 119).

FIGURE 2.1   Players will perform better if they are able to keep their minds focused on the game, not the coach's reactions.

You, as a coach, must also be willing to work. Summitt, who has coached her team to six NCAA championships, tells what it takes: "Make work your passion.... They know that I'll work as hard as they do, and they know that I love my work. I'd better, I've been coaching longer than they've been alive" (1998, pp. 125–126). John Wooden believes that "winners are usually the ones who work harder, work longer, and as a result, perform better" (1997, p. 42).

Michael Jordan of NBA Chicago Bulls fame said: "If you do the work, you get rewarded. There are no shortcuts in life" (1998, p. 131). Who deserves the victory? What does that mean, deserving a victory? Pitino puts it this way:

> According to Churchill, victory comes only to those who work long and hard, who are willing to pay the price in blood, sweat and tears. Hard work is also the basic building block of every kind of achievement.... You can start with a dream or an idea or a goal but before any of your hopes can be realized, you truly must deserve your success. This may sound old-fashioned in this age of instant gratification. (1997, p. 1)

He goes on to say, "You want to succeed? Okay, then succeed. Deserve it. How? Outwork everybody in sight, sweat the small stuff, sweat the big stuff. Go the extra mile. But whatever it takes, put your heart and soul into everything you do" (1997, p. 3).

TEACH DISCIPLINE

You must be disciplined yourself before you can teach it. If you want your players to follow the rules, you must follow them. If you want them to be prepared, focused, on time, and so on, you must be first.

Summitt sums it up:

> Have few team rules that all the players buy into, sign and obey. No excuses, a "better the ball" attitude. They learn to be on time, follow directions and are more self reliant and successful. They learn to take responsibility for their actions and not blame others. Teaching discipline creates players who have self-discipline.... Self-discipline is a matter of how hard you are willing to work when no one is watching.... It is essential to success. (1998, pp. 92,97)

ENCOURAGE TEAMWORK

When you come to practice, other interests and problems stay outside. You cease to exist as an individual; you become part of a team. It is amazing how much you can accomplish when no one cares who gets the credit. This attitude also engenders loyalty and puts self-interest in the proper perspective.

Phil Jackson, coach of the Los Angeles Lakers, former coach of the Chicago Bulls, and the owner of nine NBA championship rings (two as a player, seven as a coach), has this to say about teamwork:

> But working with the Bulls, I have learned that the most effective way to forge a winning team is to call on the players' need to connect with something larger than themselves.... It requires the individuals involved to surrender their self-interest for the greater good so that the whole adds up to more than the sum of its

parts. This isn't always an easy task in a society where celebration of ego is the number one national pastime. (1995, p. 5)

John Wooden agrees:

Team spirit is also an important block in the heart of the structure. There is an eagerness to sacrifice personal glory for the welfare of the group as a whole. It's togetherness and consideration for others. If players are not considerate of one another there is no way we can have the proper team-play that is needed. It is not necessary for everyone to particularly like each other to play well together, but they must respect each other and subordinate selfishness to the welfare of the team. The team must come first. (Wooden & Jamison, 1988, p. 90)

BE PREPARED

Here is what some coaches feel about being prepared. John Wooden says: "Confidence comes from being prepared" (Wooden & Jamison, 1988, p. 94). Pretend you are a member of a choir that has practiced a number only a few times before it is asked to perform it. There will be a lot of stumbling, missed notes, words mispronounced, and little cohesiveness. You and the other members of the choir won't come in on the same notes together or end together. Hesitation will be apparent, and free-flowing energy and spirit will be absent from the performance. The same happens in an athletic performance. Lou Holtz sums it up: "Preparation dispels pressure because it builds confidence" (1998, p. 139). Coach LaVell Edwards of Brigham Young University football fame takes this idea a step further: "When you expect to be successful, it follows that you'll plan ahead. You'll prepare yourself, you'll make certain that you follow all the steps that have helped you be successful in the past, or you've watched others who have found success. When opportunity presents itself, you'll be in a position to open the door. That's your focus. That's your game plan" (1995, p. 150). John Wooden sums it up simply: "I will get ready and then, perhaps, my chance will come" (Wooden & Jamison, 1988, p. 157). He also goes on to say: "Remember it's the perfection of the smallest details that make big things happen" (Wooden & Tobin, 1997, p. 72). He believed this wholeheartedly, so much so that he even taught his players how to put on their socks correctly to prevent blisters.

KNOW YOUR PLAYERS

No one cares how much you know until they know how much you care. It is essential that you get acquainted with your players and their likes and dislikes. Get to know some personal things about them and their families (see Figure 2.2). Don't be interested only in what they do in your particular area. There is so much more to your players than their athletic ability, and it all contributes to who they are and how they tick. Lou Holtz has written that "leaders must know what motivates their people. Some will not do their best until you kick them in the butt; others need continual pats on the back" (1998, p. 12).

How do you get that sort of knowledge about your players? Pat Summitt meets individually with her players four times each year. "We look eyeball to eye-

FIGURE 2.2   Look eyeball to eyeball and talk about everything.

ball and talk about everything from her fears to her ambitions. I spell out what her role is and what's expected for her, but more important, I ask what she wants.... Listening has allowed me to be a better coach" (1998, pp. 68–70).

So do you get to know players just so you can win? What should the motivation be? According to Wooden: "People want to believe you are sincerely interested in them as a person, not just what they can do for you. You can't fake it. If you don't mean it, they know it just as you'd know if someone were pretending to be interested in you" (Wooden & Tobin, 1997, pp. 33–34).

Edwards adds: "You have to sense things; you have to know your players.... As much as anything, I think what coaching really comes down to is putting the right people in the right places, providing them with a decent game plan and letting them run it. Once you've taught them the principles, be smart and get out of their way" (1996, p. 85).

COMMUNICATE

Players need to know their roles on the team and what is expected of them. Too many times we coaches just assume players know what we are thinking. It is very apparent to us, why shouldn't it be to them? Many studies of human communication state that well over half of our communication is achieved through body language, not verbally. Because of this, there can be a considerable amount of miscommunication if our players misread our intentions. We need to be very clear with our players and verbally tell them what we are thinking, instead of assuming they know.

Here is what John Wooden says about communication:

The individuals who aren't playing much have a very important role in the development of those who are going to play more. They are needed, and you must let them know it. Everyone on the team, from the manager to the coach, from a secretary to an owner, has a role to fulfill. That role is essential if the team is to come close to reaching its potential. The leader must understand this. Every single member of your team needs to feel wanted and appreciated. If they are on the team, they deserve to be valued and to feel valued. Do you want someone on the team who doesn't feel necessary and appreciated? How do they find out unless you let them know? (Wooden & Tobin, 1997, pp. 139–140)

Dave Odom, who piloted Wake Forest University's men's basketball team to seven consecutive NCAA tournament appearances, believes that: "Identifying important roles, and helping them feel these roles, gives them the best chance to succeed" (1998, p. 87). That is our ultimate goal—to help our players succeed.

The following strategies are more specific to volleyball, though they could also be used in other sports. If you implement these philosophies in your practices, it will make a tremendous difference in your players' attitudes. Your athletes will become more competitive and positive, and your practices will also be more productive.

USE GAMELIKE SITUATIONS WHENEVER POSSIBLE

In the 1970s and early 1980s many top coaches conditioned their players with a thirty-minute running/station program at the beginning of practice. This took time from their ballhandling skills and did not have a lot of retention value. Players learned less when they were physically and mentally fatigued.

Now, all conditioning programs should be gamelike situations using the ball. Your players not only enjoy it more (and consequently put more effort into it without you hounding or driving them) but also improve their physical and mental skills and reflexes. Using consequences at the end of each game also teaches your players to hate to lose (a nice motivational technique).

TELL PLAYERS WHAT YOU WANT TO SEE THEM DOING, NOT WHAT THEY ARE DOING WRONG

If you tell players what they are doing wrong (e.g., bent arms on pass), that is the last picture they have in their heads and it acts as a negative reinforcer. If you tell them what you want to see (e.g., keeping arms straight), that is the last thought and it becomes a positive reinforcer. In addition, experience shows that there are inherent differences between coaching males and females. Females tend to be holistic. This means that if you criticize a skill, female players might take it more personally than would male players. In other words, female players may feel like *they* are being criticized, not just the skill. Using a positive approach eliminates a lot of hurt feelings and thoughts of inadequacy.

Use a player who is performing a skill correctly to demonstrate whenever possible because a correct picture is very important. It is much easier to emulate a visual image than a verbal step-by-step instruction. Besides, it gives the exemplary player a boost and encourages the others to achieve that level also. They see that the skill is an attainable one.

USE PLAYER-CENTERED DRILLS

If you are doing a lot of serving and spiking at your players, you need to question how many ball touches you are depriving them of and how much better they could be with as much practice as you are getting. Also, if you are not directly involved with the drill, you can observe and give feedback to your players. Taking one player out of a drill (as it continues) and giving that player one or two pertinent cues is a great coaching strategy.

A good place to observe and coach any six-on-six drill is from behind the middle of the end line. You can tell a lot about your defense and transition from there, and your players aren't always looking at you after a mistake or great play. They tend to focus more on each other.

ENCOURAGE AND ALLOW YOUR PLAYERS TO TAKE RISKS

To risk nothing is to gain nothing. Your players are unable to reach a higher level of skill if you don't allow and encourage them to risk failure. You need to allow them to fail without censure and encourage them to try again if you want the maximum amount of growth to occur. You must give them the courage and your permission to leave their comfort zones and try something new. Everyone will fail—it is what one does after the failure that counts. As a coach, your belief, support, and encouragement in your athletes can give them confidence to expand their abilities. The opposite can stifle them. You don't need to punish failure; the gamelike situation does that. Coaches and players both need to understand that without failure there would be no success.

Do you realize that simply stepping on the court, becoming a member of the team, or playing in front of peers and family is a risk for your players? Placing their ideas and dreams before a crowd constitutes a risk of exposing their true selves and of failing or succeeding.

Summitt has written: "When you choose to be a competitor, you choose to be a survivor. When you choose to compete, you make the conscious decision to find out what your real limits are, not just what you think they are. Competition trains you to accept risks and to endure set-backs" (1998, p. 214).

Encouraging your players to risk is encouraging them to succeed, and not only in volleyball.

SUMMARY

Danforth sums it up: "I dare you, whoever you are, to share with others the fruits of your daring. Catch a passion for helping others and a richer life will come back to you!" (1998, pp. x–xi).

CHAPTER 3

Before You Teach
a Skill or Drill

Do you want to use the best and most efficient way to teach a skill? There are many teaching methods for motor learning out there. What you need is one that is proven to have the best retention value and provides the most success.

Many motor learning experts believe that the motor program is a type of central representation (an image in the mind) that controls actions and movements. So, the actions and movements of volleyball players (serving, passing, spiking, etc.) are controlled by their motor programs. Obviously, making certain that athletes develop effective motor programs is one of the most important tasks facing coaches.

What we have found from research and from observing our own teams is that the best way to teach a skill is by

- Using a correct example in a demonstration (by putting an image in players' minds) (see Figure 3.1).
- Having players practice that skill and giving immediate feedback using a few important cues.
- Practicing the skill in a very simplified drill with many repetitions.

FIGURE 3.1 The best way to teach a skill is by demonstrating it correctly.

- Placing the skill in a gamelike situation where it is repeated many times, but randomly. For example, if you were learning to spike, the progression would be similar to this:

1. Demonstration with key words
2. Simplified drills: You go, I throw (approach, jump, and spike)

   I throw, you go (timing is now added)

   Spiking lines, setter sets balls (random ball placement)
3. Random drills: Serve-pass-set-hit

   Block, transition, and spike

   Three-on-three or Queen's court

This is the simplified version. To delve deeper into methods of developing motor programs and skills, it will help if we examine the issues of specificity versus generality; transfer; whole versus part practice; state-dependent remembering; and random versus blocked practice.

SPECIFICITY VERSUS GENERALITY

Does general athletic ability really exist? Most people believe it does. They believe that someone who can play baseball very well should be able to play golf very well, that someone who can play basketball very well should also be able to play volleyball very well, and so on. Back in the 1920s and '30s, several prominent physical educators even went so far as to develop a number of general athletic ability tests. Modern physical educators, led by scientist Franklin Henry, no longer accept the notion of general athletic ability. Instead, they believe that abilities are specific to the task or activity. The following statement by Henry (1958), even though it was written more than forty years ago, is typical of current beliefs: "It is no longer possible to justify the concept of unitary abilities such as coordination and agility since the evidence shows that these abilities are specific to the task or activity" (p. 126).

TRANSFER

How much will the pepper drill (two players hitting back and forth) help backcourt defense? If the conclusion that motor programs are very specific is accepted, then it is possible to make a number of predictions. One of the predictions is that there will not be very much motor transfer from task to task. Pepper might not transfer very much to backcourt defense. The issue of transfer is of crucial importance to coaches, because every drill players perform and every practice a coach designs is expected to produce large amounts of transfer to game situations. But, if playing pepper does not do much to improve the skill of digging hard-driven spikes, it may be because there is not enough transfer between the drill and the competitive activity.

The research here is very clear. There is not as much motor transfer as we might think. Schmidt (1975) summarizes: "There has been a great deal of research conducted concerning transfer from one variation of a task to another variation of the same task.... One is forced to the conclusion that the amount of motor transfer is quite small" (p. 63). The prediction of little transfer is upheld. What prediction could be made about whole versus part practice?

WHOLE VERSUS PART PRACTICE

Should your players practice all of the spike or only part of the spike? This area is fairly complex, because there are problems with the definitions of *whole* and *part*. In spiking, the whole is the approach, the jump, the arm swing or contact of the ball, and the recovery. A part might be the approach or the arm swing. It is beyond the scope of this chapter to go into all the issues. It is possible to say that if motor programs are specific, and if there is not much transfer between various tasks, then when we are trying to develop a motor program, whole practice should be better than part practice. Nixon and Locke (1973) studied the research in this area and discovered that "in the 30 whole-part studies reviewed, not one favored teaching methods that used the part or progressive part methods of instruction. In the majority of studies, some variation of the whole method was associated with superior learning" (p. 1216). I have seen coaches break spiking into parts for instruction. First they work on the spiking action or arm swing against a wall. Then they work on the approach without a ball. Finally they combine the two. According to Nixon and Locke, it would be better to start with the whole spike in the beginning and, as we have already recommended, use keys (performance cues) to teach the arm swing and the approach.

STATE-DEPENDENT REMEMBERING

What things do our athletes remember? Cognitive psychologists have shown that remembering is very state dependent. *State dependent* is a complex term, but what it means is that when a person learns something and it becomes a part of memory, information about the mood of the learner and the surrounding environment is also stored in memory. Performance is significantly better when the mood of the learner and the environment in which performance must occur matches the mood and environment in which learning occurred. No wonder an inexperienced athlete has great difficulty performing before a large audience. No wonder there is a home-court advantage.

RANDOM VERSUS BLOCKED PRACTICE

Should practice be blocked or random? In other words, should there be variability in practice? Armed with the knowledge of specificity, little transfer, the superiority of whole practice, and the state dependency of learning and remembering, it seems logical to make one last prediction. Drills that introduce the variability we normally find in a game (this would be random practice) transfer better to game conditions than drills where the trials are blocked. For instance, the forearm pass is an essential volleyball skill, but it is often practiced in a situation where the ball comes from the same place and goes to the same place. This would be blocked practice. Lots of successful repetitions occur in this type of practice. However, the skill is rarely performed under such controlled conditions in a game, so blocked practice does not transfer very well to game conditions. It is clear that players need varied practice situations to prepare them for actual games.

APPLICATION

The preceding information forms a remarkably cohesive body of knowledge. There are five converging lines of evidence, and this convergence makes the recommended applications even more compelling. The foregoing concepts apply to two main coaching areas: progressions and drills.

Progressions

About a year ago, I attended a volleyball clinic that specialized in setting and attacking. The coach who instructed the setting portion of the clinic recommended the use of a fairly lengthy progression to teach players the skill. The progression started with players kneeling on the floor with their hands on the floor in the correct overhead passing position (thumbs 3 cm apart and forefingers 8 cm apart). Next, a ball was placed on the floor, and the players' hands were placed on the ball in the correct overhead passing position. The next position required players to bend at the waist and bounce the ball repeatedly from the floor to the hands. Other parts of the recommended procedure had partners facing each other while sitting, kneeling, and lying on the floor on their stomachs. It wasn't until progression number 15 that the players actually stood facing each other and passed a ball back and forth, and finally, on progression number 22, three players passed a ball around in a triangle.

The problem with progressions such as this is that they are an inefficient and ineffective way to teach motor skills, and they certainly don't follow the principles of specificity, transfer, and whole practice that were outlined earlier in this chapter. Extensive progressions, like the one used in the setting example, can be used if there is fear or danger, but there isn't much fear or danger associated with setting.

It is clear that progressions must be used to teach motor skills. If I want to teach my young son how to spike a volleyball, I can't start by having two imposing blockers block every ball he hits, but the principles of motor learning dictate that I shouldn't start with the ball on a spiking tee, either. So what rules can be outlined for progressions? There are two:

1. Progressions should be limited in number. Appropriate regulatory stimuli are necessary.
2. The stimuli that are used should resemble those that players will encounter in actual games as much as possible.

Setting the ball while lying on your stomach is not a gamelike situation. Nixon and Locke (1973) support the idea that extensive progressions are not effective: "Progressions is a near-sacred principle in physical education and is taken most seriously in teacher training. Evidence indicates that the faith…may be misplaced.… Progressions generally appear not to be significant factors in learning many motor skills" (p. 1217). If you want to teach players to set the ball, the first thing you should have them do is set the ball. If you want them to learn to attack, the first thing you should do is have them attack the ball.

Remember the recommended teaching method? Have players set with emphasis on a cue, or have them attack with emphasis on a cue, and work through the three or four cues that will be used to teach the skill. Please don't waste their time by having them perform all sorts of activities that are not in any way going to develop the specific motor programs required for volleyball. There isn't much transfer from lying on the stomach to setting an actual ball, and if your practices have a greater percentage of transfer to actual game play each day than your opponents', it won't be long until your team is much better than theirs.

Drills

In a similar vein, drills, like progressions, must be gamelike. Drills should be designed to develop specific motor programs. Many coaches think that pepper is a great drill to use when they are trying to teach their players individual defense. In reality, if a coach wants to teach his or her players defense, there are many drills that are better than pepper. Marv Dunphy (the 1988 Olympic men's volleyball team coach) used to say that the best passing drills are pass, set, hit (P-S-H), the best setting drills are P-S-H, the best hitting drills are P-S-H, and the best digging drills are P-S-H and dig. Marteniuk (1976) explains: "Anything less than a game situation, unless very well planned, has the possibility of introducing artificial situations, and complete transfer to the game situation might not occur. When drills are developed, the teacher should carefully consider the way the skills are performed in a game to determine that the drills are as close to the game as possible" (p. 219).

To ensure gamelike drills and increase transfer, coaches should consider these factors:

- Players' positions on the court
- Players' movements on the court
- Players' orientation to the net
- The sequence of events and the timing of the sequence
- The stimulus to which players react (a coach standing on a table is not the stimulus that a player will have to react to in a game)
- The natural termination of the ball in play (let most rallies come to a natural termination; don't catch the ball)

IMPROVING RESPONSES TO DRILLS IN PRACTICE

Coaches should try to organize practices in which their athletes experience many successful responses (see Figure 3.2). Success can be increased by proper scheduling of work and rest times.

Massed or Distributed Practice?

The main question here is how the work and rest in practice should be distributed. If a coach wants to practice serve reception for 30 minutes every practice, how should the time be scheduled? Would it be better to do all 30 minutes at once (massed practice), or should the time be broken up into smaller blocks of perhaps

FIGURE 3.2 Organize practice to ensure many successful responses.

10 minutes each (distributed practice)? These and other questions have prompted extensive research for almost 90 years. There have been conflicting findings, but there is recent evidence that massed practice reduces effectiveness of both the learning and performance of a motor skill (Lee and Genovese, 1988).

So the best procedure for a coach is to provide distributed types of practice. For example, it would be better to do smaller bouts of serve reception than to do a long 30-minute session. In fact, instead of simply inserting rests between serve reception practices, it is wise to insert other activities such as serving or spiking. With this system, the advantages of distributed practice (no depressed performance or learning) and massed practice (many opportunities to respond) are both realized.

Physical Fatigue

I have seen many coaches start practice with long warm-ups involving ladders or "suicides" and other types of physically demanding routines that actually produced physical fatigue in their athletes. When I first started coaching, I had my athletes go through a 45-minute circuit-training program before every practice. We were fit, but could we play? (Actually, the team was never very good until I stopped the routine.) Research indicates that physical fatigue impairs both performance and learning. Some coaches argue that athletes have to play when they are fatigued, so they need to learn skills when they are fatigued. However, research reveals that this belief is not justified. It appears that practice under ideal conditions is best for learning regardless of the conditions under which the task is to be performed. So the best place for circuits, ladders or "suicides," and most types of fitness activities is near the end of practice, probably just before the cooldown (see Figure 3.3). Of course, practices can still be demanding, but heavy fatigue will reduce the amount of learning that takes place.

WHAT INFORMATION SHOULD PLAYERS RECEIVE ABOUT SKILL AND DRILLS?

Information obtained after a response is called *information feedback* (IF) and is generally viewed as the most important variable for determining learning, except for practice itself. Here are several IF guidelines:

FIGURE 3.3   Save conditioning for the end of practice.

- The information that is presented must not overload the information-processing ability of the athletes. Coaches who do not use cues (discussed earlier in this chapter) are more likely to overload their players than those who do use them.
- Two types of information can be given: knowledge of results (information about the outcome of the response; e.g., "that was a straight-down spike") and knowledge of performance (information about the way the response was performed; e.g., "your four-step approach was perfect that time"). Because knowledge of performance is not easy for the learner to obtain alone, it is especially important for the coach to provide it in the early stages, when the learner has not yet developed an internal standard of correct performance.
- Players like practices in which they get lots of positive feedback because it is very motivational. So, coaches should do everything in their power to increase the amount of positive feedback they give in practice.

Because information feedback is generally viewed as the most important variable for determining learning, except for practice itself, players need practice trials in order to get that feedback. Many studies have shown that the number of times players practice a skill (at an appropriate level of difficulty) is the best predictor of their improvement. So coaches should do everything they can to make sure that the number of practice trials, or the number of opportunities to respond, is maximized.

There are four main ways to increase opportunities to respond:

1. Skill Warm-Up.   Instead of starting each practice with a warm-up that requires the players to jog around in circles, start the warm-up with ballhandling drills. The drills do not have to be intense; they can be at a level that will allow gradual warm-up. After this game-specific warm-up, add any stretching activities that you want to employ (to guard against injury). The 10 minutes or so that you devote to ballhandling will give your team a competitive advantage.

2. Tutoring.   Tutoring is an activity where the coach and one, two, or three players work together in a session designed to practice a specific skill. Because there are only a few players at a tutoring session, each player has numerous opportunities to respond and receives a great deal of good feedback. Virtually every practice should be preceded by a tutoring session, and it doesn't hurt to end every practice with a similar session.

3. Small Groups.   It is true that a certain percentage of practice time should include six-on-six gamelike drills, but when your athletes are playing six-on-six, the number of chances they have to play the ball is diminished. It makes sense to schedule a number of small-group games, like doubles or triples. If a team of twelve players plays three games of doubles, the athletes will play the ball three times as often as when they are playing six-on-six.

4. Wash Games or In-a-Rows.   Bill Neville and Doug Beal devised many different types of practice situations in which their players had to win two or sometimes three, four, five, or more rallies in a row. The routine was as follows: Every time a ball was served and the rally terminated, a coach would immediately throw another ball into play. If the objective was to win two in a row, the team that won the first rally would also have to win the second rally. If first one team was successful and then the other, then no points were scored and it was a wash. It is possible to set any number of in-a-rows as the goal, so if the goal is to win five in a row, then after the serve, four balls would be thrown into play one after another (as long as the same team kept winning the rallies). In this system, because of all the extra balls thrown into play, there are a much greater number of opportunities to respond.

A combination of all four of these procedures can have a dramatic cumulative effect and give a team a real advantage over other teams that are not using these notions.

TEACHING PLAYERS HOW TO PERFORM THE SKILLS OF THE GAME

Now that you understand the motor basics of learning, how do you teach the skills? You teach by

- Not overloading the athletes with information
- Demonstrating
- Using cues
- Applying a teaching method that facilitates learning

Reducing Information Overload

One of the most important concepts of motor learning is that learners have a limited ability to process information. Coaches can facilitate learning by reducing the amount of information they present when they are introducing a goal. If we present a great deal of information all at once, our athletes will not be able to remember most of it. Many volleyball coaches talk too much. They know so much about volleyball, and they want to share all their knowledge with their athletes. Other coaches may not know so much, but they still like to talk. When you are talking, your athletes may be receiving more information than they can handle, and they are also not practicing. There are two main elements coaches must employ when presenting goals to make certain that they don't talk too much or give their athletes too much information to process: demonstrations and cues.

Demonstrations

Motor learning studies have found that movement information is retained in memory in the form of an image. Therefore, it makes sense to give the information in the form of an image in the first place. A demonstration will provide the image. Other work has shown that most tasks are learned at a faster rate when repeated demonstrations are shown. Gallwey (1974), in his fascinating book *The Inner Game of Tennis*, writes, "I was beginning to learn what all good [teachers] must learn: that images are better than words, showing, better than telling, and too much instruction worse than none" (p. 7).

Cues

Demonstrations alone are not enough. Researchers have discovered that learners will attend to task-irrelevant information when their attention is not directed. One way to help overcome this problem and improve learning is to use keys, or performance cues (cues are short, concise instructions given by the coach to the athlete). Cues serve at least four very important purposes. They are

1. Condense or chunk information.
2. Reduce words, thus reducing information processing requirements.
3. Encourage athletes to attend to important elements of the skill.
4. Enhance memory.

A very important part of coaching is deciding which cues to use to teach the skills of volleyball and the order in which they will be presented. There is some evidence that more successful teachers make better decisions about using cues than less successful teachers do. It is also important to combine the demonstrations and the cues into an effective teaching method.

Teaching Method

If coaches realize that their athletes have a limited ability to process information, they will be concerned about presenting the right amount of information at the right speed. Because words have little meaning to beginners, coaches must avoid constant talk and keep learners active. (Several studies have found that students experience on-task performance only one-third of the time or less in a typical physical education class.) Remember, athletes learn best by seeing and doing.

One way to get athletes to see and do is to follow a method of goal presentation that includes the following steps:

1. Demonstrate the skill.
2. Have athletes attempt the skill so you can assess their abilities and determine what cues need to be given. (If the coach already knows the abilities of the athletes, these first two steps can be omitted.)
3. Demonstrate the skill with attention focused on a cue.
4. Let the athletes practice and give them feedback about the cue.
5. Demonstrate the skill with attention focused on the next cue.
6. Let the athletes practice again and give them feedback on the new cue.
7. Repeat the process until all cues have been covered.

It is difficult for coaches to know how to choose cues, how to present them in the proper order, and how to give the right amount of information at the right speed. Coaches usually agree on the concepts, but they seldom agree on the cues or the order in which they should be given. Here is an example from our experience. When we teach forearm passing to beginners, we have five cues that we want them to learn, and they come in this order:

1. Wrists and hands together
2. Straight and simple
3. Face the ball, angle the arms
4. Shuffle
5. See the server, see the spin

Most skills can be taught with four cues or less. Continue to work on each successive cue until the athletes have experienced some success at each.

SUMMARY OF THE STEPS IN TEACHING SKILLS

1. Preassess (ask or have players perform the skill).
2. Briefly state the objective and the reason why the skill is important. Don't talk longer than 30 seconds.
3. Give three to five full demonstrations.
4. Give one cue for players to focus on.
5. Practice. Give players many opportunities to touch the ball.
6. Give specific feedback on the cue—tell players what they did right, or re-emphasize what you want them to do.
7. When players have mastered the first cue, give the second cue, repeating the process until all cues have been given.
8. Use gamelike drills—pass, set, hit, and so on.
9. Add scoring, targets, goals, or combinations of the three in each drill. (See Chapters 14 and 15 for ideas.)

KEYS TO BEING A SUCCESSFUL TEACHER

1. Do not allow any of your players to talk while you're teaching. It displays a lack of respect for you and what you are teaching. Also, others get involved in the conversation or can't hear because of it.
2. Do not allow bouncing or tossing of balls or other distractions while you are teaching. Players' attention will be diverted.
3. Corner or line players up so they aren't scattered all over and you can give them cues or instructions.
   - Try to teach new skills or concepts toward the first half of practice. Players have more energy and a longer attention span during the first part of practice time, allowing for better retention.
   - Practice success. When teaching a new skill, put your players in a drill situation where they are assured of having some success, such as moving up to serve or lowering the net to spike (if they are young).

KEYS TO TEACHING SUCCESSFUL DRILLS

1. Always have consequences and be sure to follow through.
2. Have a goal you are trying to achieve.
3. Have a specific purpose.
4. Try to make sure no one is out of the drill longer than two minutes.
5. Use more than one skill.
6. Use gamelike drills (pass, set, hit).
7. Change the drill by changing the way points are scored (this can change the focus).

If you incorporate these seven keys into each drill you teach, more will be accomplished in a shorter time. You should see motor skill transfer increase, and players will be internally motivated.

SUMMARY

Now that you have the fundamentals of the whole teaching process of volleyball, you will find that your players' skill will progress further during the season and they will enjoy the game more along the way. In this chapter you have discovered that demonstration is the best way to teach a new skill, and using a few simple cue words to emphasize key actions is the most helpful teaching tool to use. You now know that the best way to warm up and condition for volleyball is by playing volleyball, and that by doing this your team members will receive 100 percent transfer of their skill. So let's bring on the drills and skills—you are ready!

CHAPTER 4

Forearm Pass

There is an expression in volleyball, "The serve and the serve receive win matches." In other words, to win in volleyball, your team has to serve and pass well. The forearm pass used in the serve receive allows your team to develop an offense. The better your team can pass, the more intricate the offense. If your team does not pass well, it will have fewer offensive options.

The heart and soul of defense is the dig, which is also a forearm pass. A quick and simple pass is critical to create the opportunity to make points (convert) off of a powerful attack. The forearm pass is *the* major skill used in volleyball, and it is critical to the success of your team.

The basic concepts to remember in the forearm or underhand pass are

1. The ball "knows" angles.
2. Simple is better than complex.
3. The arms and hands respond best to the unexpected.

Here is an example of how the simple-is-better concept can be applied. Many players add an extra motion to passing called *pumping*. Instead of simply coming straight up to meet the ball from the knees, the player unnecessarily starts the arms high (around the waist), dips them down as the ball comes in, then brings them back up to hit it. This extra action slows the player's defense ability and interferes with accuracy, depending on the speed of the ball. Teach players to cut out wasted motion, that is, to simplify.

This chapter focuses on the development of the forearm pass. Short cues, or keys, to help players remember information are presented, followed by simple drills. The cues will be used to assist your athletes' skill development. Giving players short, focused feedback decreases the chance of overwhelming them with too much information.

Whys are also critical to learning. If coaches can tell their players why they use a particular cue, they gain instant credibility. Players are more apt to buy into the concept if the coach says, "By keeping your elbows straight and flat and hitting the ball with the fat part of the arm, there is more surface area to play the ball with, which will result in better ball control and direction of the ball." This makes sense and is easy for players to remember. Implement the *why* in your coaching today.

Ready Position   Figure 4.1

✦ Hands in front of knees | Slightly staggered feet, shoulder-width apart, right foot forward, hands in front of knees

Forearm Contact

✦ Thumbs and wrists together | Wrists and hands (lifelines) together

✦ Elbows straight and flat | Forearm contact with ball, fat part of arms hit ball, elbows straight and simple, make a flat surface with the forearms

✦ Platform out early under the ball | Elbows straight and flat and out early

Pass   Figure 4.2

✦ Feet to the ball | Face the direction the ball is coming from, angle arms to target, arms are no higher than waist-high

✦ Beat the ball to the spot

✦ Shuffle

✦ Face the ball, angle the arms
✦ Drop the shoulder | To angle arms, shoulder must be lower on the side closest to the intended target

✦ Pass ball over lead leg

✦ See the server, see the spin | Look at the server's shoulder and arm—is it swinging soft and slow or hard and fast?

Focus on the ball—floater or a spin serve?

Platform out early
under the ball

Elbows straight
and flat

Thumbs and
wrists together

FIGURE 4.1   Ready Position—Forearm Contact

Stay low and close to
the ground (allows more
time to play the ball)

FIGURE 4.2   Forearm Pass

WHY

+ Ready position

By placing your hands down by your knees, you are low and ready to come up and pass the ball when it comes to you.

+ Forearm contact
+ Straight and simple

The forearm (the fat part of the arms) makes a nice, flat surface for the ball to contact. This provides a smooth surface to bounce the ball off straight. No pumping action (coming down and then back up). This wastes critical time, especially on a fast spike.

+ Hands and wrists together

This makes a big surface area for the ball and provides stability of the arms and a strong surface area for the ball to bounce off.

+ Face the ball, angle the arms
+ Drop the shoulder

Facing the ball and angling the arms helps the ball go where you want it to and allows you to properly send the ball to the setter. The ball "knows" angles. Passing over your lead leg will give you the most control possible, because it provides for a large stance and gives you stability.

+ See the server, see the spin

This keeps your eyes on the ball and keeps you focused on a specific detail. If you know where the ball is coming from, you can move to the correct spot on the court; if you can see the server, you can also tell where the serve will go by watching the server's shoulder.

✦ Feet to ball or beat ball to spot ✦ Shuffle	This cue allows the player to be in the best position to receive the ball—in the center of gravity, wide stance, right leg forward.

DRILLS

Throw-Hit-Catch

A player tosses the ball to a partner, and the partner passes back. The ball is caught and tossed again. Repeat 10 times and switch.

Toss, Pass, Pass

Two players start with a toss and keep passing back and forth until 20 is reached.

In a Line of Three

Player A passes to player B, who passes behind his or her head to player C, who passes long to player A. Rotate players after 10 passes to the middle. Switch the person in the middle to give each player a chance to pass the ball backward over his or her head. This incorporates three different types of passes—one short, one overhead, and one long, which necessitates changing the angles of the arm.

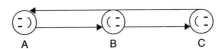

Triangle

Three players pass the ball in a triangle. This allows the passer to practice facing the ball and angling the arms. Switch directions after 45 passes.

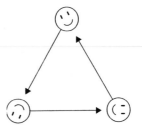

One-Sided Butterfly

Start with a minimum of six players. Coach (C) tosses ball over the net to passer (A). The passer (A) passes ball to the target (B) and target catches ball above the head. Make the passer move to work on footwork with a shuffle step. Passer moves to target's position, target runs and gives ball to coach (place ball on coach's hip), then the player runs back to the passing line. Repeat 10 times. A variation is to replace coach with a player, use half the court, and have six on each half.

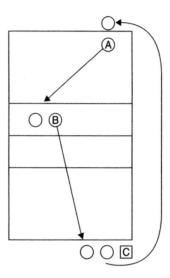

Two-Sided Butterfly

The coach can participate in this drill, depending on the players' skill level. A player or coach (A) serves down the line to the passers (B) and then follows to the passing line. The passer hits ball to the setter (C) and then moves on to the setter's position. The setter takes the ball and moves to the serving line (D) (on the same side of the court). Repeat. Run the same pattern on both sides of the court. Cue for the drill: Follow the intended path of the ball.

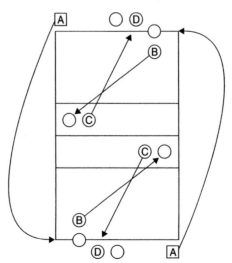

Pass, Set, Hit

With beginning players, have the coach toss or serve balls to one of three passers (A) on the opposite side of the net. In groups of three, the passers play the ball out (pass-set-hit), retrieve the ball for the coach, and then go to the end of the line (on the same side of the court). As the skill level increases, have players serve the ball. This provides the players with more serving practice and the coach can then spend time giving immediate feedback.

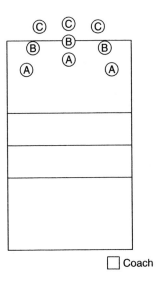

Go to 15(a)

The players are in teams of three. The coach yells "Go!" and the players run under the net and pass, set, hit. If they hit the ball in, they get a point. The first team that gets to 15 wins. Players should concentrate on angling the arms. Option: After Team A hits, have them go under the net and block Team B then run behind Team C at the end of the play.

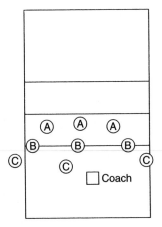

Go to 15(b)

The coach serves the ball to three players on Team 1. They play the rally. Team 1 has to win a point to get back in line. If they lose, they move over to the coach's side, and the opposing team wins a point and gets back in line. The first team that gets to 15 wins.

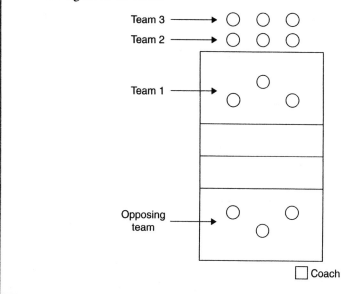

SUMMARY

Passers need to anticipate where the ball is going and get their feet there before it arrives. They also need many repetitions to get better. As a coach, you need to reinforce the proper mechanics with short cues. Early on, make it a point to have players call the ball, own the ball, or help a teammate know where the ball is. On the serve receive, cue "Call ball before over net" to help them make a decision more quickly. Indecision, or calling the ball late, is the major cause of getting aced and of dropped balls. Now, go get 'em. And don't forget, tell your players *Why*!

CHAPTER 5

Overhead Pass

Overhead passing and setting are two names for the same skill. Setting is usually defined as passing the ball to an attacker, and it is preferred in that instance because it is the most accurate of all volleyball skills. Every player should know how to perform this skill, because there are times when someone other than the setter has to set. If all players are proficient at setting, the number of attacks will increase, and the more balls a team can attack, the better their chances of winning.

Volleyball rules have been adjusted to allow the overhead pass to be used in a wider variety of situations, such as handling serve reception and spikes. The overhead pass is also recommended to be used on most free balls coming from opponents, because it is easier to control, is passed at a better angle to set, and is less likely to go over the net.

This chapter focuses on the development of the overhead pass. Simple cues, or keys, are presented followed by basic drills. If you want your players to be proficient at the overhead pass, you must play practice games such as doubles and triples that are designed to allow every player to set. Once players feel comfortable setting randomly (in gamelike situations), they are more likely to use this skill in matches.

CUES

Ready Position   Figure 5.1

✦ Right foot forward	Right foot should be slightly in front of the left foot, shoulder-width apart
✦ Face target ✦ Square to the target	Face the direction you want the ball to go
✦ Big hands	Big curved hands, the ball is round to hands
✦ Shape early	Shape early, hands up at hairline; contact is made above the hairline, elbows out; hands should be in the shape of the ball, thumbs pointing at each other or at the eyes

Arm Action   Figure 5.2

✦ Extend the arms	Extend the arms up (like a basketball chest pass, but at the ceiling)

Hands up early

Shape the ball: Big curved hands that shape around the ball

FIGURE 5.1 Overhead Pass/Set

Extend the arms

Big curved hands, shape the ball

Finger pads on the ball

FIGURE 5.2 Arm Action in the Set

WHY

- ✦ Big hands | Big hands allow you to cover a wide surface area of the ball, which gives you more control and accuracy.
- ✦ Contact on finger pads | Use finger pads instead of finger tips to provide more surface area and more control. (Ball touches all ten fingers.)
- ✦ Hands up early | Gives you more time to prepare to receive the ball.
- ✦ Extension | Full extension of the arms allows the passer to put the ball high and provides power. Also guides the ball in the proper direction.

DRILLS

Throw-Pass-Catch

One player tosses ball underhanded to a partner, and the partner sets back. The tosser catches the set ball and tosses again. Repeat 10 times and switch.

Toss-Pass-Pass

Two players start with an underhanded toss and keep passing back and forth until they reach 20.

In a Group of Three

All passing. Player A passes to player B, who back sets to player C, who passes long to player A. Rotate players after 10 passes to the middle. Switch the player in the middle to give each player a chance to back set. This incorporates three different types of passes—one short, one back set, and one long.

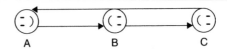

A   B   C

Triangle

Three players set the ball in a triangle. This allows the setter to develop the idea of facing the target. (Players will take the ball over their left shoulder when passing counter clockwise.) Do 45 in one direction; switch directions.

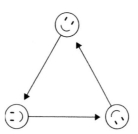

One-Sided or Two-Sided Butterfly

Player A tosses or serves the ball over the net to the passer (player B). Player B makes an underhand pass to the setter (player S), and the setter sets the ball to the spiker (player SP). The passer moves to the setter's position, the setter becomes the spiker, the spiker gives the ball to the coach or serves, and then the player runs back to the passing line. The spiker may approach and catch the ball, or he or she may attack. Repeat until a set number of good pass-set, catch-hit series are completed.

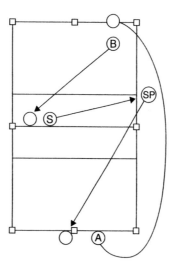

Note: To accommodate 12 players and make the one-sided butterfly competitive, divide the court with an antenna and run six players on each side of it. The first side to reach a set number of perfect series or hits wins.

Four-Corner Setting

A player is in each corner of the court, and they practice setting their partners across the court. After they set, they just follow the ball to the next spot. They can be as close to each other as needed, depending on skill level. Develop a pattern they need to follow. This drill can also be used with forearm passing.

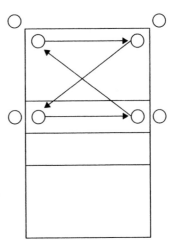

SUMMARY

Use simple cues, such as "hands up early," "feet to ball," and "extend." Once the skill is learned, use drills that all players must set in, to develop proficiency.

CHAPTER 6

Serving

A team must serve consistently to win. Serving aces is the quickest and easiest way to earn points in volleyball. Remember, the keys to success in volleyball are the serve and serve reception.

Proficient players should develop control of the direction and speed of their serves. The serving skill should be not only consistent but aggressive. Regard it as another opportunity to attack. By serving well, a team can make it difficult for its opponents to run their offense, which increases the team's ability to score.

There are four things that make a serve difficult to pass:

1. Velocity. The faster the serve, the less time your opponents have to decide who is taking it and move to intercept it. Because of the speed of the ball, if it is mishandled (shanked, too tight a pass, etc.), teammates have to react quicker and the potential for disaster is greater.

2. Position (where you serve the ball). Seaming players (going between them) creates a situation where two people have to decide who will pass the ball. If the ball is served directly at someone, there are fewer decisions to make. Adding more people to the decision process increases the potential for disaster. Deep corner serves are difficult to get to and are more difficult to control. Short serves have a greater opportunity to be passed back over the net, or into it.

3. Type of Serve. Floaters—Most passers do not focus intensely on the ball during its entire flight. A floater changes direction, sliding either up, down, left, or right.

Top Spins—Have English on the ball and will dip to the floor quicker than expected, with a downward spin.

Jump Serves—Come with more speed and a sharper downward angle than players are used to. Jump serves require a quicker decision and reaction with an unexpected and difficult trajectory to play.

4. Choice of Serve. The larger a repertoire of serves a player has, the less prepared his or her opponents will be. Mixing serves up adds the element of surprise and hinders the opponent's ability to anticipate and be ready.

To place emphasis on the importance of the serve, either add or take away points in drills or games for serving prowess, or lack of it (aces or misses). To improve a team's serving, coaches should take themselves out of the serving drills as quickly as possible. The more they serve, the less serving practice their players have. When coaches are not involved in drills, they are available to give more feedback and cues to their players.

Make sure players have many successful attempts by starting close to the net and moving back as their skill improves. Before long, they may even be jump serving!

Ready Position   Figure 6.1

✦ Bow and arrow	Hitting arm drawn back, similar to drawing the string back in archery
✦ Stand sideways	Left foot forward and pointing at the target
✦ Hold ball in one hand	Ball in left hand and up in front of hitting shoulder
✦ Hitting elbow up	Even or above shoulder height

Hitting Action

✦ Precise toss	Two to three feet in front of hitting arm, extend hand out and up with ball
	Float toss—no spin
✦ Step-toss-hit (heel of hand)	Reach, watch hand hit ball (See Figure 6.2.)
✦ Swing to target	Bow-and-arrow swing
✦ Like throwing a ball	Heel of hand to target (See Figure 6.3.)

Elbow up in bow-and-arrow position

FIGURE 6.1 Ready Position for Serve

Step-toss-hit

Right-arm swing is
like throwing a ball

FIGURE 6.2   Precise Toss

WHY

Ready Position

✦ Bow and arrow	Keeps elbow high, ready to hit ball.
✦ Stand sideways	More power to the serve, weight transfer from back to front foot.
✦ Face target	Twisting action of torso creates torque, which increases power—similar to throwing a ball.
✦ Left foot forward and pointing at the target	When your foot is pointed at the target, your hips and shoulder are pointing at the target.
✦ Hold ball in one hand	Simplifies the serve.
✦ Ball in the left hand and in front of hitting shoulder	Eliminates extra movement and allows for accurate and consistent contact of the ball. If ball is tossed on left side of body, the hitting hand will be lower on contact (ball into the net) and the crossing action will force the ball to be directed to the left, out of bounds.
✦ Hitting elbow up	Timing to contact is more efficient.

Heel of hand
to target

Hit ball with
open hand, arm
fully extended

FIGURE 6.3 Bow-and-Arrow Swing

Hitting Action

◆ Precise toss	Simplifies minimum timing, decreases decision making.
◆ Step-toss-hit (heel of hand)	Gives speed to the ball.
◆ Swing to target	Directs power through the ball, controls direction of the serve.
◆ Like throwing a ball	
◆ Have a routine you do each time you serve, like a free-throw routine	Routines develop the same motor programs for consistency.

Cues for different types of serves

1. Floater serve (like a knuckleball in baseball)
   - Toss in front of right side
   - Strike ball with flat hand
   - Hit straight through the ball
   - No follow-through
2. Top-spin serve
   - Toss ball closer to body

- Step under ball
- Hit the ball and bring your hand over the top
- Follow through
- If hit correctly, ball should drop quickly on the other side of the net with a forward spin

3. Jump serve
   - Toss ball with serving hand
   - Toss ball above your head and in front of you
   - Arm swing and approach is the same as for the spike

DRILLS

Serve at the Wall

Player picks a target above net height on wall. After contacting the ball, player follows through hand at spot.

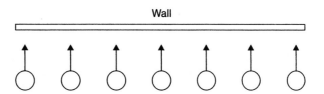

Serve from the Attack Line with a Partner

Have players move back as they develop consistency. Work on control also. Have players hit through the ball and follow through at their partners with their hitting hand. If they are successful serving the ball over the net and to their partner, they may take one big step back each time until they reach the end line.

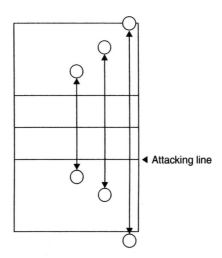

Serve and Chase

The server's goal is to serve 10 in a row. (Good warm-up or conditioning drill.) After they serve the ball over the net, they run to the opposite side of the court, retrieve a ball, and serve again. Repeat.

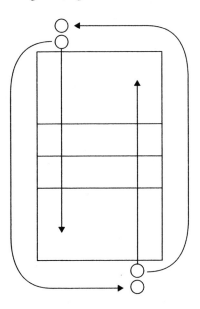

Butterfly Serve Receive

Players serve from various spots on the court behind the end line, and passers receive and pass 15 good passes to targets from three serve-receive positions on the court, starting with number 1. After they have 15 good passes to target, all passers move to court position 2. To practice randomly, players should move to a new position after each play, following the path of the ball; that is, server moves to the opposite side of the court and passes. Passer moves to the target, and the target catches the ball and moves to serve on the same side of the court.

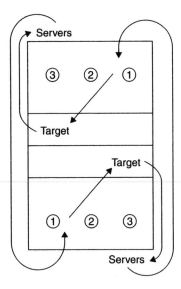

King/Queen of the Court

One team of 3 players is on the king's/queen's court. Team S is on the opposite side, with the rest of the teams behind them outside the court. Team S serves the ball and begins the rally. If team X wins the rally, they get one point and stay to play the next rally. Team S retrieves ball and moves to the back of the line on their side of the court. If team S wins the rally, team X is off and moves to the end of the line of the opponent's court. Team S runs under the net to the king's/queen's court. As soon as all 3 are in the court, the next team of 3 serves. Points may be earned only on king's/queen's court. If players miss their serves in king/queen of the court, have a consequence; for example, their team loses one point. (For more about king/queen of the court, see Chapter 14.)

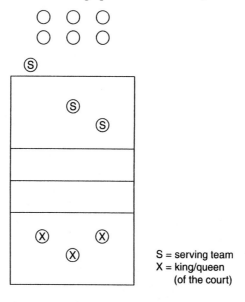

S = serving team
X = king/queen
(of the court)

SUMMARY

Have serving contests and penalties or rewards. Remind the players to be aggressive with their serving. Serve during different times of practice to better simulate a game situation. Encourage players and allow them time to learn new serves, like the top-spin or jump serve.

Serves that go in win ball games. Practice in pressure situations. Suggesting that your players focus on a place to serve the ball will improve both their accuracy and consistency, especially during intense situations. If your team misses 2 in a row at practice, have a consequence (examples are push-ups or sit-ups).

CHAPTER 7

Spiking

The spike is one of the most exciting skills in volleyball. That is why it has all the really great nicknames, like *crush*, *kill*, and *hammer*. If executed properly, it terminates a rally and swings the momentum of the match to your team. Very simply, the goal of the attack is to put the ball where the defense isn't. This is very much like a chess game, with moves and counter moves. The offensive goal is to be one step ahead and to keep the defense guessing. The team that has the best outside hitter has a definite advantage (if the team can also pass and serve proficiently).

The meat and potatoes of offense is the outside attack. The spiker coming from the left-front position has the longer approach and the better angle to hit the ball in the court. Because the setter is positioned closer to the right side of the court, the set ball will travel farther to the outside hitter, thus giving the hitter more time to approach the ball. For right-handed hitters, any set coming from their right is termed an *on-hand spike*, and the hitters will be able to hit the ball before it travels across their body. This makes the spike much easier to hit and to aim at a variety of locations on the opponent's court.

Off-hand spikes or attacks are hit from sets coming from the left. These are more difficult because the ball must cross the hitter's body before it can be attacked. Most players try to attack too early (reaching across their body), thus shortening their reach and forcing them to hit only at an angle or into the net.

Quicks (short, fast sets) are used to vary the attacks and to surprise the defense. The backcourt spike (attacker must jump from behind the attack line) adds another surprise element, utilizing the better hitters when they are in the back row. It also gives the defense an attack they are not used to taking (so they are more likely to miss-hit it). The unexpected setter attacks confuse the defense even more. Smart, consistent hitting is much more productive than a powerful kill right at a defender or into a block. Control is key, and timing is everything.

One of the major problems for players in spiking is being available or transitioning back to be ready to attack. Once the players learn the approach, it is suggested that all spiking drills be started at the net (to transition) or from a pass. This is much more gamelike and will transfer better to a real game situation. Remember, always make drills as gamelike as possible.

Following are some major problem areas to be aware of.

1. Running under the ball. The ball should be in front of the body when spiking. Many players will contact the ball above their heads, or even behind them. It is very difficult, if not impossible, to direct the ball down into the court from this angle.

2. **Not lining up with the ball.**   To get the maximum amount of power and to direct the ball in a variety of directions, the ball should be in front of the hitting arm. If the hitting arm is the right one, and the ball is on the left side of the body, the contact point will be lower and the hit will most likely be to the left. Because the contact point of the hand and ball are lower (reaching across the body), many of the hits will go into the net.

3. **Slow approach.**   Slow, faster, fastest; short, longer, longest. These are the keys for the approach. Don't let players kill their jumps by running in and stopping before they jump.

4. **Poor vertical jump and closed hitting position.**   Players tend to jump crooked and not open up to the setter or the ball if they do not swing the nonhitting arm up and point to the ball.

These are just a few tips to get you going.

CUES

These are geared for right-handed players; left-handed players do the opposite.

Hand Action   Figure 7.1

✦ Big hand

Fingers apart, hand open and firm

Hand in shape of ball

Arms out at waist

Elbows by waist

Right foot forward

FIGURE 7.1   Spiking Cues

Four-Step Approach   Figure 7.2a ◆ Figure 7.2b

There are four steps. Right, left, right, left. (Angular approach)

◆ Right foot forward	
◆ Small, bigger, biggest	Size and speed of steps increase until the last hop
◆ Slow, faster, fastest	
◆ Second step on spiking line	Swing starts on second step
◆ Arms forward (not up), back, up	No higher than waist to start
	Swing back as far as possible
◆ Brake step	The last step with the left foot is turned almost parallel with the net to the setter, shoulder length apart from the right foot in a staggered hop—(coming down quickly after right foot)
◆ Bow-and-arrow arm swing	Elbow above shoulder

Timing   Figure 7.3

◆ First step when ball is set	Trust eyes, do not guess
◆ Contact ball high and in front	
◆ Fast arm swing	Powerful wrist snap (whiplike)

Arms all the way back
at shoulder level

FIGURE 7.2a   Four-Step Approach

Hitting elbow high

Bow-and-arrow arm swing

FIGURE 7.2b Correct Spike Form

Hand open and firm, fingers apart

Focus on ball

Fast arm swing

FIGURE 7.3 Timing

Hand Action

+ Hand forms shape of ball
+ Fingers apart

Gives the player more surface area on ball, which results in better ball control.

Approach

+ R-L-R-L
+ Four-step approach

Taking four steps allows the player to adjust to the ball (e.g., inside or outside). It allows the player to get anywhere on the court. It increases speed, which converts to higher vertical jump.

+ Arms forward—back—forward

Eliminates unneeded motion and helps the player jump higher. The arms are 10 percent of the body weight, and throwing the arms straight up will help the player get higher.

+ Arm swing starts low in front

If players start with a high "cheerleader" swing, they will be slower approaching and hitting. It will be difficult for them to hit quicks.

+ Bow-and-arrow arm action

Keeps the elbow up and helps players with torque when they hit.

+ Brake

Turning last step with left foot in an almost parallel position with net will stop the forward progress of the body and help eliminate broad jumping into the net. It has a dual propose of also opening the body to the set, which helps with visibility and increases torque and power of the spike.

Timing

+ First step when ball is set

Allows players to move directly to an intercept course with the set.

+ Contact ball high and in front

Allows the player to hit the ball down into the court and above the height of the net.

+ Fast arm swing

Allows the player to hit the ball harder. Be aware that sometimes players drop their elbows to try and hit the ball harder.

You Go, I Throw

Players begin their approach with their second step on the spiking line, and the coach tosses the ball if they have performed the proper approach. The players will need to come to the coach. The coach tosses the ball as they jump. Players should jump a couple of feet back from the net and directly in front of the coach. The toss is only high enough for the hitter to swing at, eliminating the timing element. Coaches need to make sure the toss is not tight to the net. It should be one to two feet away from the net to allow the spiker room to swing without hitting the net.

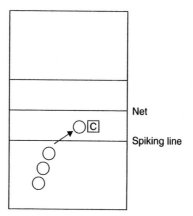

I Throw, You Go

The coach underhand tosses the ball to the outside two to three feet above the net and one to two feet away from the net. The hitters start off the court to approach the outside set. Tip: Attackers begin the approach as soon as the ball is tossed or set.

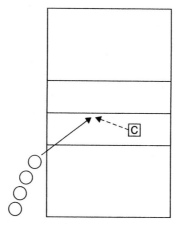

Coach Tosses Ball

The coach is standing in the back-row position and tosses balls to the setter, who sets the ball high and outside.

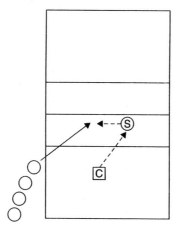

Three Line Set-Hit

The coach tosses to the setter, who then sets to one of the three hitters. Hitters stay until they hit. After hitting, they shag their balls and go to a different line. To modify this drill, passers can be brought in, and the coach can go to the other side of the court and toss or serve. If there are two nets, the coach can make this a competition, and the first side to hit 10 in the court wins.

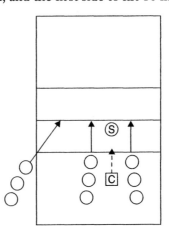

ADVANCED ATTACKS

The idea behind the spike is to beat the block and hit the ball to the floor. This can be accomplished by using faster attacks. Often these are called *quick attacks*. Commonly they are called ones, twos, threes, or slides.

A one is attacked close to the setter, and the concept is that the hitter is in the air before the setter is setting and attacks the ball quickly out of the setter's hands. This spike can also be performed behind the setter and is called a *back one*. If your middle hitter is quick enough, he or she can go from either right to left or left to right. Experiment with your setter and hitter. The timing is the tricky part, and the setter needs to get the ball quickly to the hitter. This requires extra practice on both the setter's and hitter's parts.

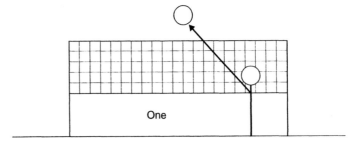

One

Here are a few tips to improve the success of a one attack:

- Attacker must be able to see the pass to the setter to judge the speed of the approach.
- Attacker must jump before setter touches the ball.

- Attacker should take off on his or her jump before being even with the setter and should be lined up with the setter's extended arms so that he or she is hitting the ball right out of the setter's hands.
- A common fault of the attacker hitting a one is jumping too close to the net and in front of the setter, thus hitting the ball from behind or above the head instead of the preferred position, which is in front of them.

The timing of the two-set is a little slower than the one. The hitter should be on the second step of his or her four-step approach when the ball is touched by the setter. This ball is set higher than for the one, but lower than the outside set.

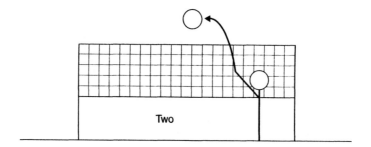

Two

The three has the same timing as the one but is farther away from the setter. Once again, the idea is to beat the block. The hitter should be up early, and the ball needs to be delivered quickly.

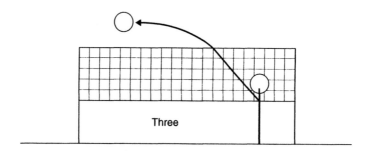

Three

The slide is so named because the player slides behind the setter and hits the ball off one foot, or left-handed players can slide in front of the setter, going from right to left. This is like a layup in basketball. The knee that is up is the same as the hitting arm. The timing is like a two-set. The attacker should be even with the setter on the second step. Slides can be attacked from different heights depending on the skill of the setter and hitter.

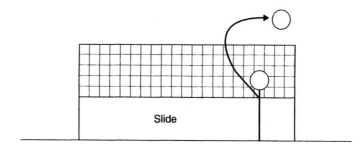

Slide

It is most beneficial for the middle hitters to be able to accomplish these spikes, though all players should learn them. These sets can also be used in various combinations to try to deceive or confuse the defense. The main goal of quick sets is to avoid having two blockers opposing the attack. Ideally, for the offense no blocks or a one-on-one situation would develop.

SUMMARY

Continue to pay close attention to the correctness of your players' footwork, position of their jumps to the ball, and arm swings throughout the season. Once the spike is learned incorrectly, it is very difficult to change, and there is greater risk of injury. If spikers are "goofy footed" (e.g., right-handed players ending their approach on the right foot), they are more likely to experience back pain and damage their rotator cuff. Ask for and demand correct form in your players' execution of the spiking skill from the beginning. To sum up spiking: Encourage your players to attack everything they can!

CHAPTER 8

Individual Defense

Your team's ability to keep the ball alive will increase their chances of winning matches. Few things are more disheartening to an opposing team than having their best hitter dug, and nothing changes momentum quicker than a great dig. There are things you can teach your players about defense, but it really comes down to their desire to not let the ball hit the floor. Great defensive players hate to let the hitters win and will do anything to get the ball up.

A player's defensive repertoire should include a variety of skills in addition to the forearm pass. High- and low-ball skills are needed to handle the different attacks, such as the run to, the sprawl, the pancake, the fist, and the tomahawk. A defensive dig doesn't have to be pretty to be effective, just up and playable. The best defensive specialists know how to hit the floor without injury and aren't afraid to. Hesitation is out, and reflexive reactions are in. "You won't know unless you go" is a prompt coaches use to encourage defensive players to try for every ball. If players do this, they will be surprised at how many "impossible" balls they do get.

CUES

Preparation   Figure 8.1

✦ Feet apart, arms ready	Feet about shoulder width apart and arms out in front about waist high
✦ Ball, setter, ball, hitter	Watch the ball (no higher than apex), setter, ball (then look ahead to its height), and finally the hitter; they will show you where they are going to hit the ball; watch their shoulders and approach
✦ Take big steps	Move quickly to the ball
✦ Stay low	Closer to the ground, more time to play the ball

Dig/Forearm pass   Figure 8.2

✦ Platform underneath ball	Be able to get the ball up in the air
✦ Absorb shock of spike	Cushion the ball

Arms like a wall

Platform
underneath
the ball

Feet wider than
shoulder width

FIGURE 8.1   Preparation for the Dig

Anticipate
spike

Arms
extended

Platform
underneath
ball

FIGURE 8.2   Dig/Forearm Pass

Sprawl   Figure 8.3

* Take a big step to the ball   Move quickly to the ball
* Stay low and turn right   Closer to the ground, more time to play
  knee out   the ball
* Hit ball, then sprawl

Get close to
the floor

Chin up

Big step

FIGURE 8.3   Sprawl

+ Extend the arms
+ Get under the ball and keep
  arms in front of you

Pancake   Figure 8.4

+ Like the sprawl	Body position on floor is same as sprawl
+ Lay body out and extend	
+ Keep hand on the floor, like a pancake	This allows the ball to bounce higher Palm contacting floor

Note: This is used only as a last option when the player can't get to the ball any other way.

Tomahawk   Figure 8.5

+ Both hands together above head	Big surface area, can interlock thumbs, palms out, cupping shape
+ Contact ball above head	
+ Use one fist if needed	Push ball up

Roll

+ Take a big step to the side	Lowers player to floor
+ Get closer to the floor— stretch out	Reach for ball, player's body should be extended

Eyes watch
the ball

Chin up

Keep hand
on the floor,
like a
pancake

FIGURE 8.4   Pancake

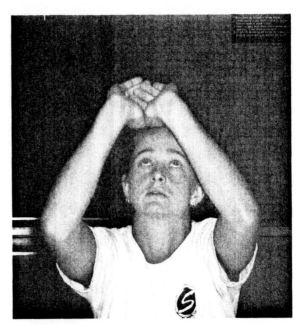

Both hands
together
above head

Make a big
surface area
with hands

Contact ball
above head

FIGURE 8.5   Tomahawk

+ Roll over your left shoulder if moving to the right

+ Roll over your right shoulder if moving to your left

+ Like a backward somersault

+ Go fast or you will get stuck

Keep head laying on extended arm when rolling over top shoulder

WHY

Preparation

+ Watch the ball, setter, ball, and hitter

Once the ball is out of contact with the player, it is not going to change direction. So it is a waste of time watching it. Instead look ahead to where the ball is going and pay attention to what the opponent is doing to prepare to hit the ball. This will give the defender more information about the direction, speed, and type of attack.

+ Anticipate spike, makes the player think ahead

+ Feet apart, arms ready

Allows the player to move quickly around the court.

Dig/Forearm pass

+ Absorb shock of spike   Dissipates the force of the ball.
+ Platform underneath ball   Gets the ball in the air.

Sprawl

+ Anticipate spike

Keeps the player expecting the hit.

+ Big step—move quickly to the ball

The player can cover more area quickly (will also lower body closer to floor).

+ Stay low, closer to the ground

Gives the player more time to play the ball (lessens impact with floor).

+ Hit ball, then sprawl

First priority is to get the ball.

+ Turn right knee out—take a big step to the ball

Prevents injury, floor contacts fat part of leg instead of bone.

+ Get under the ball and keep arms in front of you

Keeps the ball in the air and in play.

Pancake

+ Hand on the floor, like a pancake (palm touching floor)

Keeps the ball from knocking hand to the ground. Fingers spread wide allows more surface area for the ball to land on.

+ Helping hand

Left hand lowers body to ground, decreasing risk of injury.

Tomahawk

+ Both hands together above head   More surface area for the ball.

✦ Contact ball above head	Last resort to keep the ball in play on a deep attack.
✦ Use one fist	Last resort to keep the ball in play.

Roll

✦ Take a big step to the side	Will be able to cover more defensive area.
✦ Get close to the floor	Lowers body closer to floor, reduces injury.
	The lower to the floor, the more time to play the ball.
✦ Go fast or get stuck	Keeping the momentum going will help get players back on their feet quicker to play the next ball.
✦ One motion	

DRILLS

Practice each skill without the ball.

Partner Drill

Have partners toss and perform each skill. Digger should execute the skill first without the ball so tosser can see where to toss the ball to make the digger extend. Have partners toss the ball low and far away to make the digger stretch to get the ball.

5-5-5

Before practice each day have players warm up with five rolls to the right, five sprawls or pancakes to the front, and five rolls to the left. In order for the dig to count, it has to be a playable up (as high as the top of the net).

Coach to Hit at One Line

Have three people in line; the rest of the team shags and encourages. After the first player digs the ball, he or she goes to end of line. Have a set amount, such as ten playable ups, before players trade. Coach throws to each sideline, short, deep, or hard spike. Defensive players learn to read attackers' swings and shoulders to figure out where the ball will go.

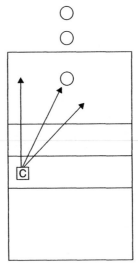

Coach to Hit at Three Lines

The player who digs, shags the ball and returns to the back of the line.

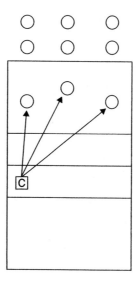

Six-Hit Partner Pepper

Two players try to continuously hit the following—one tomahawk, one fist, the other fist, and three other hits. They do not have to be in that order, but players can only hit those. Keep track of how many in a row.

Tomahawk Drill

Three players stand in a triangle using only the tomahawk two-handed or one-handed hit. See how many hits in a row they can get. This increases players' ballhandling control and gives them confidence to use this skill in a game.

Get It Up

Three hitting lines, no blockers, three back-row defensive players. This can be a team effort or individual effort, depending on goals.

Team effort.   After three combined playable ups in a row, the team is out of the drill, and three more players take their places. If they do not touch a ball, they go back to zero.

Individual effort.   When a player achieves three playable ups in a row, he or she can go over to spiking position and someone else takes his or her place. If players don't touch a ball, they start back at zero.

Keep It Up

Players are in teams of three. As long as the coach does not have to move, the team stays on the court. See how many digs in a row a team can get. At the conclusion of the drill, see who had the most digs to the coach in a row; they are the winners.

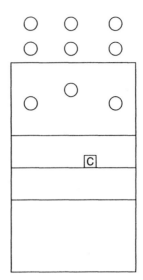

Defense Hitting

Coach is on the other side of the net. There is a permanent setter and a few hitters who will rotate. The coach hits at two diggers, and they stay until they get three dig, set, hits, then they rotate. The defenders are watching the hitter (coach) and not the ball. The first team to 15 wins. A point is earned when there is a dig, set, hit.

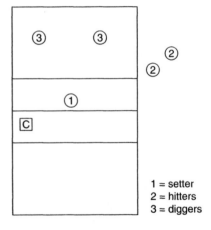

1 = setter
2 = hitters
3 = diggers

SUMMARY

Defense is played low to the ground. There are reasons for this; it gives players a longer time to play the ball, and it does not hurt as much when they have to hit the floor. Remind your diggers that they do not need to swing their arms. If they do, they are adding more force to the ball and it will rocket off of their arms. Also remind players never, never, never to quit going after a ball. If you can touch it, you can dig it. You'll never know, unless you go!

CHAPTER 9

Blocking

Blocking is a difficult skill to master. Even if your team is a great blocking team, they will not block every ball; they will not even block a majority of the attacks. The hitters always have the advantage. But the blocker's presence will direct the ball to certain parts of the court in the same way that a large rock rising out of a stream divides the water to flow to one side. Blockers need to be disciplined and realize that even though they may not touch the ball, they are protecting part of the court, allowing their team to defend a smaller and more specific area.

To a blocker, attitude is everything. Hustle and aggressiveness are the two key characteristics of a great blocker. "Owning" or controlling the net play is another aspect of good blocking. The blocker intimidates the attackers by constant patrolling and aggressively attacking any ball that comes near the net.

Performing the blocking steps in prepractice warm-ups helps players' execution become a natural, unthinking habit. Practice blocking on most attack drills to make it more gamelike for the spikers and to give the front row more experience blocking. Use every opportunity to practice this crucial defensive skill.

CUES

If going to the left, step with the left foot first. If going to the right, step with the right foot first.

Figure 9.1

+ Keep hands up at eye level in front of body

Chin down for peripheral vision
Hands are no lower than shoulders of player

+ Get loaded

Knees are bent as players move (slightly crouching)

+ Big hands

Covers more area

+ Hands up as if playing a piano

Fingers are firm and spread—Mickey Mouse ears

+ Stance is off the net

Approximately fingertip-to-elbow distance back from net

Timing   Figure 9.2

+ Ball, hitter, setter, ball, hitter

Watch what is going on on the other side of the court. Look where the ball is going.

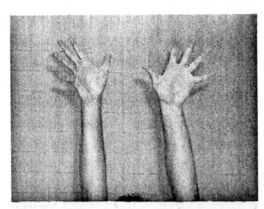

Fingers firm and
spread—like Mickey
Mouse ears or playing
a piano

FIGURE 9.1   Block

Angle hands
into opposite
court

Seal net with arms

FIGURE 9.2   Block Timing

✦ Penetrate	Reach over the net and angle hands into opponent's court
✦ Seal the net with body	Arms should be close enough to the top of net so that a ball cannot come between the player and the net. Tip: do not swing arms down; instead, reach over the net and hold. This improves timing and decreases the possibility of a net foul.

Footwork

✦ Quick step/ Two-step approach	One step (right or left), jump together

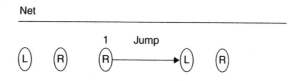

✦ Three-step approach	Big step (right or left), crossover, jump together

Net

✦ Five-step approach	Combination of both, two-step and then three

Net

WHY
If going to the left, step with the left foot first. If going to the right, step with the right foot first.

✦ Keep the hands up at eye level	Keeps the players' hands up and out of the net (not swinging).
✦ Get loaded	Allows players to stay balanced and ready to move to the block. Eliminates time needed to bend down; hence, a quicker response.

✦ Hands up as if playing a piano—Mickey Mouse ears	Creates a greater surface area to stop the ball. The quicker the set, the higher the hands.
✦ Stance is off-net	Too close forces arms to be straight up instead of at a forward angle.

Timing

✦ Ball, hitter, setter, ball, hitter	Helps players know in which direction the ball is going to be hit. Helps players have a specific focus. Players can anticipate what will happen ahead of the ball.
✦ Penetrate	Sends the ball straight down to the other side and aids in keeping the ball on the opponent's side instead of rolling down players' arms
✦ Seal the net with body	The blocked ball will go down on the opponent's side and not between blockers and net.
✦ Hips into the court	Square body to court—prevents balls from being blocked out of bounds.

Footwork

✦ Quick step	One-two quick step allows the blocker to move efficiently along the net and cover distance fast.
✦ Three-step approach	Three steps allows the blocker to move efficiently along the net and cover greater distance.
✦ Five-step approach	Three-two allows the blocker to move efficiently along the net and cover the greatest distance.

DRILLS

Footwork

In pairs, across the net from each other and mirroring actions, players do various footwork patterns along the net.

Six Trips

A. 5-3-3
B. 5-2-2
C. 3-3-3
D. 3-2-2
E. Q3-3-3
F. Q3-2-2

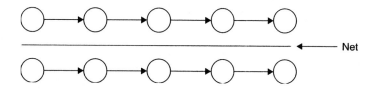

Two Coaches and Tables

Coaches are positioned on outside hitting positions standing on tables. Some players are shagging and handing balls to them. Players are lined up in the middle of the court with one blocker opposite each coach. One coach slaps ball, and the middle blocker moves to outside blocker and attempts to block ball hit by coach. As soon as the middle player moves to block, the next player moves up from the middle line and the second coach slaps the ball. After the pair have attempted to block the ball, the outside blocker goes to the end of the line, the middle blocker moves to outside, and play continues.

Ball, Hitter, Setter, Ball, Hitter

Two players block ball off of one hitting line. They are concentrating not on watching the ball's flight, but instead on looking ahead to the intended target.

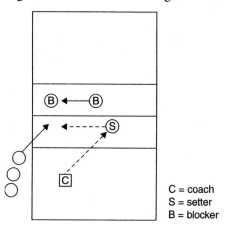

C = coach
S = setter
B = blocker

Players block ball off of three hitting lines.

Two-man block outside. Option of three-man block middle.

Two-man block where ball is set. Third block pulls off net to defensive spot. Practice ball, setter, ball, hitter.

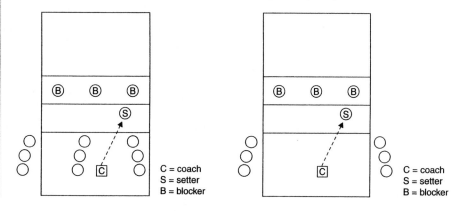

C = coach
S = setter
B = blocker

Wave Through

The setter tosses a ball to the coach, who forearm passes the ball back to the setter. The setter sets, hitters hit, and volleyball ensues. Teach ball, hitter, setter, ball, hitter (watch blockers' eyes). Go for a certain period of time, then the offense hits until they lose 15. Quick score. Wave through.

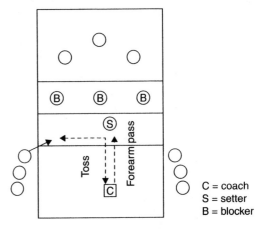

Rapid Fire

There are three hitting lines. Coach or other player tosses ball to setter. One player blocks all three positions. Three trips up and back, consecutively (as players' conditioning improves, add more trips). Blocker starts outside left, then middle, then right, middle and left. Continue rapidly until blocker has made three trips. Work on ball, setter, ball, hitter. Give three points for stuffs, two points for blocks, and one point for touches.

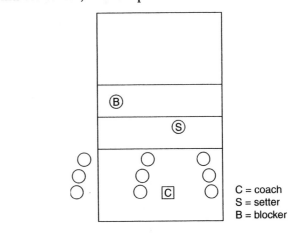

SUMMARY

Your players will likely get frustrated, but remind them that blocking is the most intimidating defensive skill and is crucial for your team's success. Back row defense depends on blocking skills.

CHAPTER 10

Serve Receive

Receiving the serve is crucial to a team's success. It's the most important element in volleyball. A team can have the best hitter in the league, but if they can't pass the ball from a serve, that hitter will have very few opportunities to attack. Because of the magnitude of its importance, at least half of practice every day should be involved with serve and serve receive.

BASIC SERVE-RECEPTION CONCEPTS

Create a Platform

For optimum passing, it is best to have all the keys of underhand passing, but the most important is the platform. No matter what kind of contortions the rest of the body is in, if the platform is there with the correct angle, a perfect pass can be made. A coach can't overemphasize how important the platform is.

Center the Pass in the Middle of the Body

The majority of the world's great passers take the ball in the center of their bodies, with their feet slightly staggered. This allows them to get behind the ball quickly and efficiently.

Get the Feet to the Ball

Players should move to intercept the ball before it gets there. They should be waiting for it. A passer needs to have quick feet to get to the ball early. This is one of the most important aspects to serve reception and one of the greatest faults. Players will often wait until the ball reaches them before they take one step. The butterfly up-and-back drill in Chapter 14 is an excellent one to use to get your players to decide and move quicker.

Simplify Serve Reception

The three most common serve receives are the W (five-person), the box, (four-person), and the three-person. We recommend the three-person. With fewer passers, you have less misunderstanding, fewer decisions that have to be made, and more practice passing serves. The majority of balls are served in the black area of the court (see the diagram on the next page), and most of those are in the center of that (gray area). This area is adequately covered with the three-person serve receive.

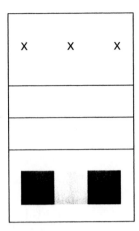

The W puts players in the way and leaves the area of the court that is served at the most (the area inside the circle in the diagram below) in a seam (between two people). It could be used at the beginning levels, where players do not move or make decisions quick enough.

The box, or four-person, again puts a seam right where most of the traffic is (see the diagram below). There is also a question of who should take the short-middle balls and deep-corner serves. There are more people, and more potential miscommunications.

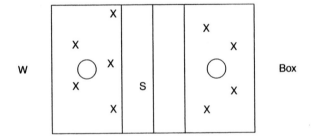

Any of these three styles can be used successfully if they are practiced enough and everyone's responsibilities are made clear. The bottom line is, use what you feel comfortable with, but we will focus on the three-person configuration.

Place the Passers Effectively

Most teams stand too deep. In order to cover the court adequately, home position should be two-thirds of the way back from the net (halfway between the spiking line and the endline). There will have to be slight adjustments made for each server and any alignment maneuvers.

Clarify Players' Responsibilities

Front-row players, usually the middle blocker, should verbally identify the opponent's front-row players and the position of their setter (front row, back row). Setters will communicate their own attack strategy to their teammates. Passers call balls as soon as the ball is served (letting teammates know they are taking the ball), and the rest go call them and open up. This is how they physically acknowledge who is responsible for passing the ball, by backing away a step and turning toward the passer. That way there is no confusion about who is responsible for taking the ball.

Another key to preventing misunderstandings in the serve receive is calling the ball early. When players wait until the last second, either no one attempts to hit the ball, or they all do. Cue players to call the ball before it is over the net.

Have All Players Not Passing the Serve Call "In" or "Out" for the Passer

The passers should be focusing intently on the pass, and they need their teammates' help in judging if it is in or out (especially the hidden players who are usually close to the boundaries of the court).

Clarify Who Should Take Served Balls

It is primarily the person on the left's responsibility to pass the ball when it is served between two players (except the deep serves). The setter is to the right of the left and middle passers (or two-thirds of the court). It is natural to pass to the right when the left passer moves to the right to contact the ball. The only exception is deep serves. The player on the right is in a better position to pass this ball (with a backward bump to the setter) than the player on the left is. Your players' passing responsibilities can be explained by having them point their right hands at a two o'clock position and their left hands at a seven o'clock position. Everything within those arms to the player to the left of them is theirs.

Use Effective Passes

The best kind of pass is low, a couple of feet above and off of the net carrying a small amount of spin. The higher the pass, the harder it is to set, and the slower the offense. Passes that are too tight on the net decrease the setter's options, sometimes forcing a tip, which most likely will be blocked because it is expected.

Guide Players to Err Away from the Net

It is better for players to pass to the spiking line than over the net. If passers are going for a difficult serve, it would be more advantageous for them to hit the ball to the setter at the 3-meter line than have it passed over the net and have no attack at all (and have it crushed back at them). Have your team keep the ball on their side to attack. In practices, penalize the balls passed over the net.

Clarify Where Team Members Should Be Focusing

All players, even those who do not pass and who are transitioning to attack, should focus on the server. All team members must keep the ball in sight the entire time it is on their side of the net.

Put Players Who Are Not Passing to Good Use

Have players stay out of the passer's line of sight. Too many times, players will inadvertently block the passer's view of the incoming serve. If opponents are observant, they will use these people to serve over. Have players duck down or move.

Start Front-Row Attackers Who Are Not Passing Off The Net

There is no advantage to keeping front-row attackers at the net during serve reception. Pull outside hitters back and to the sidelines to clear the view for the passers and to prepare for quick attacks. But don't pull the middle blocker too far back, because he or she can get in the way of a short serve and hinder the passer's vision. One exception would be if the player has to stay there to prevent overlapping.

Practice the Serve Receive with a Set Lineup

Players need to get used to who is passing next to them. Each person covers different territory, and some are more aggressive than others.

If you are stacking or moving people out of their normal rotation pattern to serve receive, they need to know who they can overlap and who they can't. This complicates passing and must be practiced to prevent a possible side-out caused by misalignment. This also prevents you from subbing freely. Players must know the positions they go in for well and the possible overlapping situations.

ALIGNMENT

To place your players in their optimum positions on the court, you need to understand the alignment or overlapping rule. The serve receive is governed by this rule, which is very similar in all levels of play. Once you understand it, you can then manipulate it to your advantage. The rule is:

> At the moment of serve, players have to be in their correct serving order and have at least part of one foot closer to their sideline, center or endline than the adjacent player's two feet. (National Federation of State High School Associations, 1999)

Right and left players only have two people to worry about—the ones directly next to them. Middle players have three. Left back has to be concerned about overlapping with left front and middle back. Middle front should be aware of left front, right front, and middle back (see the diagram).

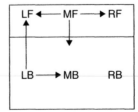

Stacking

What if you want to move your left front (who is your second-best passer) to the right-back position to serve receive (then you would have your three best players passing)? Okay. The LF must stay above the LB and to the left of the MF. This is called stacking, because the three front-row players are stacked to the right side of the court, and the three back-row players are arranged to the left of the court.

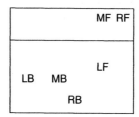

Notice the position of the right-back player. When you have a player that you don't want to use as a passer, you "hide" that player; in other words, take him or her out of the serve receive. The right back is hidden. Tip: If you can possibly place the hidden player in the corner of the court, he or she has an excellent perspective from which to call the endline and the sidelines in or out for the passers.

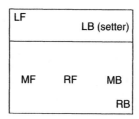

Stacking works great when your left back is a setter and you want to move him or her as close to the setting position as possible (left back is the most difficult position for the setter to come from during the serve receive). Move the middle and right front back to pass and leave the left front in the corner (a left stack). Now move all the back-row players to the right (keep them in order); this is a right stack. To avoid misalignment, the middle front has to be closer to the centerline than the middle back, and the setter must stay below the left-front player. The rest is easy. Now, after the opponent contacts the serve, anyone can move anywhere on their side of the court, or the extended boundaries.

Specializing

Your team is composed of specialists (players who are better at a certain skill than others). Setters are specialists, and there are defense specialists and attack specialists. So why not have passing specialists? Since about 60 percent of the serves go to the number six (middle-back) position on the court, why not have your best passer there and increase the number of good passes? If your top three to four passers receive the serve every time, you will give up fewer aces to your opponents and increase your passing percentage, which will improve your offense.

It is possible, within the overlapping rules, to place your number-one passer in the middle-back portion of the court (number six) in all six rotations (depending on what your lineup is). Of course, three of those times they will be front row and attacking, but if you practice it enough, they will be able to pass and go right into hitting. Coming out of the back row from passing to hitting will give them a number of spiking options and attacks at different positions on the net.

Why not use the best as much as possible? Once you have decided on a lineup and are working on your serve receive, your passing specialists will improve even more rapidly, because they are getting much more practice at passing than their teammates. Look at your match statistics. You will see that the player who is in the number-six position on the court is receiving two to three times more balls than anyone else. Because of all this extra practice, he or she will improve even more.

An example of how to manipulate the positioning of your best passers is included with the next concept.

Where to Place the Setter

Your setter touches more balls than any other player on the team. That means the setter uses more energy running than anyone else. It is critically important for the setter to be in the right position to take the pass. It is possible to place your setter close to the seam of the number-two and number-three areas of the court (the player's home setting position) in all six rotations. Doing this will reduce the amount of movement the setter is required to do (decreasing his or her fatigue) and will increase setting accuracy. It will also give your opponents one less target to serve at (when the setter is transitioning) to try to cause problems with your serve receive.

Where you place players in your line-up will determine how often you can place your setter and best passer where they need to be. If you choose to have your best passer and setter in their ideal positions each rotation during the serve receive, the number-one passer must be placed two people away from the setter. In other words, if the setter is the right back in your lineup (serving), your number-one passer must be either middle front or left back.

Here is one example of a possible serve reception lineup in each of the six rotations. In at least five out of the six rotations, all players are in their optimum positions. Only one time do you have to compromise and either put your second-best passer in the middle (the setter goes to his or her best spot) or put your best passer in the middle (his or her best spot), and the setter transitions from the front-left side of the court. It is your preference.

You have an extra benefit if your best passer is a middle blocker, because that player will come straight to the middle front from the middle-back spot, unless you want to run combination plays or swings. Put your best player in his or her best position as often as you can and your team will profit.

This example is based on a 5–1 offense (one setter) and three-person serve reception (see the diagram). The concepts will be the same in any type of serve-receive formation or offense.

O1   outside attacker number one (your best)
M1   middle blocker number one (your best)
S   setter
OP   left-side attacker, the player who is opposite the setter
O2   outside attacker number 2 (your second-best)
M2   middle blocker number two (your second-best)

Notations accompany each rotation to alert you to the players who are in danger of overlapping (moving the most from their original serving order). A suggestion to prevent unnecessary overlapping calls by the officials: If you have a complicated serve-receive lineup using stacks, it is a good idea to show the offi-

Serve-Receive Chart _____

(circle: M2, S, O2, M1, OP, O1)

_____
_____
_____
_____

1

O1	M2	S

Serving order

OP	M1	O2

M2   (S)

O1 [M1] O2
OP

Serve reception

O1 must stay left of M1 and above OP.

2

OP	O1	M2

M1	O2	S

OP   M2   (S)

O1 [M1] O2

Setter must be below M2 and to the right of O2.
O1 has to be above O2 and to the right of OP.

3

M1	OP	O1

O2	S	M2

OP   (S)

O1
O2 [M1]
M2

M1 has to stay above O2 and to the left of OP.
S must be between O2 and M2 and below OP.
O1 has to stay in front of M2 and to the right of OP.
Notice an added benefit in the first three rotations. The three passers are the same (increases consistency) four times out of all six rotations.

4

O2	M1	OP

S	M2	O1

O2   (S)

OP   O1
[M1]
M2

This is a stack—front-row stack is left and back row- right.
M1 must stay between O2 and OP and above M2.
S has to be below O2 and left of M2.
OP must be above O1 and to the right of M1.

5

S	O2	M1

M2	O1	OP

(S)
O2

O1 [M1] OP
M2

Setter must be above M2 and to the left of O2.
O1 has to be below O2 and between OP and M2.

6

M2	S	O2

O1	OP	M1

M2   (S)

O1 [M1] O2
OP

M1 has to stay below O2 and to the right of OP.

cials a copy of your serve reception formation in each rotation before the match begins.

Copy the serve-receive chart in the appendix of this book. Use different line-ups and arrange your serve reception formation several different ways until you find the one that gives you the best options in the most places.

SUMMARY

The most important way to improve your team is to help them become proficient at serve reception. Since aces are the quickest and easiest points to get, preventing them by passing well is one of the best and fastest ways to gain an advantage. Use serve reception when you practice setting and spiking to keep everything gamelike and to facilitate better motor-skill transfer. We can't emphasize enough how important this skill is to the success of your team. Drills and games to help in your practices are listed in Chapters 14 and 15.

CHAPTER 11

Offensive Guidelines and Strategies

An offense in volleyball is like the proverbial chain, only as strong as its weakest link. The basic links in an offense are

- Serve reception
- Setting
- Spiking
- Spiker coverage
- Defensive digs (create)

The material from which an offensive chain is constructed comes from the philosophy of probability. This philosophy is simple, but execution is very difficult. To be successful, an offense must be based on probability or percentage. Simply stated, you shouldn't do things you are not good enough to do, and you should capitalize on things you do very well. The idea seems rather straightforward, but many teams do not play as well as they could because either they are unaware of or they do not consider the probability of the success of the choices they make.

A young or inexperienced team will be much more successful if they get very good at a few things, rather than being mediocre at many. In other words, find out what attacks your players are good at or capable of executing and use those extensively. Your players should still practice new techniques to step up a level and add to their repertoire, but the majority of every team's attack practice time should be spent on using what they are good at and making it better.

A team's offense will be the most dominant characteristic it develops. It will most likely determine which athletes will play most often and the nature of their roles on the court. Working on the offense will probably occupy the majority of time during practice, but remember to incorporate attacking off of passing from serve reception. Many teams practice too much on offense and neglect serve reception, then find that they seldom have an opportunity to spike because of poor passing.

The better the pass, the better the offense. The premier teams in the men's NCAA leagues will pass two out of three balls perfectly and will be aced 6 percent or less.

KEY COMPONENTS IN CONSTRUCTING AN OFFENSE SYSTEM

- The offense must be structured around the passing skills of the team. It is impossible to run a more complex or difficult offense than the passing skills allow.

- The offense must maximize the strengths of the individuals. Specialization is the most likely way to achieve this goal.
- The choice of offense must take into consideration the skills of the setter(s) on the team. The setter must be able to technically and mentally master the offense.

Do you have an offensive system and then put players into it, or do you develop a system depending on your players' abilities? Do you always run certain plays or combinations, and are you known for a signature offense? What happens if you just don't have the quick hitters that you've had in the past—do you keep running it anyway? You've already learned that a system should be developed *after* you've seen what players you have to work with. With these overriding general principles in mind, here are the core components for building a successful offense.

PUTTING YOUR LINEUP TOGETHER

What System Are You Going to Play?

There are three major offensive options (and many variations on them). A description of each option follows.

4-2 (Four Hitters, Two Setters)

This is the simplest offensive pattern. The setter sets the ball from the front row to two attackers.

The original 4-2 has the setter moving to the middle of the front row after the serve and setting to two hitters, front and back. Remember, before the next serve, all players must go back to their correct positions in the rotation.

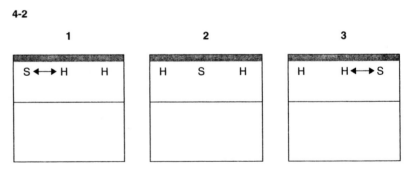

(The next three rotations are the same.)

The international 4-2 has the setter moving to right front and setting to attackers positioned left and middle front. This is an improvement on the original 4-2, because it delivers the ball to two on-hand hitters, whereas the beginning 4-2 had one on-hand and one off-hand hitter. The ball is harder to hit effectively from the off-hand side, because it must cross over the body before it is attacked. The best attacking position is the on-hand side.

International 4-2

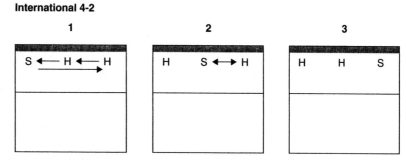

(The next three rotations are the same.)

This is also a superior system to use because setters do not set back as much as they do forward. A back set's accuracy is not as good as a front set's (being a blind set), and the forward-setting motion is easier than the back-setting action. Because of this, the right-front position in the original 4-2 received fewer balls to spike than the on-hand left-side position. Using the international 4-2 will almost double a team's offensive power.

To use this system, you should have two strong setters who are both excellent blockers (they are blocking the opponent's left side or on-hand) and passers. This is an excellent system for beginning programs because of its simplicity.

6-2 (Six Attackers, Two Setters)

This offense always has three hitters in the front row (called a *multiple offense*). Both setters (who are opposite each other in the lineup) will transition from the back row to the front to set after the serve and become attackers when they reach the front row.

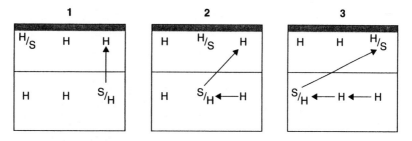

(The next three rotations are the same. The attackers can switch hitting positions, as can the defense.)

If a team has two good setters who are also excellent spikers, this system will work well for them. It is also a good offense for younger teams to use, because it isn't clear which players are going to be the best setters or hitters yet. This allows players to do both until it is decided who is going to specialize in which area and learn the multiple offense system.

The term *multiple offense* was coined to describe an offense that had three front-row attackers, with the setter coming from the back row.

The 6-2 offensive system gives a team the advantage of always having a multiple offense. The disadvantage is that the setters only get half the practice setting and spiking that they normally would. This tends to make them mediocre at both skills unless they are exceptional athletes.

5-1 (Five Spikers and One Setter)

Three rotations will have a multiple offense (three spikers), and three rotations will have only two attackers, with the setter in the front row. One person (the setter) runs, or has control over, the offense.

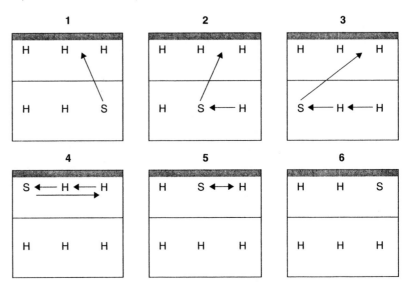

Attackers can switch hitting positions also. And the same goes for the back-row defense players.

The 5-1 offense is popular in high schools and colleges. Under this offense the setter becomes very proficient in assisting kills (because of the number of repetitions). An attacking setter has the added element of surprise, because the opponent doesn't know if he or she will set or hit. Because the setter must play defense when in the back row, if he or she digs the ball, a back-up setter or the right-front player (called an opposite) will have to set the pass. This necessitates having an opposite who is a good, confident setter.

Which Players Are Going to Play Where?

How do you decide where to put your players? This is one of the hardest decisions to make. Here are some ideas that might help you determine that.

Offensive Positional Characteristics

1. Outside (left):

Best spiker	Powerful	Good approach
Excellent control	Aggressive	Correct hitting mechanics

2. Middle:

Quick	Good reflexes	Good jumper
Excellent blocker	Intelligent (placing ball)	Reaches high

3. Opposite (right side):

| Best blocker | Quick hitter | Angle around |
| Confident setter | Left-handed player is ideal | |

4. Setter:

Smart	Quick	Leader (quarterback)
Good hands	Control	Communicator
Left-handed is ideal		

Try to put your closest-to-perfect lineup together with the following considerations:

- Your best outside hitter should start front left. This player gets more attacks because he or she is in the front row more often and longer than all other players.
- Position your best middle hitter with your second-best outside hitter in the front row to balance out your attack.
- The best and most consistent servers should start one, two, three in the service rotation. With your best hitter in the front row, the team will have more opportunities to make points.
- Put your best blocker in the front row, right side. This player will then be facing your opponent's best hitter.
- Place your best passer two positions away from your setter. The passer can pass in the number-six position more often if you do (if you want your setter in the front row every time).
- Start your best defense specialist in the right-back position (playing middle back). Better chance of digging your opponent's number-one attacker's hits.
- Try surrounding your setter with your number-one blocker and your number-one-hitter. This helps when your setter is in the front row and you only have two attackers. It will give your team the best attacking options during the three rotations in which your setter is in the front row. You need to have at least one consistent go-to person in the front row on every rotation.

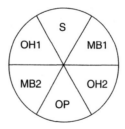

Where Should Your Best Athletes Be?

Many coaches believe that their three best athletes should be their two outside hitters and the opposite. Others argue that your setter is so important for quarterbacking your offensive attack that he or she should be the best. Try to put players in the position that fits them best and that they want to play. They must buy into the role you want them to play in order to give it their all. Studies show that the team with the best outside hitter has a distinct advantage.

Middle Blockers Do Not Have to Be Tall

Too many coaches think they must have their six-foot-plus players in the middle blocking position. Not so, as long as they are good blockers and can act and think quickly.

It Is Best Not to Have Short Setters

Many junior high and high school teams will use short setters because they are quick and have good hands, and coaches need their tall players for spiking. This can be a costly mistake, for the following reasons:

- The front row position that the setter plays is opposite your opponent's best hitter. You should match up your best blocker for the best defensive coverage. You are just asking for trouble if you put your shortest player against your opponent's best hitter, unless your setter has an incredible vertical jump. And even then the setter will have trouble blocking quick hits.
- A taller setter can save many poorly passed balls from serve receive and defense by intercepting them before they go over the net. A tall setter can turn what would have been an overset into an attack on his or her side.
- A taller setter (and one who can jump set) will speed up the offense (how quickly the attackers get the ball).
- Taller setters are usually better attackers. Tips and dumps are quicker.

Because the setter touches more balls than any other player on your team, he or she will have more opportunity to help or hurt you. Saving just a few oversets off of the serve receive usually means the difference of a couple of points each game. That is an important fact to take into consideration.

Don't Overlook the Right-Front Player

Note: This position is also known as the opposite, right side, or off-hand. This player is blocking your opponent's best hitters and should also be hitting one out of every four sets. You need the right-front player to distract, diversify, and help take the heat off of your main on-hand hitter, making that player more productive.

If the right-front player were left-handed, that would be perfect. That would make his or her sets on-hand, and you would then have three on-hand hitters instead of two. (A set coming from this player's on-hand side improves his or her ability to attack.)

Because the majority of sets go to the left side of the court, a defense gets many more repetitions in practices and matches blocking and digging the left-side attack. Because of this, most teams are not as proficient defending the right-side spikes. Take advantage of this, and put one of your best hitters on the right side.

The Outside Hitter Should Be a Strong Power Hitter

Outside hitters don't necessarily need to be as quick as the middles or the setter, because they have more time to approach the set. They will be hitting over half the sets, so they need to be in good condition and consistent.

All Offensive Players Need to Know How to Play Defense

There is no room on your team for a player who can only spike the ball. All players will have to dig and set sometimes, and if your opponents know they are incompetent, they will attack their positions.

Look for Offensive Players Who Have Well-Rounded Skills

The more players your team has who can play all the way around, the more continuity you will have. Momentum is a huge factor in volleyball. Subbing constantly can interrupt that. It is good to have a few core people who can play all six rotations and hold the team together.

Who Is Most Consistent?

What if that spiker can put the ball down better than anyone on your team can, but only one out of four times? If that's the case, substitute the spiker until he or she is more consistent.

Using the serve-receive chart in Chapter 16, experiment with several different lineups to find the best choice. The right lineup can make or break a team. Make sure you use your players' skills to their best advantage.

Once you have chosen your lineup for the season, the following tips will help you use it effectively.

OFFENSE TIPS

- Design your offense to deliver the ball to the best (hottest) hitter the most.

- Your offense must be flexible enough to adapt to different defenses. Coaches tend to teach their players how to attack only against the same defense they use. This is a mistake; it can mentally shake a team up if they are not prepared for a variety of defenses.

- Teach your hitters to be proficient at attacking a variety of sets. Hitters need to feel comfortable attacking from different positions on the net, and they must have enough control to hit the ball to many places on the opponent's court.

- A major element in a successful offense is surprise. Give the defense what they aren't expecting. Attack first and second balls if the opportunity is there. That is one reason setters can have such a high kill average; the defense isn't expecting the attack on the second ball. Everyone tends to get into a 1, 2, 3 rhythm.

- If the other team is expecting a tip off of a tight pass, don't tip. Turn and hit it, or push it deep, or one-hand set it for a quick hit. Don't be predictable; keep the defense guessing. Don't let an opponent know where the set is going. All hitters should be available to add to the confusion (that is, ready to attack).

- Motion attracts blockers and can be used to open up a desired hitter. It is a good tactic to have more than one attacker approaching to distract the defense. The more a blocker has to think, the less time he or she has to react to the set. You could have a back-row player come in for a fake one (quickset) to confuse the defense.

■ It is often desirable to set the gap in front of (or next to) the worst blocker. In other words, where blockers aren't. They have to move to get there.

■ Quick hitters should try to hit so that the opposing middle blocker has to move. This creates more gaps and decreases the possibility of being blocked.

■ Quick hitters should try to be in the air before the ball is set. Combinations around the quick hitters should be second-step sets. Back-row sets should be second-step sets.

■ Setters should jump set as much as possible and especially on all perfect passes. It is wise to help players get really good at a few things. Don't spread your offense too thin. Pick a few plays or types of attacks and perfect them.

■ Better the ball. All players should have a "better the ball" attitude. No matter what type of pass comes to the setter, he or she should put the best ball up for the attacker to hit. No matter what type of set the setter is able to give the hitter, the hitter should do something smart with it. Instruct your players to always put the ball in a smart spot, even a free ball.

Never let your players catch a poor set in practice. Players get poor sets in games, and they need to learn how to make the most of them. Make sure players let the setter know they appreciate good sets. The setter doesn't get the attention the hitters do, and the compliments will spur them on to greater efforts. Also, the setter needs to know the type of sets the hitter likes most. Never let your attacker blame the setter for a poor hit (the set probably came from a poor pass, anyway). Blame won't win championships. Bettering the ball will.

■ How many steps do your attackers take in their approach? Some players start their approaches almost on the endline. For most players that is a little too far back. But the point is that most attackers need a longer approach. Four steps is the average, but that doesn't mean left-side hitters can't take more. The further back they start, the more speed they can get (which converts to a higher vertical) and the better the chance the hitter will be behind the ball, and not under it (which is a major problem with most attackers). A good rule of thumb here is, you want your players to be able to step on the spiking line with three steps left.

What about using a three-step approach for the middle and right-side hitters who have less time to approach the ball? Many successful teams use this to speed up their attack. It works, but it will also decrease the speed of the approach and thus the vertical. Our suggestion is to keep the four-step approach but have hitters start earlier on their approaches. Whereas the outside hitter starts after the setter releases the ball, the middle and opposite should be on their second step when the setter touches the ball. The timing of the approach is, of course, different for a variety of attacks, but for the basic high sets, a four-step approach will increase the vertical, give hitters more angles from which to approach the ball, and allow hitters to get to more places along the net to hit from.

■ Hitters must get available. If two of your hitters get tangled up in the serve receive and only one is ready to attack, that is a dead give away to the defense. Learning to transition correctly is a major key to getting available. Practice transitioning in most, if not all, spiking drills to make it a deeply ingrained habit.

■ How do you decide whose sets are whose? To prevent attackers from crashing into each other, a ball that is set between two right-handed players belongs to the person on the left. The ball will be on that player's on-hand side, so it will be easier to attack.

TRANSITIONING

Transitioning means moving from one stage to another. In volleyball it means moving from offense to defense and from defense to offense. When referring to the front-row players, it is usually from defense to offense. More specifically, it is a set number of steps spikers use to move off the net (from a block) to prepare to approach and attack the ball. This is the most important way for players to get available, and it is a major skill attackers need to develop. Remember, the more hitters available, the more attacking options, and the harder it is for the defense to key on one player. If coaches fail to practice transitioning with their teams, the results often are that

■ Players run under the ball and have difficulty putting the ball down into the court, which usually results in deep hits with little power.
■ Players are not ready to hit.
■ Players have no power or speed on the approach, which results in a low vertical.
■ The hitter doesn't expect the set.
■ Players have little choice as to the type and direction of the spike.
■ It is much easier to block (because of fewer choices available).

The keys to transitioning are

1. Players should always turn toward the ball when they transition.

2. Instruct players to keep the ball in sight the whole time it is on their side of the court, even as they transition.

3. The further back the pass is to the setter from the net, the further back the attacker should be.

4. The deeper in the court the attacker is, the faster the approach should be. Speed is built up, and the vertical is higher.

5. Left-side hitters need to angle out of the court, middles usually angle to the left, and right-side hitters stay about on the sideline (unless they are left-handed, and then they angle out of the court, too).

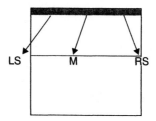

6. Keep steps low and quick and long. The higher the step, the slower the approach.

Now, how do players transition? Very simply, just about like they approach, only backward, and they have to get turned around to go back to the net at the end. It will speed up the transition (and speed is an important commodity in transitioning) if the blocker can come down on the outside foot only and turn and start the transition with the inside foot (for very strong players only). As players become more skilled, they need to learn to transition from both sides of the court, because they will be blocking and attacking from a variety of net positions. For a left-side hitter, it would look like this: angling outside the court to well behind the spiking line—right, left, right (twist), left (facing the center of the net). This leaves the right foot forward to begin the approach (see the diagram).

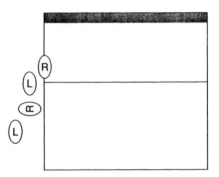

The middle hitter's transition is more complicated. The ball does not always go to the right of the player, as almost all do for a left-side hitter. Many times it goes right over the middle hitter's head and the hitter must decide which way to open to and which steps to take. On middle-of-the-court hits, most hitters will still open up to their right and angle to the left sideline, because that opens up two-thirds of the court for them. Then they can watch the ball and take it in the on-hand hitting position. It is critical that these players learn both transition steps as quickly as possible.

Middle hitters have the added complication of passes coming to the setter that are too close to their position. The priority is for the setter to take the ball, so the middle blocker/attacker needs to get out of the way and let the specialist do his or her job. A quick transition helps the middle hitter stay out of the setter's way.

Right-side hitters should turn to their left. Unless they are left-handed, they do not need to go back as far or angle as wide as left-side hitters. Their steps are left, right (twist to face middle of net), left (one less than the left-side hitter). That leaves the right foot forward to begin the approach again (see the diagram).

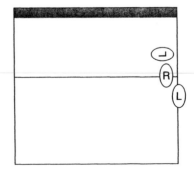

TYPES OF ATTACKS

There are as many names for and types of attacks as there are teams playing volleyball. Each team invents its own names for plays and combinations, sometimes just to confuse the defense. Many teams even change the basic numbering system to further baffle their opponents. The set numbering system changes as players' abilities improve and they are able to attack at more places along the net. We will give you a basic idea of how most offensive coaches number their attacks.

Numbering System and Names

Numbers will start from the left and increase to the right. The first number called is the position on the net; the second is the height of the set.

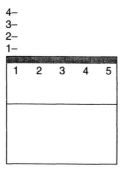

Some common sets using this numbering system are

- (14) high, outside
- (12) shoot set to outside (quick set along top of net)
- (23) lob, quicker set between outside and middle
- (31) quick set middle of court (a "one")
- (32) a second-step set in the middle of the court (commonly known as a "two")
- (55) high back to right side

More net positional numbers equal greater choices of attacks and require consistent control of the serve receive and more skilled hitters and setters.

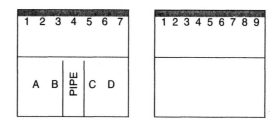

Back-row designations: Starting from the left side, they are A, B, C, and D. The term *down the pipe* refers to the gap between B and C (see the diagram).

Timing

All of these timing suggestions are very general and depend on a number of things, such as the size and speed of the hitter, the speed and distance of the set, and whether the setter jump-sets or not. Your team will have to practice to get it just right, but these recommendations will give you a starting point.

1. Fours (high outside sets).   The hitter should take the first step after the ball leaves the setter's hands. The taller the attackers (and the longer the strides), the later they start their approach. Depending on the height of the set ball, try to start the approach just after the ball leaves the setter's hands.

Make sure the player opens up to—that is, turns and faces—the setter to increase the spiking torque (speed created by twisting the body). This will also give the player more options as to where to place the ball.

2. Outside Shoots (quicks that are just above the net).   The attacker should be on his or her second step and should be at the spiking line when the setter touches the ball (called *second-step set*). The attacker should swing high. Once the arms are up in the air from the jump, keep the arms high and swing fast—use this technique on most quicks. This speeds up the attack.

3. Lobs between Outside and Middle Hits (quicks).   This is a second-step set. Be careful to direct setters not to lob it too high or too slow in the gap, or it will be easy for the defense to get two blockers there.

4. Ones (short, one- to two-foot sets above net).   A slow one is when the attacker should jump when the ball touches the setter's hands. On a quick one the spiker should be in the air when the passed ball gets to the setter. The attacker should go to the setter and jump before they are even with the setter (at least a couple of feet away). The attacker should not get too close to the net, as it will be difficult to swing at the ball without hitting the net.

5. Twos (slow quicks, between ones and fours).   This is a second-step set usually in the middle of the net. Again the attacker should go to the setter.

6. Back Slides.   The second step of the attacker should be even with the setter when the setter touches the ball. This approach is just like that of a basketball layup, going off of the opposite foot of the hand that is hitting.

7. Fives (back sets, similar to a two by the antennae).   This is a second-step set. A big key to its effectiveness is to line up with the ball (in front of the hitting arm).

8. Tandem.   Combination play of a one and a two. The player hitting the two is slightly behind and off the left shoulder of the one hitter. This is usually hit out of the middle.

Vocabulary Terms

Spread series.   A set of plays featuring sets to the outside of the court. It is the best series to use against a bunch-read defense.

X series.   A set of plays featuring quick and combination plays in the middle of the court, usually a left-x series and a right-x series. It is the best series to run against a middle blocker who commits on the quick or against a spread-read defense. When the block is spread, the middles should be able to hit past a middle who is committing, so a set to the quick is a good option. Of course, another good option is a set to the combination hitter, who should be able to attack the middle blocker who has just jumped.

Double-quick series. A set of plays featuring two quick hitters, with the third hitter swinging to hit combinations off of both quick hitters. It is the best series to run against a stack blocking system. It is designed to attack a single-commit blocker who has a stack blocker behind him or her.

Combination plays. A combination of quick and second-step sets in close proximity. It is important for the combinations to be low combinations.

DESIGNING SIMPLE PLAYS AND COMBINATIONS

It is important to understand that the setter dictates the offense, but each hitter needs to study the defense that he or she faces and give recommendations to the setter that will enhance the hitter's own effectiveness. Here are some ways to start putting plays and combinations together for your team.

Free Balls

One of the easiest and most effective ways to introduce plays to a beginning team involves free balls. Since free balls coming from the opponents are the easiest balls to pass, there is a better chance that your team will be able to run a simple offense. To free up the attackers for a quick approach, your back-row players should take all the free balls they can. It is best if they use an overhead pass, because it is quicker and more controllable. Have players speed up the offense by passing the ball fast and low. Because it is a free ball, the attackers should already have transitioned and should all be available.

Have some set options or plays designed so that every time players receive a free ball they will run a quick attack. For instance: shoot to the outside player or a tandem to the middle, or if there are only two hitters front row, run a back slide. It is a good idea to have an escape set in case of a poor pass or to have attackers call plays.

Serve-Receive Plays

The next step up the offensive ladder is plays from the serve receive. As soon as your team can pass consistently, have designated quick sets or combinations in place, with options available for poor passes. Setters should signal the plays just before the ball is served. And even though they are using set plays, it is a good idea to remind the hitters what their sets will be so there are no miscommunications. Hitters, with two possible options, can call an "audible" to designate which one they prefer.

Develop new plays for each serve-receive rotation. Pay special attention to where the attackers and the setter are coming from. Be tricky and use some back-row players as fakes on some combinations. (Just make sure the setter doesn't set the ball to them.) Be aware that if an attacker passes the ball, he or she may be coming in later to attack, so you might need to adjust and have a slower option, too. Remember, in order to be successful, have players do what they do best.

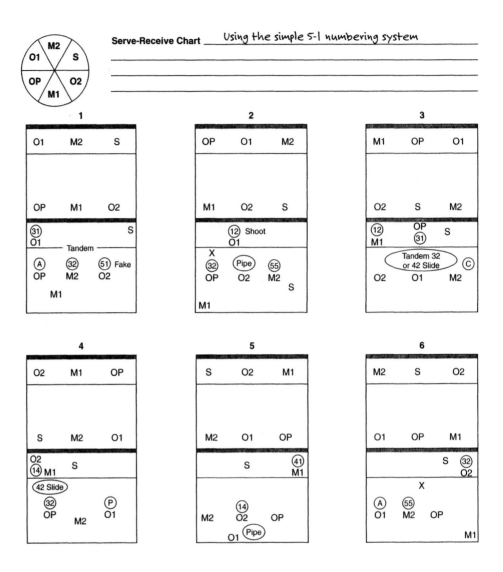

Serve-Receive Chart _Using the simple 5-1 numbering system_

HITTER COVERAGE

This is really a defensive skill, but it is tied closer to the offense, so we will cover the concept here. Another term for this skill is _blocker coverage_. Its purpose is to defend against spiked balls that are deflected off your opponent's block. Your hitters will get blocked. This is a given, so be prepared to defend the possibility. There are three major positions on hitter coverage (see the diagram). It is important that your players cover both close to the hitter and the middle of the court. Their focus should be on the blockers' hands, not on their attacker. Similar to the ball, setter, ball, hitter idea, doing this will give them more time to react. Your players should expect a blocked ball every time, and then they won't be surprised.

As the set is being made, all players not attacking are moving into position with their arms extended in a defensive position. Because of the quickness of the deflection (it is faster the harder the ball is hit), there will be very little reaction time. The closer the player is to the floor to dig the ball, the more time the player has to react. If the hitter coverage is done correctly, it will be similar to the spokes of a wheel, with three players evenly spaced around the attacker (see diagram). The three players are the setter, the middle hitter, and the left back-row player. The two other players' places (middle and right back) are in between the spokes. The players covering the hitter need to be careful not to come in too early and hinder the attacker's approach.

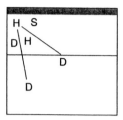

How many players "cup" on hitter coverage will vary, especially with quick attacks, because the front-row players will be jumping, trying to distract or split the blockers, and won't be able to get to their positions for hitter coverage. It is very important that players move to their home positions as quickly as possible when the ball goes over the net. Here is an example of the positions for the three basic coverage patterns:

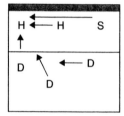 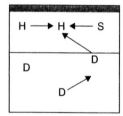 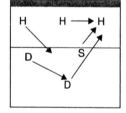

Have fun playing with all the possible options. Once you have a good idea of the serve-receive lineup and plays you would like to use from each rotation, you need many repetitions for your players to become comfortable with them. To accomplish this, try playing the game 120 Serves (see Chapter 15).

SUMMARY

Remember, the biggest key to a successful offense is passing from your serve reception. Your choices in attacking all depend on your passing. How many aces you give up depends on your passing. You want a good offense? Then pass, pass, pass! Here's one more point to emphasize in offense: Have your team get really good at a few things. Be the best at whichever attack you choose, instead of mediocre at several. These two suggestions alone can make mountains of difference in every team's attack. Now, kill the ball!

CHAPTER 12

Defensive Guidelines and Strategies

The philosophy for defense should be the same as the philosophy for offense—probability of success—only now you have two teams to worry about, yours and theirs. To play good defense, you need to answer these two questions: (1) What things are we good enough to do? and (2) What things are they good enough to do?

Once you come up with answers for both questions, you are ready to start designing your own defense. We will give you the basics, but remember that each team and its opponents have different strengths and weaknesses, and you will need to adjust your defense accordingly. An important part of coaching is the ability to adapt and modify offensive and defensive concepts to meet your own team's needs.

MAJOR DEFENSIVE CONSIDERATIONS

Before we give you suggestions for your defensive lineup, we need to cover home positions (where players go as soon as the ball passes over to the opponent's side of the net). Home positions should be consistent for all defenses. It is critical that players get to their positions quickly and keep the ball in view as they are transitioning. Players are placed strategically to optimally defend against setters' dumps, tips, or quick hits.

The starting position for blockers is called a *bunch*, or *cluster position* (see the diagram). The outside blockers are approximately two-and-a-half yards (or three steps) in from the sidelines (closer to the middle blocker than to the sideline). This position will help blockers defend against a setter or quick attack. Because the blockers have more time to get to an outside set, it is wise to start them closer to a possible overset or quick play, which is usually in the vicinity of the setter.

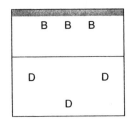

The left and right back-row defensive players are in a 2 × 2 defensive position. Simply put, they are approximately two steps in from the sidelines and two steps back from the spiking line (younger and smaller players will not be able to cover tips as quickly if they are this far back and should be adjusted close to the spiking line). The center back is in the middle of the court, approximately three steps in from the endline. This player is prepared to cover middle and deep corner dumps from the setter.

Choosing the Type of Defense System

Rotation Defense

The features of this system are

- Tip coverage behind the block on left- and right-side hits.
- Middle-back player swings to cover the line hits.
- Off-front-row player (not blocking) comes back behind the spiking line to cover the sharp-angle hits.
- Left and right backs either move up to take tips (if the set is on their side of the net) or move over to dig the corner shots. If they have a read defense, they can adjust up and cover the angle shot.

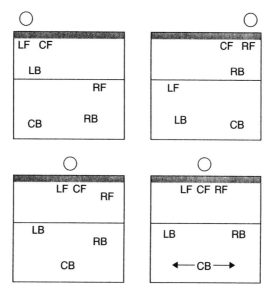

(Choice of two or three blockers)

The *assets* of this system are that the tip and corner areas are covered. The line is also covered, but many times the players do not go all the way to the line or get there fast enough. The liabilities are that the power angle (unless they adjust), the middle of the backcourt, the sharp angle (in front of the spiking line), and the center of the court are not covered.

This defense is excellent to defend against teams who tip quite a bit, but it leaves the middle of the backcourt open. This is where most seams in the block are, and it is statistically the area where most defensive balls fall. You have also moved your best defensive player to the line, and the majority of balls do not go there. It does not cover the hard-down line shot or the off-speed to the middle of the court, either (unless adjustments are made). It does cover the angle and deep corner. If you have an excellent two-person block that seldom has gaps and teams that do not run quicks, this defense works well.

Man-Back Defense

The features of this system are

- Angle coverage
- Line coverage
- Middle-back coverage (which can read and adjust to corner)
- Sharp-angle and middle-tip coverage
- Corner coverage

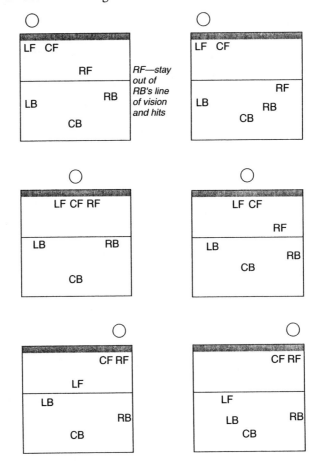

The assets of this system are that there is excellent line and power-angle coverage; the middle of the backcourt is covered (where the majority of balls are hit); and sharp-angle and center-of-the-court tips are covered. The liabilities are that the far corner is often open (unless the middle-back reads and adjusts or the off-blocker pulls back and the angle player drops down); there is poorer tip coverage; and the sharp angle (above the spiking line) is open for tips or hits.

The man-back system has excellent hitter coverage and also takes care of balls hit through the seam in the block. This system works well against quick attacks because players are closer to their home positions. It is not as effective against tip coverage, unless the tips are high and you have tall blockers who can jump. Unless the off-blocker is adjusted to pull in and be responsible for tip coverage.

Placing Players for Each Type of Attack

Statistics taken from men's NCAA matches show that 83 percent of the balls were played in the front two-thirds of the court. Consequently, most of the players should be placed in that area. Do not place your defense too deep.

Placing Players for Defense

Your best defensive player should play middle back all three times he or she is in the back row. Because that position takes the most balls, it makes sense to use your best defensive person there.

A multiple-offense setter should play the right-back position to facilitate transitioning to the front-row position. The opposite, who also plays this position, should have very quick reflexes, because there are a greater number of down-the-line hits from the opponent's best and hardest hitter. These players are also usually responsible for the line tips.

Your best blocker should match up against your opponent's best hitter on the right side of the court. Your quickest blocker should be in the middle.

Specialization allows your players to improve their consistency and to develop quicker response times, because they know which balls are theirs. Playing in the same defensive spot will also help them become more aware of their boundaries in calling balls in or out.

Digging Hard-Driven Spikes

Hard-driven spikes should be dug to the spiking line. If your players are going to make an error, they should err to the 10-foot or 3-meter line. It is better for the ball to be too far back (your side can still play it) than over the net to the opponents.

Using Ball, Setter, Ball, Hitter

This concept cannot be stressed enough, because it benefits your defense so much. Everything revolves around it. It is explained here and referred to again throughout the book.

The defensive players watch the ball go over the net to their opponents. Once the ball is in flight, its path will not change until it is hit again. Because it is obvious where the ball is going, the defense need not waste its time watching the ball but instead should direct its attention to the intended target, the *passer*. Learning to read that person's actions can give an early clue as to what he or she is going to do with the ball. After the *ball* leaves the passer's arms, the defense should look ahead to the *setter*. (Blockers should glance quickly at the hitters to see if any are on their way in for quicks.) The defensive players might notice if their opponents are going to attack, backset, or tip the ball by their preliminary actions. As soon as the defensive players know where the set is going, they should tear their eyes away from watching the *ball* the whole flight to look at the *hitter*. The set is not going to change direction in the middle of the air, and they are wasting precious moments that would be better spent observing the spiker's approach and arm action. Looking at the approaching attacker can tell them the probable speed of the hit, the direction and type of hit, and where their opponents are going to hit from, all of which can prepare them for the attack.

Being forewarned in volleyball is everything to the defense. Outguess the attackers. To do that, the more pieces of information your team can obtain, the better the odds. This is called reading the offense, and the best defenses do it. They seem to be just waiting there to dig your team's hit.

Coaches need to watch their blocker's eyes and see if the blocker is watching the set or looking ahead at the hitter. There are drills in Chapter 14 that will help your players understand this concept. One very simple drill that will help is just having two hitting lines, left and right, with three blockers opposite. The setter tosses the ball to the coach, who passes it back, and the setter sets (the players are looking ahead of the ball each time). The ball is set in order, first to the left and second to the right. The blockers already know that the ball is going to the left and right, so they don't have to watch the set. Coaches need to take themselves out of the drill in order to see where their blockers are looking. Help defensive players get over this useless habit of watching the complete flight of the ball.

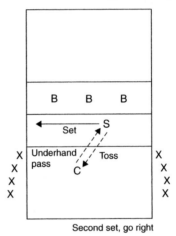

Second set, go right

Practicing Defense

Because you practice against your own team's attacks, your defense will learn how to defend those types of hits. If your offense never hits quicks, your team will have a difficult time with the blocking skill or timing of that hit from an opponent.

Instilling a Winning Attitude

Encourage your players to make an effort to touch every ball that comes over to their side of the court. They learn quickly that if they can touch it, they can dig it. If you penalize "no touches" in practice games, the desire to win will push your players to touch every ball and to create "no touches" on their opponent's court to penalize them. Hustle and aggression will ooze out of your players.

Defending Free Balls

Free balls are easy passes over the net, and they usually go to the back two-thirds of the court. They can be over- or underhand. They usually result from a saved hit that couldn't be set up to attack. There are two basic defensive formations you can use to prepare for these hits, depending on the position of the setter (that is, whether the setter is in the front row or the back).

Because the free ball is easy to defend, the setter releases from defense as soon as a free ball is apparent. If the setter is coming from the back row, the center back must move over to divide the court in half with the left back. Many teams forget to do this, so the number 1 court position is an excellent place to free-ball it to. The front-row players should back up at the same time the setter is moving in to prepare to attack. To speed up the offense, a back-row player should take the free ball, preferably with an overhead pass.

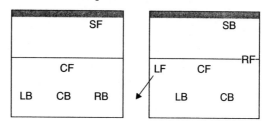

SF = setter front row
SB = setter back row

Handling Down Balls

Down balls are attacks hit with a spiking motion that originate away from the net and possibly from behind the spiking line. They require different defensive positions than attacks close to the net. How different depends on your level of play and on the attacker's jump and skill.

The timing and direction of the ball are difficult to judge for spikes hit off of the net. If you set up a two-person block to defend against that kind of spike, your back-row players are usually screened from seeing the ball (because of the distance the hitter is off of the net) and will have a harder time digging it. Attempting to two-man block down balls also has a lower percentage of success. Attackers tend to use the block more (the ball deflects off of the blocker's hands). Most of the time, down balls are hit deeper into the court, similar to serves. It is more advantageous, then, to play this ball for a dig, unless yours is a college team that can put up a solid three-person block.

Have your back-row players back up to a serve-receive pattern in the middle of the back two-thirds of the court. You could leave one blocker up to defend against any balls coming low over the net. The two front left and right blockers should back up to the spiking line and stay inside the sideline a couple of steps to handle short hits. The primary responsibility for passing this type of ball will be with the three back-row players. If the setter is in the back row, he or she should stay back and dig, and the opposite must step in and set it.

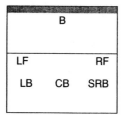

Defending Oversets

There are three options your players can use to deal with oversets: crush them, crush them, crush them!

The overset is the easiest ball to hit, because it is coming straight on to the attacker. But in order to be successful with the attack, it is very important that a decision be made early as to who is going to take the ball. It is usually the player on the left of the ball (who would be taking it on hand), unless the player on the right is better at crushing it.

There really are three options for dealing with an overset. The best option is usually to spike it straight down, away from the defenders. The possibility of this happening depends on how far the set is from the net. If it is too close, an attempted spike could result in a net violation, and a two-handed block would be the best option. Have your players always block away (at an angle) from the defense. A third option is a one-handed tip, again, away from the opponents. Be aware, however, that the opponents should be scrambling to block you, too.

Using the Court Numbering System

You need to know the designations for the different zones of the court for better communication in offense, defense, serving, and serve receive. The court is divided into six equal parts (as shown), with the number-one zone being the back-right corner, where the number-one rotation starts. The numbers follow the order of rotation (the second server in the top right-hand corner is number two). The areas between the numbers are called *seams*. To designate an area, use the terms *seam 5/6*, or *4/5*, and so on. That way it is easy to communicate the area you want to attack or serve to.

4	3	2
5	6	1

BASIC BLOCKING CONCEPTS

Blocking is a valuable asset in defense. In addition to preventing the ball from coming over the net, it defines the area the back-row players should defend. A good block will take out a certain part of the court that needs to be protected, allowing your players to cover other areas where the ball will probably be hit.

Blocking Philosophy

The following is basic blocking philosophy you need to be aware of to build a successful defense.

Blocking tactics should be based on what you know about the opponent's offense. Offenses can be designed to defeat a team that uses only one blocking system, but if the systems and tactics are interchanged, then the offense has to react to the block rather than the block reacting to the offense. It is often desirable to put the best blocker in front of the most likely hitter. Matching players up this way is not a new strategy in sport. The basic concepts of match-up blocking are:

(1) Put your best blocker in front of the opponent's best hitter; and (2) Put your best blocker in front of the position where your opponent sets most often. In many cases, these two principles point to the same location.

If there are three blockers at the net (as there usually are), it is possible to position them in several different ways. In high school, it is often possible to simplify a very complex issue and do three things: Front, trap, or dedicate. The key to the success of the system is in scouting. Every team has offensive tendencies; that is, things they like to do and players they like to go to. The discovery and utilization of this information is the key to matching up your blockers with their hitters in the most effective way.

Key Blocking Vocabulary

There are key words you need to know to understand the different types of blocking available.

- **Read.**   The blocker reads the setter and reacts.
- **Commit.**   The blocker jumps with the hitter no matter what (with quicks).
- **Dedicate.**   The blocker moves slightly in the direction of the potential hitter.
- **Front.**   The blocker gets completely in front of the potential hitter.
- **Trap.**   Two blockers front and commit on a hitter (usually a quick hitter, but it is also possible to trap an outside hitter).
- **Bunch block.**   The starting position of the outside blockers is about a stride and a half away from the middle blocker. The players are bunched closer to the middle.
- **Spread block.**   Players are evenly spaced along the net.

Foundations of Blocking

- **Read blocking.**   Ball, hitter, setter, ball, hitter. In other words, your blocker should determine where the *ball* is going, then glance quickly at the *hitter* he or she is responsible for blocking to see if the hitter is already approaching for a quick hit. Then the blocker should look at the *setter* to determine the type of set that is coming, then look to see where the *set ball* is heading, and lastly look at the *hitter* and notice the speed and angle of the hitter's approach and arm swing. The blocker should also use peripheral vision to remain aware of the actions of the other attackers.

- **Commit blocking.**   Ball, hitter, setter, ball, hitter (same as read blocking).

- **Never quit.**   Players should have the desire and commitment to always block, even if they are not in their desired positions. They will still take out a part of the court that the ball can go to. Sometimes it is necessary that players jump twice.

- **Lead with the hands.**   Remind players to press their hands over the net to the ball and hold. They should not move their arms down on the net or toward the ball; their arms should be in the correct position as they go up and over.

- **The better the pass, the higher the hands.**   To block quicks effectively, the blocker's hands should be higher while waiting (this speeds up reaction time). If the pass is right on target, blockers should expect a quick and prepare with higher hands.

- **Turn hands and shoulders in.** The block should be directed into the court. This will help prevent out-of-bounds deflections.

- **Seal the net.** Make sure the blocker's extended arms are close enough to the top of the net that a ball won't be hit between the arms and the net on the blocker's side. Remind blockers that their arms should remain still once they are up, not come down to the ball.

- **Penetrate.** Have blockers reach over the net at the ball.

- **Square.** It is important for blockers to square the feet, hips, and arms to the net. When blockers have to move quite a distance in a short amount of time, they tend to not swing their last step all the way around and square to the net, and the following things can happen: If going to the right, the blocker's last step (right foot) will be further behind the centerline than the left foot. This will angle the body away from the net, and the right hand and arm will be lower and farther off of the net. Consequently, the ball can be trapped between the player and the net, or the ball can be deflected off the hand into the blocker's own court or out of bounds. Emphasize bringing the last foot down (right foot when going right) even, or closer to the centerline than the other foot. This will turn the body and arms into the net.

- **Jump hip-to-hip and shoulder-to-shoulder with the other blockers.** For the major types of blocking, your players should be close enough that they have lower- and upper-body contact. This technique decreases the chances of having seams, or holes, in the block.

- **Get on the hitter soon.** Remind blockers to be aggressive and to be ahead of the hitter's approach, in the same way that a defending basketball player stays between the player he or she is covering and the basketball hoop.

- **5-3-3; 5-2-2; Q3-3-3; Q3-2-2; 3-3-3; 3-2-2.** Blockers need to know these series of steps to be successful. The steps must be executed automatically to be effective. The blocker's attention is on where the set is going and the timing of the block. He or she does not have time to think, "right, left, jump," and so on. (See Chapter 9 for more on this.)

- **Don't jump with the setter.** If the setter jump-sets, middle blockers have a tendency to jump with them, especially if they have attacked a time or two. For three rotations, the setter is in the back row and cannot attack the ball, and the majority of the time the setter is in the front row, he or she will not attack. If blockers are drawn into jumping with the setter, they will be late blocking the real hit. They need to be prepared to block the setter when they are in the front row, and if they practice the defense technique ball, hitter, setter, ball, hitter, they can usually tell if the setter is setting or attacking, and then block.

- **There is a time to block and a time not to block.** Too many teams block all the time, to their detriment. If a set is not a good set (that is, if it is off the net, too low, or out of bounds), it would be smarter for the blocker to stay on the ground (down). Blocking everything can cause more problems than it helps. Blinding the defense, deflecting balls, diverting balls out of bounds, or trapping balls between themselves and the net can hurt a blocker's team more than an occasional blocked ball will help.

■ **Identify where the offense is.** Blockers need to identify the opponent's hitters and determine whether the setter is coming from the front or back row. The outside blockers must identify the hitter's movements.

■ **Decide how many blockers you are putting up on each hit.** Always try for at least two, even on quicks. If the middle attacker is a good hitter, put three blockers up. If not, put the left-front and center up, and pull the right-front back (unless the middle is left-handed). Most on-hand hitters hit more balls to their right. Bringing in the left-front to block will take that angle away.

Technical Information on Read Blocking

The basic concept behind read blocking is that we want to defend against the things that happen most often. It is usually true that few, if any, teams run the middle quickly and repetitively.

This is the starting position for read bunch blocking. The opponent's setter is in the back row.

```
  LB    LB    RB


   X           X

         X
```

The blockers are inside. The left- and right-front blockers are a three-step from the sideline, and far enough away from the center blocker (CB) so that the CB can take a first step without being hindered. The CB is in the middle of the court.

The blockers are in these positions to defend against fast and combination plays. When it becomes evident, because of a bad pass or style of play, that the opponents cannot set the ball in the middle zones, the outside blockers must release by moving to the outside of the court.

The left-back and right-back players are about two steps from the sideline and two steps from the 3-meter line. The center-back player should be about three steps from the baseline.

This is the starting position for read bunch blocking. The opponent's setter is in the front row.

```
  LB    LB    RB


   X           X

         X
```

The blockers are in the same position as before. The left-back player is closer than he or she was when the setter was in the back row (one step by one step). The right-back player is still a two-step by two-step. The center-back player is much closer than in the preceding example and has significant setter-tip responsibility (about four to five strides in from the baseline).

Here are some other read blocking options:

- Read, read, dedicate.

```
├──────┼──────┼──────┤
   R      R         D
```

- Dedicate, read, read.

```
├──────┼──────┼──────┤
   D          R      R
```

- Spread, read.

```
├──────┼──────┼──────┤
   R        R        R
```

- Read, dedicate, read (tell the left-front blocker).

```
├──────┼──────┼──────┤
   R        D        R
```

- Read, front, read (tell the left-front blocker).

```
├──────┼──────┼──────┤
   R        F        R
```

Communication

Front-row players (usually left or middle) should identify the hitters before the ball is served; for example, they might call "All three, two split, stacked right, stacked left." Outside blockers must identify the hitter's movements (back-row players can also help with these calls); for example, "Inside, around, crossing." Identify the setter's attack; for instance, "Hitting, dumping."

The goal is for the defense to spend as much time as possible watching the setter before he or she sets the ball and then as much time as possible watching the hitter before he or she hits the ball.

Focus of Attention

This is the key aspect of blocking. Because of its importance, we will explain this concept once again. Ball, hitter, setter, ball, hitter. The blocker should watch the pass to its peak. If it comes over, the blocker should call for it and hit it very hard. If it is not coming over, blockers must watch the hitter to see where he or she is going, then watch the setter (continuing to see the hitters out of their peripheral vision). On a good pass, blockers must get their hands and body in a position so they can get up fast on a quick set in the middle. After blockers see where the setter is going to set the ball, they need to watch the ball. If it is quick set, they can jump and "late block" it; if it is a combination or high set, they'll want to watch the ball to its peak, then watch the hitter and try to make an adjustment to his or her signals and stuff the ball. Remind players to move their hands to the ball when blocking.

Eventual Placement of Block

Basically, the blocker's job is to block the ball, but to some extent the placement of the block is determined by the depth of the set (the tendencies of the hitters are also important).

If the set is deep, the line should be left open and the angle blocked (both hands are inside the ball). If the set is perfect, the outside blocker (one hand in front of the ball) must guard the line. If the set is close, the outside blocker (both hands in front of the ball) must cover the line. The outside hitter should block the line on all balls he or she thinks could not be dug if they were hit down the line.

On outside sets, the outside blocker (OB) will set the block, and the center blocker (CB) must come to him or her. On inside sets, the CB must set the block, and the OB will come to him or her. When blockers are reading the hitters, they don't need to jump hip-to-hip and shoulder-to-shoulder (they can split block), because they will be able to move their hands into the intended hitting angle. Sometimes, when the CB is late and not far enough outside and he or she reads a hit into the seam, the CB should try to react to that hit by reaching into the seam with a soft block.

No Block

If the hitter doesn't have a really good swing at the ball, there are times he or she should not be blocked. Anyone can call this, but it is better for the blocker to just quietly stay down. It does help if one or two designated players take the responsibility so that there are not conflicting calls. When the hitter has a marginal swing at the ball, the blocker should yell "No!" and then go ahead and block.

BACK-ROW DEFENSE

Basic Philosophy

- Defensive tactics should be based on the probabilities of the opponent's offense.
- It is desirable to put the best defensive players in positions to which most balls are hit.
- What players do before the ball is hit is at least as important as what they do after the ball is hit.

Foundations

- Back-row defense must be coordinated with the front-row block; that is you cover the area the front row doesn't block.
- The ingredient required to make a great defensive player is a burning, intense, determined, focused, courageous desire to be a great defensive player.
- Someone must have tip coverage on every play.
- Defensive players are responsible for defensive areas, not just a precise spot.
- The defensive players should get to their spots early and stop when the offense contacts the ball so they can move in the direction of the hit. Of course, some attacks will have to be dug on the run, but the optimal choice is to stop.
- Balls hit between two positions should be taken by the player shorter in the court (who goes in front), and the deeper player should go behind (called scissoring).
- The angle digger should be able to see the ball. If he or she can't, it is most likely because he or she is behind the block, and therefore useless. This player should be a "third" blocker. If he or she were to walk right up from the usual position, he or she would be next to the inside blocker.

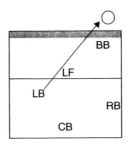

- If the ball is set tight, have players move up. If it is off the net, players should move back.
- Know hitters tendencies, whether they hit deep, short, line, angle, tip lots, and so on.
- If the angle area where the ball could be attacked is covered by a blocker so that a hitter can't hit to that area, the angle back-row player can release and move to the back corner for a possible deep hit.

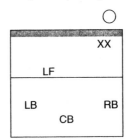

Basic Recommendations for Man-Back Defense

The line player's (left or right back) outside foot is on the sideline. Hits come to this player so quickly that there is little time to react. If the player's foot is on the line, then any ball outside of it is out of bounds. The blockers should be taking out the space between this player and the center back. How far back they play depends on how fast they can move forward to help with tip coverage on the line. If there is a solid block, they could release and move in for a tip.

The center back's main responsibility is the seam, or hole in the block. This player needs to angle with the approach of the blocker. If the attack is quick, the center back should move up.

The angle player (left and right back) has the power angle and should watch the hitter's approach to gauge what position to take. If the set is tight, this player needs to move up; if it is off the net, this player needs to move back. If angle players cannot see the hitter and the ball, they are probably too deep in the court and behind the block.

The off blocker (left or right side, front row) can either pull back to take the sharp-angle shot or move in to dig tips. If the off blocker moves in to dig and gets too far back, he or she will be in the angle digger's way. Off blockers should not reach back and take the hard hits but should just defend between them and the net (in the spiking area) and the tips behind the block.

Generic Defensive Positions for Read-Blocking Options

Here are bunch read starting positions (starting positions for all systems). The opponent's setter is in the back row.

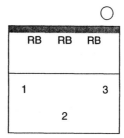

Number 1—In a position to dig one-sets hit between the left- and center-front blockers.

Number 2—In a position to help with oversets that come into the middle of the court.

Number 3—In a position to dig one-sets that are cut back and travel to the right of the center blocker.

Here are bunch read starting positions for when the opponent's setter is in the front row.

Number 1—In a position to cover setter tips and dig one-sets.

Number 2—Much closer than when the opponent's setter is in the back row. Significant setter-tip responsibility.

Number 3—In a position to cover setter-tips and dig one-sets.

ATTITUDE

Nothing can take the steam out of a team faster than having their best hit dug or blocked. Technique cannot compensate for attitude on defense. The best defense is one that will not let a ball touch the floor. Instill that desire in your players, and you will be surprised at how many "ungettable" balls get got!

SUMMARY

The ingredients of a great defensive team start with the players' attitude that all balls are playable. The second most important ingredient is the ball, setter, ball, hitter technique. Developing this technique into a habit with all your players is vital for a successful defense. The last crucial ingredient is to place your best defensive player in the middle back, where the majority of attacks come. Using just these three concepts will make a tremendous improvement in any team's defensive abilities. Now dig it up!

CHAPTER 13

Setting Guidelines and Drills

The setter has the most important role on your team. This player touches the ball more often than any other player and runs your offense in the way that a quarterback on a football team does. The setter takes every second ball, decides who attacks, and determines the type and speed of the attack. Setters are extremely important to your offense and defense, yet they are often overlooked in the search for that great hitter or blocker.

A good setter can make or break a team. As in football, you may have the best receivers (hitters) in the league, but they won't even begin to reach their potential without a good passer (setter) behind them. Too little practice time is spent on improving setters' skills, especially considering the pivotal role they play on a team. In football, the quarterback gets a lot of attention and credit for delivering the ball and calling the right plays. Not so in volleyball, because most people are awed by the power of the kill or stuff block and do not even notice the great set or the brilliant choice of play.

No other position or player can affect the performance of your team more than the setter. Your decision in choosing a setter is critical to the success of your team. And yet, few coaches run drills in practice that are specifically designed to help the setters, and often coaches don't give setters as much individual feedback or as many cues as they do hitters. We will try to rectify that in this chapter.

CHOOSING A SETTER

To begin with, you need to select the right athlete to be a setter. Here are the ideal attributes to look for in an athlete:

1. Well Conditioned: The setter touches almost every second ball and during half the match must transition from the back row to the front. This player moves more than any other player on the team and, in order to perform consistently throughout the match, needs to be in the best physical condition of any team member.

2. Right Attitude: The setter must be emotionally stable. This player must be able to handle pressure, be consistent, and learn from mistakes without becoming overwhelmed. The setter also must be able to handle playing the role of a behind-the-scenes player. Very few kudos go to setters, just like the front-line blockers in football who create the holes and protect the quarterback don't get a lot of attention. And yet, what they do is critical for the success of the play.

3. Coachable: Because the setter runs the team, he or she needs to work closely with the coach. The setter must be able to absorb and use what you teach.

4. Problem Solver: The setter needs to quickly discern whether an attacker is struggling or being shutdown by the defense and how to circumvent that; which of the hitters is hitting best; and what type of sets each attacker can hit best. Setters have to make split-second decisions about which sets they can use, depending on the type of pass they receive, and they have to set to an ever-changing cast of hitters.

5. Observant: Setters need to know who the opponent's best blockers and defensive players are and what offense is best to bypass them. They want to contrive an attack that will put their hitter one-on-one with a blocker.

6. Team Leader: The setter runs a team's offense. This player controls not only who gets the set but the type and speed also. If the setter is confident in his or her role, the rest of the team tends to be confident, too, and everything will run more efficiently.

7. Physically Strong: The majority of sets should go outside, to the left of the court. The setter must be able to push the ball repetitively to the sideline with accuracy.

8. Good Blocker: The setter's front-row, right-hand position pits him or her directly against the opponent's best outside hitter, so ideally the setter is also a strong blocker.

9. Quick Reactions: Setters typically play defense on the right side of the court. The majority of the opponent's attacks come from this side of the court also. The line shot is the quickest hit to defend. Also, the line tip is one of the most difficult to dig. These both are the setter's responsibilities to get. The setter must also transition to the net from defense quickly whenever the ball does not come to him or her to pass.

10. Good Server: If setters are not good servers, they are much more difficult to substitute, because you must put another setter in to serve (if you are running a multiple offense with the setter coming from the back row to set).

11. Good Communicator: Setters need to call the balls they take (to minimize crashes), talk to their hitters, call free balls and down balls, and direct the opposite or other players to step in when the setter has to take the first defensive hit. Quiet setters allow chaos to reign on the court. The other players don't know who is getting which balls or what is expected of them.

A good communicator can remind the team to cup for hitter coverage and can tell his or her hitters how many blockers are up or give them a key to help them hit better. Setters can help their hitters to be more productive.

12. Hustler: Setters are expected to take every second hit they can get to, because they are the best on the team at what they do. Also, being team leaders, their example will have a Pied-Piper effect on the rest of the team.

13. Team Player: It really helps if the setter is congenial. If the players have confidence in the setter's abilities and respect his or her decisions, the team will be more successful. The setter is choosing who gets to attack the ball and what kind of attack is implemented. The setter's job is not to make everyone happy but to run an effective attack.

14. Tall, or a Great Vertical Jumper: Many coaches choose shorter players as their setters, probably for two reasons: they are quick, and coaches want the taller players to attack. This is not the best choice for several reasons.

- Many passes that come from the serve receive and defense are too close to the net. A short setter usually only has two options—to tip it over or dig it out of the net. The tip will be expected by the defense (because of the tight pass) and easy to block or dig. If the short setter opts to dig it out of the net, it is a low-percentage play. Because of different net tensions and unpredictable actions of the ball coming out of the net, this is a difficult hit to make successfully. Remember that the dig out of the net will be the second hit, so the next hit needs to be the attack.
- A taller player, or one who has a great vertical, can intercept many passes that are too tight or are going over the net and can set them up a for an attack.
- A taller player will usually be more successful attacking, blocking, and tipping.
- Tall players will also have a larger range of motion on defense and better leverage serving because of their height. You want your setter to be one of your best servers, especially in a 5-1 offense when there are three attackers on the front row.

15. Left-Handed: This is the most ideal characteristic of all for a setter. Some coaches have had their right-handed setters use their left hands to eat and write in order to improve their dexterity.

Because the setter's position is the right side of center, the majority of passes come from the left side of the court. Having a left-handed setter creates a situation where most passes come to his or her on-hand side for an attack. To be most effective as an attacker, the setter should approach the pass just as he or she would a jump-set, and then turn and swing. Attacking unexpectedly or taking the defense by surprise gives the setter a better chance for success. Another reason it is advantageous to have a left-handed setter is that most dumps (tips) should be attempted with the left hand. This makes the tip harder to block, and it has a better chance of staying out of the net.

GENERAL IDEAS AND CONCEPTS

Now that you have selected your setter, how do you help him or her become proficient? Correct repetitions, correct repetitions, and correct repetitions. So, what are the correct basics to teach a setter? To start out with, setters need to follow the steps and drills outlined in Chapter 5 for the overhead pass. Once they are proficient at the overhead passing skill, they can move on to the setting techniques.

One major concept that affects all skill development, putting the greatest distance between the great player and the poor player, is discipline. The more exact athletes drive themselves to be in performing each skill, the more accuracy they will have. As Chuck Erbe, who has won nine national volleyball titles at various levels in twenty-six years of coaching, notes, setters "must have discipline before creativity." Encourage your setter to be exact. After they have perfected the fundamental techniques, setters can develop their own unique styles. Following are the most important keys for setting correctly.

Feet to the Ball

- Get to the ball quickly; anticipation and quickness is important.
- Shuffle to place the right foot forward always. This helps prevent balls being set over the net and gives stability and power to the set.

Face and Square to the Target

For most sets the player should face the on-hand (left side of court) antennae or just to the left of it. This is a target that stays consistent on all courts. The setter's shoulders and hips should be perpendicular to the net. Squaring to the target is extremely important for consistent sets. If the setter is not square (dropping the inside shoulder, or turned slightly) and pushing the ball at an angle, instead of straight ahead, the ball will float, or drift. This causes the hitter to head for where the ball appears to be going, but when the hitter gets there, the ball has drifted closer to the net.

Transition to the Net from Defense

Many setters release from defense either too quickly or too late. The sequence should be as follows:

- Transition to defense position and stop.
- As soon as they can tell the ball is not being hit to them, they should leave as quickly as they can to transition to the net (their offensive position, which is to the right of the middle and about a yard away from the net).
- If they leave too soon, it is called *cheating*, and smart opponents will take advantage by hitting to that empty position.
- If they release too late, any pass that is even slightly close to the net will have to be dug or tipped over. The setter will not be in position to set the ball to the hitters.

Anticipating the direction of the ball and releasing at the right time are the most difficult skills a setter has to learn. These skills need to be practiced repetitively.

Hands Up Early

Encourage your setters to bring their hands up earlier than they think they have to. The hands should be above the forehead. Many setters' hands come up late, and they catch the ball chin or chest high. A ball that is set from that position will have a low trajectory and will be more like a shoot set, which is harder to hit.

Big Hands

The setter's hands should be curved round, in the shape of the ball. Many setters have their hands slightly closed, or pinched. The hands should be big and open, with fingers spread wide. The hands should be tipped back as far as the wrists will allow so that the hands form a platform (like a pedestal for the ball to rest on) above the forehead. The eyes will be looking through a window that is formed by the thumbs and forefingers. If the ball were to come through the hands, it should land on the forehead, or directly between the eyes.

All five fingers of each hand should touch the ball. The more fingers on the ball, the more control. The majority of the ball's weight is on the thumb and the first two fingers of the hand, but all fingers should be used. The thumbs should face each other, or be directed toward the setter's eyes. Make sure they are dropped down so the hands have a ball shape. One of the biggest causes of sprained thumbs is incorrect position.

Quick Release

No "deep dish." That means allowing the ball to come down further than the point of contact. This is an illegal set, because there is too much time in the contact. The hands usually are not the cause of the problem; the decrease of angle between the upper arm and the forearm is the culprit. It is helpful for the setter to concentrate on releasing the ball quickly.

Extend Up

The setter should push the hands upward to the ceiling and hold the follow-through (until the partner touches the ball). This is an exaggeration, but it will help setters get the point.

The follow-through should be similar to a superman/woman pose (if flying vertical), with no breaststroke action. The follow-through is in the direction of the apex (or height) of the set. The hands remain open with fingers extended toward the ceiling. There should be *no* pinching motion.

THE PERFECT SET

What are the characteristics of a perfect set?

No spin—it should be a floater. In other words, if the name of the ball were on the top at contact, it should remain on the top the whole time until it is hit.

Sets should be at least an arm's-length from the net.

The timing of the set should allow the hitter to be able to complete a full swing.

The ball should drop close to the spot where the hitter is supposed to approach (except any shoot sets).

There should be very little sound when the set is hit.

It should be accurate. The overhead pass is the most accurate way in which to direct the ball. It is used primarily to set up the attack and to pass free balls. An underhand pass can be used for an attack, and there are times when that skill is the best choice. But because the overhead pass involves a higher level of contact and a better angle, it is the preferred offensive attack skill.

Types of Sets

Jump Set

Jump-setting speeds up the attack and can be used to confuse the middle blocker. When setters are in the front row, the jump set can be part of their attack strategy. It forces the blocker to remain in position longer, because it is not clear whether the setter will attack or set. The jump set is also an excellent technique to use to save passes that are too tight on the net or are going over the net. Quick sets are more successful and faster if hit off of a jump set. Young players can be taught to jump-set, but it takes good coordination and strength. The keys to jump-setting are

1. Get to the ball quickly.
2. Hold hands high above the forehead.
3. Contact the ball at height, or pause at the height of the jump.
4. Release the ball quickly.

Back Set

The back set is a blind set, because it travels behind the setter, so many teams do not use it as much as they should. Because most teams do not use the back set very much, they do not usually defend a hit from that position very well, either. Using the back set will give you more attackers, which will divide your opponent's block even more. Because of that, and the inferior defense, you should incorporate the right-side attack into your team's offensive strategies. It is especially helpful if you have a left-handed hitter, because that would make spiking from the right side of the court an on-hand hit also.

Back setting can be quite accurate if practiced correctly and repetitively. Some specific techniques to practice are

■ Setters should set directly behind them. This will improve accuracy. Their shoulders should be squared to their target. This will also decrease the "floating" tendency.

■ The ball should be contacted the way a front set is contacted. If setters catch balls farther back on their heads, that is an early giveaway to the defense that the set is going back.

■ The hips should be thrown forward in order to get the ball all the way to the antenna. That type of set makes the middle blocker travel farther and creates holes in the block for the attacker to hit through. It also gives the hitter more court space to hit the ball into.

■ A quick release will also push the ball farther. The faster the hands and arms extend, the more speed and power the set has.

■ The hands should be up and back; how far up and back depends on the distance the ball needs to travel. Usually the hands will follow through above the middle of the top of the head.

Quick Set

The bread and butter of a team's attack should be the high outside set. Quick sets are used to add variety and a surprise element to a team's offense. They can also set up the outside (left) hitter's success.

One of the offense's goals is to decrease the number of blockers a hitter has to face. Only one blocker will usually be on hand to defend a quick set. If a team is very proficient at this technique, players coming in quickly in a fake hit (as if going to attempt a quick hit) can delay the release of the opposing blocker long enough that the blocker will not be on time to put an effective block up outside.

Another advantage to quick sets is the surprise element for the defense. Many teams are not able to defend against it, especially if they do not practice it. The timing of the block has to be right, and the back row has to be ready sooner (move in closer).

A word of caution here—do not sacrifice your high outside attack in order to develop a quick attack. The majority of sets and the main brunt of your attack should still be high and outside. The quick is used to enhance that attack, not replace it. In other words, it opens the door for the most important hitter, the left. Once a defense understands the principles of defending the quick, it can do so easier than the high outside attack. Also, the quick is riskier and fails more often than the outside.

A few keys to help a setter be accurate on quick sets.

1. Keep hands high.   This speeds the set up and leaves less room for error. Contact the ball 9 to 12 inches above the forehead. The follow-through cue is "wrist flick." The body motion is straight up.

2. Jump-set.   This draws the blocker with the setter, so the blocker is on his or her way down when the hitter attacks. The set has less distance to travel to the attacker's hand and is more accurate. The jump set also draws attackers into jumping on time, which increases accuracy.

3. "See" the hitter approaching and put the ball into the hitter's hand. Each hitter has a different arm swing, jump, and so on, and the setter needs to adjust the speed and position of the ball to improve hitting success.

4. Place the ball.   Ideally, the ball should be placed directly in front of the setter's body and be contacted by the attacker on its way up.

5. Pass correctly.   If the ball is passed too tight on the net, set the ball back to the middle hitter to give him or her a swing. If the ball is too close to the net, the hitter cannot swing full or hard for fear of hitting the net.

6. Do not set any quicks close to the net. Quicks that are set close to the net are the easiest to block, even by one blocker, because there is little time or room to change the direction of the ball. Setting quicks too close will also draw your hitter into the net. The hitter is coming in quickly to hit the ball and does not have as much time to change the direction of his or her approach to vertical.

Two-Set
This is between a quick and a regular set. The height is anywhere from 2 to 4 feet above the net. Setters should tilt their heads back farther, extend their arms straight up, and set the ball right in front of them.

Backcourt Attack Set
This set should be a high set to allow the attacker time to approach and jump. Where it is depends on the leaping ability of the player. The rules state that the back-row player must leave the court from behind the 10-foot or 3-meter line to attack legally. If the approach is fast and the jumper has a great vertical, the set can be placed halfway between the line and the net. Most players prefer the ball to be set slightly in front of the 10-foot (3-meter) line.

Lob Set
Also called a *number-three set*, this is a soft set halfway between a high and a short set. The contact is a little lower on the forehead, and the follow-through is out and forward. It is usually set between the blockers on the net.

Shoot Set

This set is just above the net. It is a fast outside set, designed to divide the blockers and create a one-on-one situation with the blocker and attacker. Do not set this tight on the net, because that makes it easier to block and gives the hitter few options as to direction.

One-Set

This is set directly in front of the setter, straight up. A jump set speeds the timing and helps hitters with their timing. The setter's arms should be almost straight at the moment of contact, and the movement is really a flick of the hands. If the pass is too close to the net, the ball should be set back to the hitter as he or she comes in.

Slide Set

Very similar to a lob or three-set, depending on the speed, quickness, and height of the attacker. It can be placed anywhere from a few feet behind the setter to the right sideline. The setter's hands should be extended high, as for the one-set. The further back the setter wants to go, the quicker the flick of the hands must be and the bigger the step and hip thrust required.

Tandem

This is a play where two attackers are hitting a combination of a one- and two-set. The one attacker approaches first, and the two attacker jumps just after the first one and slightly behind and off of the left shoulder of that attacker. The setter chooses which hitter to set to. It is best to use this play after the one quick has been successfully established. Ideally, the number-one attacker draws the middle blocker to jump with him or her and also screens the approach and hit of the number-two attacker from the defense.

There are countless combination attacks you can use, depending on the talent of your attacking personnel and your setter. To be successful with quick hits and plays, much time needs to be dedicated to practicing them to perfect the timing.

SETTER ATTACKS

If your team uses a 5-1 offense, it is to your advantage to have an attacking setter. This is an unexpected attack, out of the usual 1, 2, 3 rhythm, and it takes the defense by surprise. If the setter always jump-sets, then when he or she is front row, the blocker will not know whether to expect an attack or a set. Even when the setter is in the back row and cannot attack, jumping to set will often draw blockers to jump also. Often the setter will have a better attack percentage than the hitters do. This also helps your attackers, as it splits the blocker's attention and does not allow the blockers to cheat to the middle when the setter is in the front row.

The setter should practice these skills in drills and practice games. The options for setter attacks are spikes, power dumps, and tips. Because a setter's approach is different from a hitter's, there are specific techniques to practice for each attack.

Spike

The setter must choose the pass to attack carefully. If the pass is too close to the net or in the middle of the net, a blocker will be there. The pass that works best is a medium pass—one that is between blockers. What makes it best is when it is a pass the other team is not expecting the setter to attack. It helps if there are other diversions, such as a middle hitter coming in calling a one or the left-outside hitter calling a shoot. The diversions help draw attention away from the setter.

Power Dump

This hit typically goes to the deep corners (1 and 5) of the court. The higher the setter jumps, the more effective the dump. To dump to the number-one corner, it is recommended that the setter use his or her right hand. To dump to number-five, the setter should use his or her left hand. It is important that at the time of contact the ball is between the setter and the net (not behind). This will decrease the risk of being called for an illegal hit (throw). The hand is spread wide open, as in a set, and flexed back. The ball will be contacted on the bottom half, and the setter's arm should be fully extended. Hold the follow-through at the intended spot.

Tip

This is a short, quick hit. To be effective, it must be unexpected and have a low trajectory. If the tip is too high, it will allow the defense time to get to it. The setter should jump as high as possible and hit the tip with his or her arm fully extended. This will shorten the distance and time the ball travels to the floor. If the hit is directed mainly with a flip of the wrist, and not from the motion of extending the arm, it is less likely to be detected or called as illegal.

It also helps if the tip is between blockers, or hit away from them, to decrease the chances of their blocking it. A tip hit to the front of the setter, in the number-two area, can be hit with the right or left hand. A tip hit to the number-four area (behind the setter) is best hit with the left hand, unless the ball is too close to the net, and then a right-handed tip is best. The number-three area is a setter's preference. Usually the left hand is most effective to use because it catches the ball farther away from the net and has less chance of hitting the net or being blocked.

SETTING SIGNALS AND PLAYS/COMBINATIONS

The strategies and choices of developing plays on offense are covered in Chapter 11, along with the numbering system of attacks. This chapter deals with the setter's responsibilities in this area.

Signals

It is up to the setter to use hand signals before each serve to notify all the hitters of their options. These hand signals are as diversified as each setter. The most common place signals are flashed is on the lower back of the leg. Some setters use their bodies to hide the signal by turning and showing the hand signal in front of their abdomen or behind their back.

The most common signals are numbers such as one, two, or three. Some other hand signals are C, L, X (crossed fingers), or a closed fist. The setter can also differentiate which sets are front or back by using the first three fingers as front sets only and the ring and pinky fingers as back sets. Signals shouldn't be too complicated; there isn't a lot of time to recognize the call, and a miscommunication can be costly.

Serve Receive

The setter is primarily responsible for calling the plays before the ball is served. However, if the attacker disagrees, he or she has the option of changing the play. Usually, each serve-receive rotation will have set plays already established. (Examples of how to set up serve-receive plays are in Chapter 10.) There will be different options available, depending on the quality of the pass, the defense, and the attacker. It is up to the setter to choose the option, depending on the blockers' and hitters' capabilities. Sometimes, if the hitter or setter notices defense anomalies, they can override the set plays with verbal or hand signals.

The complexity of combinations and plays will depend on your team's passing, setting, and attacking capabilities. Begin with simple plays, and as your team progresses, add some quicks. It is always good to have a relief set (high-outside or back) in case of a poor pass. The intricacy of combinations and freelancing increases as the skill level climbs.

Transition

It is the attacker's responsibility to call the choice of hit when transitioning from defense to offense. This lets the setter know who is ready for what set. Setters can talk to attackers before the serve and suggest possible options, but attackers carry the most weight in calling sets in rallies.

Free Balls

Because a pass from a free ball (an easy return over the net) should result in a near-perfect pass to the setter every time, combination quick plays can already be in place. The more advanced a team's skill, the more options and verbal calls should be used.

SETTING TACTICS/PHILOSOPHY

All players should be confident in their setting ability. This will increase the number of attacks your team will be capable of producing and decrease free balls, if they are not afraid to step in and set when the setter is unavailable. For this to occur successfully, players need to step forward with confidence, knowledge, and experience (where to set it to, how close to the net, what positions people are hitting, and so on).

The best way to accomplish this after players have acquired the skill of setting is to make them use it in a gamelike situation. A few drills to set the stage are

- Queen or king of the court—when warming up, have players practice a number of combination hits, using the overhead passing skill. Examples are: Set three in a row for 3 minutes off of a throw or underhand server, then two sets and one bump for 3 minutes, and then one set and two bumps for 3 minutes (in any combination).

- Triples—everyone has to take a turn setting.
- North Pole, South Pole—playing doubles for warm-up, start out with 2–3 minutes of setting only, then two sets and one bump, then two bumps and one set, and so on.
- Butterfly—serve, pass, and set. Target catches and runs to serve. Everyone follows the pathway of the ball and plays every position.

Position the setter as close to the front-right position as possible.   This is critical for a number of reasons. Setters run more than any other player on the court. Placing them close to their offensive position decreases their movement and saves their strength. Also, if they are transitioning from the back row, several negative things can happen:

1. Servers can direct the ball into their pathway.
2. When the setter is transitioning during the serve, he or she can block the passer's view of the served ball.
3. The setter loses sight of the ball if transitioning from the left side and the ball is served to the left side, unless he or she runs backward all the way.
4. Setters have a harder time setting balls passed tight on the net.
5. It is easier for the defense to recognize the front/back row status of the setter.
6. Setters are often late getting to the pass from a short, jump, or fast serve.

Setters can be placed in or very close to their offensive positions on the serve receive if you understand and use the overlapping rules. Stacking front- or back-row players is one example. It is possible to position the setter in the two and three court positions all six rotations without compromising your serve receivers (keeping your best passers passing). Examples can be found in Chapter 10.

When in doubt, set it higher.   Always set the ball high enough to allow the hitters time to get a complete swing at the ball. Many transitions from defense to offense do not give hitters the time in their attacks to take a full approach or swing. This results in a poor attack, such as a forced tip, half hit, or hit into the blockers. If the attackers are ready and are asking for quicks, go ahead. When a setter isn't sure if the hitter is ready, it is better odds to set the ball higher and give the hitter time to approach and swing aggressively.

If you err, err away from the net.   This helps prevent oversets (balls that are set over the net) or balls set too tight. The setter always wants to give the attacker an opportunity to swing at the ball. If the setter is moving after a difficult pass and doesn't have time to square up to set (creating a guessing situation), it would be better if he or she set the ball off of the net than too tight or possibly over the net.

Set to all hitters at the beginning of a game to find out who is hitting well that day.

The best hitters get the highest percentage of sets.   Just as Michael Jordan was given the most opportunities to shoot the basketball, so should your best player be given the majority of the sets. Half to two-thirds is an appropriate amount. Your best hitter should be your outside hitter for several reasons:

- That position gives the most room to hit the ball in the court.

- It is a longer set, allowing more time for a big approach, and the ball is in the ideal position for a right-hander, coming from his or her right side.
- If the set is on the line, it will give the hitter a better opportunity to hit around or through the blocker, as many middle blockers won't get all the way out, which leaves gaps in the block.
- The ball has a better chance of being blocked out of bounds than when blocked from the middle of the court.

Every play, assess opponent's front row.   The setter tracks the ball the first third of its path. He or she then can focus on hitters and blockers. The setter should also collect data when the ball is on the other side of the net, when attackers approach, and when each team is transitioning.

Establish quicks soon to divide blockers.   This slows down the blockers releasing to get outside to block, because they have to make sure your team is not running a quick first.

Do what you do well.

Attack weak blockers.   Know where the shortest and poorest blockers are. Notice if they are slow moving (you can use more quicks, like shoots) or have poor skills, like not sealing the net or not squaring to the middle of the court. Set to those positions more often.

The poorer the pass, the higher the set.   When the pass is poor, the setter has less control, and it would be a much higher gamble to try a quick. You want to minimize the mistakes, and you do that by playing smart odds.

When in doubt, don't.   Volleyball is a game requiring consistency. It isn't the one big hit that wins games, it is all the little successful hits that accumulate. Consistency is the key to success. Go with plays and sets you are most comfortable with, especially in tight situations.

Setter should maintain a neutral body position on all sets.   That way the setter can threaten all sets all of the time. If the setter gives away where the set is going, the defense has time to read it and get prepared earlier.

Make the opponent's blockers stay home.   When the setter is in the front row, he or she needs to attack every once in a while; otherwise the blocker can release and "cheat" over to block middle and on-hand. To help out the middle hitter, the setter needs to be a constant threat, thereby forcing the blocker to stay where he or she belongs until the set is made.

Don't do what they expect you to do.   If the pass looks like the setter will have to tip it, don't. Punch it up with a one-handed hit or set it, tip it deep, or turn and hit it. Always try to come up with the unexpected. Set quicks on an average pass.

Establish the best hitter first.   The best hitter is the best for a reason. Starting out with your big guns sets a precedent and a challenge. Many times it is intimidating, and that is just what you want your team to be.

Make the long set.   The easy, expected set, especially when transitioning from defense, is the middle or back set. Do the unexpected, and set it outside to the line.

Set opposite from the movement of the ball.   The defense tends to drift to one side of the court during rallies. Set away from the concentration of players.

Do not set someone who is not ready.   The players should call for a set. It helps when they communicate, especially during quick exchanges or rallies.

Don't set someone because it is their turn.

Push the pace.   If you can set the first ball when transitioning, do so. Teams get into a 1,2,3 rhythm, or rut, and attacking the ball on the first or second hit throws in the unexpected. The same type of thing occurs if the setter speeds up the set.

Take advantage of another team's mistakes or poor defense.   If your opponents only block one up in the middle, run a barrage of hitters from the middle in twos or tandems.

   The setter could also dump on the second hit to the middle of the opponent's court or to an area not covered because of the server coming back slowly to defensive position.

Audibly change your team's attack if you give up two points in a row.   The setter needs to throw your opponents out of their rhythm or stop their momentum and give a new look to your team.

Go back to the same hitter.   If a hitter makes a mistake, give him or her another chance. The setter should let the hitter know in advance that you are going to him or her. This will prepare the hitter and help build his or her confidence.

When games are close at the end of a match, don't tip.   Encouraging hitters to tip begins a passive attack, and the aggressive attack will almost always dominate. Most teams pull their defense up into the front half of the court as rallies and matches progress (because they neglect to go home when the ball goes over the net). If your players swing instead of tip, the ball comes faster and usually farther back, catching opponents unprepared.

Know and use the hot hitter.

Jump at everything close to the net.   This keeps blockers honest and prevents them from putting an umbrella block on the ball. It will also usually draw the blocker to jump with the setter, expecting a tip or hit. This sets your hitter up with one less blocker or a good hole in the block to hit through, because the blocker is usually late getting over to them after jumping with the setter.

Setter should find reference points to aim for or establish positions on the court for sets.   It helps pinpoint sets if the setter can use visual targets, such as lines or different colors on the court, to set to. One of the easiest and most consistent targets is the antenna. Setting accuracy will improve greatly in unfamiliar courts if setters will find reference points to use and practice using them during warm-ups.

MENTAL CHECKLIST FOR SETTERS

To help setters mentally prepare for matches, it is a good idea to have them answer the following questions about decisions they will have to make during the match. Committing their opinions to paper helps setters clarify their options.

There are three different groups of questions. The first group should be used before the league play begins and then repeated sometime later, as players' skill levels change and progress during the season. The second set of questions should be used before a match, and the third set, after a match. Copies of these questions are included in the appendix of this book. Many of the questions were taken from a Stanford University coaches' clinic handout.

SETTER EVALUATION

There are several methods of evaluating a setter's effectiveness. Here are some you can use:

- Set/kill ratio. Known as assists, or kill assists. All sets are recorded in the following ways:

  1 = The attacker hit the ball over the net and it is kept in play.
  K = The attacker killed the ball.
  – = Setter missed hits, such as illegal hits, unhittable sets, or oversets.

  1. Total all kill sets, then subtract all minus hits from that total.
  2. Total all sets (minuses, kills, and ones).
  3. Divide number 2 into number 1 (the total of all sets into the total of the kills with the minuses subtracted).

- During a practice scrimmage, keep track of the number of kills in one game, then switch setters only and repeat.
- Notice the number of sets to the left, middle, and right of the court. Are they following your game plan?
- Compare hitting statistics.

DRILLS WITH SETTING EMPHASIS

Many drills can be adapted during practice to give setters more opportunities to improve specific skills. Even so, we recommend that extra time before and after practice, at least two to three times a week, be spent working primarily with the setters for the first half to two-thirds of the season.

As your athletes' skill levels increase and you are able to select the athlete who will be the primary setter, they need to specialize. That means they should spend most of their practice time doing only what they will be doing in games: setting, serving, blocking, defense, and attacking from the setting position. Relatively little of their time should be spent on skills they will use only occasionally, like passing and attacking.

Try not to use too many drills. Just a few are enough, as long as they give multiple repetitions for the specific skill your setter is trying to learn. Drills should also replicate gamelike situations. The success of the drills depends on

- Correct execution
- Specific goals and consequences
- Immediate feedback and simple cues

The following basic drills can be used to improve your setter's skills. They can be made simple or complex, depending on your setter's skill level.

1. Triangle Pass.

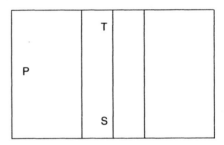

This drill involves three players: one at the net (setter), one on the left sideline (target), and the third in a passing position in the court (passer). The ball starts with the target, who throws the ball at the passer, who passes it to the setter, who sets it to the target. Variations:

- For an easier drill, have the passer toss the ball to the setter (vary where it is being passed from and the speed of the pass).
- Move the passer to different passing positions on the court.
- Have the setter transition from the defensive position to the net on the throw from the target.
- Have the setter jump-set.
- Change the position of the target.
- Have two targets outside in a line. One is at the net, and the other is tossing the ball to the passer. At the toss, the target transitions off the net, then approaches and catches, or hits, the ball. The hitting target then retrieves the ball and gets back in the target line to toss the ball to the passer. This will work hitters on transition steps, learning the approach, swinging both arms up, and keeping the ball in front and to the right of their bodies.
- Instead of target people, have players set at ball carts placed on the left sideline, and count the number of sets that drop into the cart.
- Use two setters. Pass the ball to the seam of the number-one and number-two positions on the court. The setter must come from the net and pivot in the air to square his or her shoulders to the target before setting.

2. Bounce Set with Partner (50–100 before practice).

This drill helps setters get to the set quickly and put their hands up early. Setters are to put their hands up when the ball bounces on the floor. Only one bounce is allowed before the setter sets to the partner or target. Two cautions: The higher the toss or set, the bigger the bounce will be; also, make sure balls are inflated properly.

3. Butterfly. The setter stays in the setter position. Everyone else rotates around the setter. See Chapter 14 for a full explanation of the Butterfly drill.

4. Shuttle.

There are three players in one line, and two in the opposite line. The ball starts in the line with the most players. Players set and run right to the back of the opposite line. Without catching the ball, players continue to set it back and forth. Count how many sets in a row. It is a good idea to do most setting drills along the net (for reference). Work on having players place their right legs forward in a shuffle step before setting and having them bring their hands up early.

5. Transition from Defense.

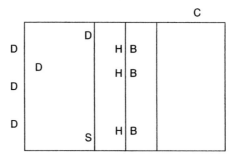

In this drill, there are three hitters at the net and three blockers opposite the attackers across the net. The setter is coming from his or her defensive position (right back) on the hitter's side of the court. There are two other defensive players in the back row. The coach tosses or hits the ball over the net to the back row of the hitter's side. The setter either passes the ball or transitions to set. The setter must touch the net before setting the ball (this makes the setter transition closer to the net) or do two push-ups. After the attackers spike, they retrieve the ball and either give it to the coach or put it in the ball cart. The defensive players move in to fill the spot left open by the last attacker.

This drill helps players make quicker decisions about releasing from defense. Have the blockers trade when they have X number of blocks. You can run this drill with one setter or with two setters taking turns.

6. Three Hitting Lines.

The coach or player tosses, sets, or passes the ball to the setter. Hitters transition off of net and call the set they want.

7. Transition from Blocking.   This drill emphasizes the setter's quickness in finding the ball and getting to the offensive position from blocking. There is a setter, a target, and a coach on each side of the court. Both coaches have two balls.

- Coach tosses ball to setter.
- Setter sets ball to hitter.
- Hitter approaches and hits or catches ball (then returns ball to coach).
- Opposite setter (across net) blocks (work on ball, setter, ball, hitter).
- Second coach tosses ball to second setter right after the block.
- Cycle continues.

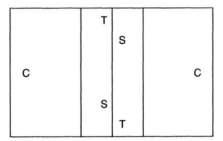

SUMMARY

Don't neglect the one position on your team that has the most effect on your offense's success, the setter. Tall, quick-thinking setters are a premium to have on your team. Jump-setting is an important skill to teach to step up to another level of competition. And last, your setter's attitude influences your team like no other player's does. Make sure you choose someone you are compatible with.

CHAPTER 14

Making Drills Work

Anyone can be a coach, but the good ones have the ability to analyze their teams' weaknesses and practice skills that have high game transfer. Like with putting together a puzzle, a good coach knows what the pieces should look like, then fits them in place. At the end of the season, all the work will have been worthwhile when the picture presented is a unified whole. This chapter discusses the following items:

- Knowing what skills your team needs to improve
- Making drills competitive
- Getting the most out of drills
- Creating drills specific to team needs
- Scoring systems
- Drills for each skill

KNOWING WHAT SKILLS YOUR TEAM NEEDS TO IMPROVE

Every team is different and each requires a specific emphasis. What worked great last year probably won't get the job done this year. Following are some suggestions for determining the types of drills that are needed.

1. **Review practice and match statistics.**   They may reveal what is lacking and who is not producing.
2. **View match video tapes.**   Pay particular attention to each individual's movements away from the ball.
3. **Notice team trends.**   Poor team attack statistics could reveal setting inconsistency.
4. **Practice observation.**   Coaches should not be so absorbed in the execution of drills and games that they are unable recognize what help their teams need. This is a common mistake. A huge key to avoiding this problem is to stay out of drills. It is very hard to be objective when you are involved directly in the drill.
5. **Observe off-the-ball movement.**   Coaches need to watch the movement that is going on around the ball. (This advice applies for a good defense as well.) Are players transitioning to hit, cup, or play defense? What happens before the ball is hit is more important than what happens after it is hit.

You must have a standard by which to measure your team and a direction in which you want to go. Do not use a drill unless you have an objective in mind.

("This drill will enable us to..." or "This is what we want to accomplish with this drill.") If you can envision the drill done properly, your players will be more apt to get it right (much like having the puzzle box to look at).

All drills should be gamelike. Lying on your stomach, setting is not very gamelike. Playing two-man pepper is not very gamelike. Spiking against the wall is not gamelike (and can create bad habits). The drills that you use to develop particular skills should simulate a slice of the game, and with a few twists of the criteria for using those skills in a game, new rules will make it work in drills.

Now that you have the first two keys to making drills work (deciding what your team needs to work on and choosing the right drill).

MAKING DRILLS COMPETITIVE

The best way to motivate players is with competition. How do you make something competitive? What drives athletes? It helps if each drill has the following characteristics:

- A goal that players can use to measure progress that is within their reach.
- Consequences.
- A natural conclusion. It gets frustrating if the coach keeps interrupting.
- Fun. Every player needs to be successful in some ways.
- Involvement. Each player should actively participate.

GETTING THE MOST OUT OF DRILLS

Here are some other important concepts that will help your athletes gain more from each drill.

- **Keep the coaches out of the drill so they can coach.**   Coaches can usually serve harder and more accurately than any of their players. They have had more practice than the students. As the coach, you should let them practice the repetitions while you give immediate individual feedback and positive cues. This is hard to do from the other side of the net while you are thinking about executing the skill, getting the next ball, and its destination. Do not divide your attention. Focus as intently on your players as you want them to focus on the ball and the game.

- **Make your drills build on each other.**   After working a new skill in a static (very specific) drill, such as transitioning from the net to hit, go to the next step by putting it in a butterfly drill. (You could set certain criteria such as players don't get to hit unless they transition behind the spiking line.) Next, play a game where the focus is on transitioning. If they don't transition behind the spiking line during the game, their sub goes in. Use each sub to help (you can be sure they will be watching intently).

- **Simplify.**   Don't get too complicated and overwhelm the players. Allow them to focus on one important part of the skill while executing the whole. Perfect that one part and then move on to the next problem.

■ **Be exact in your expectations.**   Don't allow sloppy performance. When you notice a lackadaisical attitude in practice, put a bite into the drill. For example, the players with the five lowest scores do 10 push-ups; or every time two serves are missed in a row, all servers do two high knee jumps (and the next time it is three high knee jumps).

■ **Attitude.**   You want your practices as gamelike as possible to facilitate better match transfer, and that includes intensity. The closer the practice atmosphere is to a match, the more comfortable your players will be. "You play like you practice" is an unrefutable truth.

CREATING DRILLS

Now that you know what to fix and how to run the drill effectively, how do you adapt this knowledge to your team's specific needs? Following are some examples that will give you some ideas.

1. Are right-side attackers getting too few sets? If so, it is usually because the setter doesn't feel comfortable back setting, so use a drill in which all they can legally do is back set and they can't set the same person twice. It will challenge them.

2. Are hitters not attacking down the line? Put a target down the line (such as the ball cart or a chair). If they spike the ball and it hits the target, they become part of the chair club. The first one is the president, the second is the vice president, and so on. After a set amount of time, whoever doesn't get in the chair club pays a consequence. (There are lots of appropriate consequences included in Chapter 15.)

3. Are servers hitting to number 6 (middle of the court, where your opponent's best passer is) too often? Put markers (such as cones) out cordoning off zone six. The first one to 20 wins. Each serve in the court gets one point, unless it is to zone six, which gets minus two.

Evolution of Creating a Drill

Now that you have a good idea of how you want to proceed, let's examine the creation of a drill to improve a team's serving and passing. Specifically, this team is not serving aggressively and is giving up too many aces on serve receive. The goal would be to develop a drill that rewards serving aces and penalizes receiving errors.

What type of serve receiving or passing should you have the players practice? It would be wise to stay with a three-person passing formation to keep it gamelike (more retention). It would be even more gamelike if whoever passed the serve approached and spiked the ball. Thus, the consequence is built into the drill: If the serve is passed well, it is more likely there will be a good set to hit, and there is the reward.

The setter might need practice transitioning to the net on serve receive and defense. Have the player start behind the spiking line for each serve and run and touch the net before setting the ball (for a specific, measurable goal).

Spiking against blockers would be even more realistic, teaching your attackers to hit around them. Put three blockers up opposite the passers. This also will keep more players active and fewer waiting to serve or pass. Every team needs practice blocking and hitting against a block.

The drill should look like the accompanying diagram for 12 players.

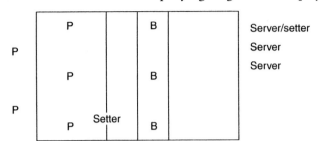

Every drill must have rules to define the parameters. For example, this drill might include the following:

1. Allow the passers to stay on the passing side if they can hit the ball into the opposite court without being blocked or dug. (reward)

2. If the passers get aced, have a miss-hit (out of bounds or in the net); if they get blocked or dug, they go to the block side. (penalty)

3. The blocker who blocked or dug the hit, or who was the longest there, moves to serve. (reward)

4. The server who got the ace or served last goes over to pass (reward). If the server keeps missing the serve, he or she will stay and keep serving. (consequence)

5. If the passer/hitter is successful, he or she stays on the passing side and keeps passing and spiking. (consequence and reward)

6. The setter needs to practice serving too, so a second setter might serve until he or she gets an ace or the hitter is out on a serve. The serving setter might switch with the setter on the passing side. Another passer will have to be added to pass in order to keep it even.

This drill has quite a few natural consequences built in, and good drills will, such as the following:

1. Passer can't pass; they won't get to hit, so they will work hard to get a good pass.
2. If servers misses their serve, they keep serving.
3. The smarter and tougher they serve, the better the chance of moving to the serve receive/attacking side. They will start to think, Who is the worst passer over there, and where is the most effective place to serve to?
4. Because spiking is one of the favorite things a volleyball player likes to do, the reward and consequence for successful spiking will be to stay on the passing and hitting side.
5. The spiker will be looking for holes in the court and the shortest blocker to hit over and will be calling for sets like shoots and slides to get away from the blockers or to create a hole in the block. This drill encourages players to be innovative in order to be successful.

If you want a concrete way to measure success and stay positive, you could have the players score each time they successfully stay on the passing side. Then ask for the high scores and give a reward for the highest.

In summary, when you are creating drills, keep the following in mind:

1. Have a purpose.
2. Keep the drill as gamelike as possible.
3. Involve as many players as possible. (The goal is that no one sits out more than two minutes.)
4. Encourage repetitions.
5. Provide individual feedback.
6. Simplify; focus on a few things.
7. Provide measurable goals.
8. Allow for natural consequences.

SCORING SYSTEMS

A variety of scoring systems are available to assist you in creating drills for your team.

X in a Row

Example:

10 good passes in a row with one team competing against another team
10 consecutive pass-set hits in a row by a receiving team

Wash

- 2 balls = 1 served ball and 1 tossed ball by the coach at the end of the serve rally.

Example:

If the serving team wins the rally, they get one point.
If the receiving team wins the toss ball rally, they get one point.
If each team gets one small point, it is a wash or the score is cleared.

- The team to win the rally for the serve point and to win the rally for the toss ball play gets two small points or one big point.
- Play scrimmage games to 5, 10, 15.

Big Points, Little Points
(Emphasizes consistency, intensity, and making fewer mistakes and smarter choices.)

Example: Queen's court

3 little points equal one big point; play to 15 big points
5 little points equal one big point; play to 10 big points

(+) and (0) and (–)
(Decreases the number or errors.)

Example: "You get to go, you have to stay drill."

(+) = ace spike
(0) = hitting the ball and receiving team returns it
(–) = spiking into the net or out of bounds (errors)

Rules
After three accumulated (–), player drops out of the drill
(+) and (0) players stay in the drill
Compete to see how many (+) one player can score

Fast Scoring–Rally Scoring (one point for rally)

Example:

Scrimmage play
The team who wins the rally gets one point
Play games to 10 or 15

Catching Up Drill

Example:

One team starts with 5, 10, or 12 points, and the other team has to catch up
Handicap the better team

Start Scrimmage with Tied Scores
(Teams play out the games.)

Scrimmage

The coach tosses a ball to the winning team at the conclusion of the rally that began with a serve. This scoring system emphasizes passing skills and keeps players focused and alert in drills.

Options:

Best servers on a team to serve to the team
Teams of two, three, four, five, or six players

Going Out Backward (negative points)

Example:

Each missed hit is one point, and when team reach 15 points, their turn is over (say, spiking).

Note the following suggestions:

- End games at 15 points unless scores are tied at 14–14 (then game will have to continue until one team wins by 2), or finish out the game until there is a winner.
- Adapt the scoring system to fit your players' skill levels and the talents of your players.
- Be flexible; not all drills will work. Adapt them, or drop them.

The next section covers a few basic drills in each skill category to get you going. Each of the drills can be adapted in a variety of ways to accommodate your team. That part is up to you.

DRILLS FOR SKILLS

Server and Serve-Receive Drills

Butterfly Drills

One of the best gamelike drills that is a must for all teams to have in their repertoire is the butterfly drill. It is flexible enough to be beneficial in practicing almost all the skills in volleyball, with a little change in emphasis and requirements. Its primary focus is serve/serve receive. The name comes from the positions of the players during the drill, which is similar to butterfly wings. The basic single butterfly is a simple serve, pass, target pattern. A cue to help the players understand how it works is to tell them to follow the path of the ball (server to passer, passer to target, target takes the ball over and serves it). There should be two players at each position to begin the drill and two balls. It is a great conditioning drill as well. Add a setter and an attacker (who has to transition), and you will work other skills in a very gamelike method.

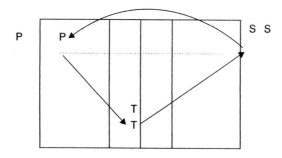

Some great options with this drill include the following:

- Divide the court in half with an antenna in the middle of the net and compete against a second set of six players. The first team to 15 perfect passes wins (subtract one for each overpass).
- Put the full team together to play a double butterfly. (Now you can see how it got its name.) Compete against time or another team, such as the JV (require the better team to get more passes).

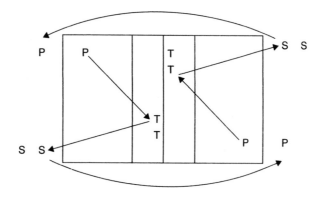

- Not all balls go to number five; servers need to practice hitting to other parts of the court, and passers need to change their platform angle depending on their court position. So after your team reaches a set amount, say 15, have the passers move to number six and start again; then to number one. Take points off for oversets or no-touches on the ball. Keep a running total of the whole team's score.
- Butterfly up and back. If you have trouble with passers moving to the ball quickly enough, try starting passers on the endline. They must remain until the ball is served. The serve should be hit short. Give the whole team five good passes from that spot before they move up to the spiking line. There the server serves deep and the same rules apply. After five good passes, they move to the endline in number six, and so forth.
- Move servers against passers as a group. Servers rotate with servers and passers with passers. The first one to 15 wins.

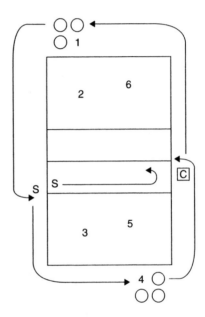

Two-on-Two, Three-on-Three, or Four-on-Four
The court could be divided in halves or thirds with antennas, which allows for more repetitions in a shorter amount of time. These drills are great for warm-ups and learning new skills. Give a few rules to emphasize what you want accomplished, such as three sets, three bumps, jump tip, backcourt spike. If your team lacks hustle, try the following: If a ball reaches the floor with no touches, the team that allowed it to happen does one roll. Players will become proficient at rolling, and the team will start to go call each other after a while. Set time limits and rally score; winners move up and losers down.

In-a-Row, Serve-Receive Ladder
The goal is to score three points in a row, which equals one big point; college serves get two points, and passers get five. Targets keep score. When a person scores one big point, he or she trades places with the target. Only one side will score little points (in-a-row, remember).

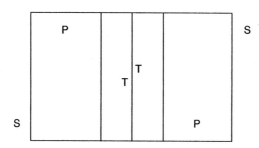

To add more teams, divide the court in half. Players are grouped by number; that is, three numbers 1s make up one group and so on. Player number 1 serves to passer number 1, and the number 1 passer directs ball to the number 1 positioned close to the net. Here is an example using two courts and twelve players.

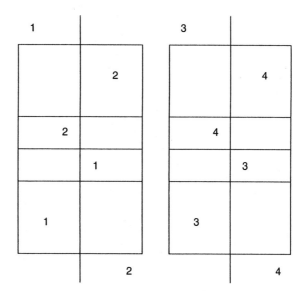

At the end of 10 minutes, winners move up and losers down. Play three rounds. If servers are less accomplished, they may move closer to the net, and in-a-row scores for passers may be increased. You might keep track of players' positions in the ladder on a bulletin board in the locker room, and each week start players where they ended the previous week.

Another option is a tournament (only one net is needed for this drill), which includes groups of three 1s (numbered 1, 2, 3), three 2s (numbered 1, 2, 3), three 3s (numbered 1, 2, 3), and three 4s (numbered 1, 2, 3). The groups take turns serving to each other for a predetermined period of time (for example, 5 minutes). The players play a round robin in their own group until each player has served and passed to each other player. The format is: 1 serves 2, 1 serves 3, 2 serves 3, 2 serves 1, 3 serves 1, and 3 serves 2. There are six rounds at 5 minutes each for 30 minutes total. When the players have completed the entire round, the winners move up and the losers move down. You can record everyone's new positions and continue this tournament throughout your season.

```
        1  |  1
      ┌─────┬─────┐
      │  2  │  2  │
      │     │     │
      ├─────┼─────┤
    3 │  3  │     │
      │     │ 3   │ 3
      ├─────┼─────┤
      │  2  │  2  │
      │     │     │
      └─────┴─────┘
        1  |  1
```

Ten-in-a-Row

At the end of practice, try to get a certain number of passes (10 or 15) in a row. Set a time limit, for example, 10 minutes for 10 or 15 minutes for 15. Passers might get bonus points for scoring in-a-row more than once, or for scoring more in a row. If passers are less proficient, you might count in-a-row perfect passes, but don't count the poorer passes, and start over if they are aced.

Fours, Throw One

The teams (four players) should be comparable to one another in fours, throw one. Begin the game with a serve and, after the rally terminates, give a toss to the receiving team. If the receiving team wins the serve and the toss, they capture the serve (otherwise, the same server keeps serving). Rotate servers for every new serve. The game should move quickly. Play to five for a big point. Losers leave the court, and the new team has five seconds to get on the court and serve. The match ends when one team scores 15 big points. Only setters can block. The team coming in serves.

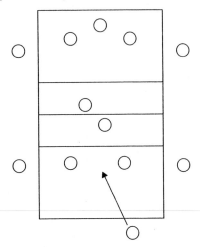

Half-Court Doubles Ladder

In half-court doubles ladder, there are four players on a court: two against two. After five minutes, players switch to compete with another player in the same foursome.

Keep track of the total points from each round. The highest scorer moves up, and the lowest moves down. Rank players randomly, or use the standings from your serve-receive ladder to make up the teams. If you have 12 players and no extra courts, you may want to have steady setters who always play on the receiving team. Quick score. Allow five minutes per pair for three rounds. If there is an extra court, make setters part of the tournament. If there is no extra court, two players will have to sit out the first round.) In round 1, players 1 and 2 play against 3 and 4. In round 2, players 1 and 3 play against 2 and 4. In round 3, players 1 and 4 play against 2 and 3.

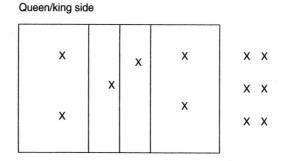

Queen/King of the Court

Queen/king of the court is played in groups of three. One side of the court is designated as the queen or king side. Players score points when they successfully remain on that side. When a player loses, he or she runs off the court, and the winning team members run under the net. Once the last team member has passed under the net, the next threesome begins serving. The first team to score 15 points wins. Some variations include the following:

- Use for warm-ups, or to incorporate new skills into a gamelike situation. Run a series for two to three minutes and then go to the next one.

Examples of game rules for skill progression are

Three overhead passes in a row (toss or underhand serve over).

Three overhead passes in a row.

Two under and one over.

One under and two over.

Two hits plus a back-row attack (must jump).

Two hits plus a jump and tip.

Two hits plus a front-row spike.

Anything goes.

Add rules, such as each person must call ball or his or her team is out.

If players pass the serve over the net their team loses one point.

If no one touches the ball the team loses one point.

Queen/King of the Court, Throw One

Queen of the court can be played three-on-three (on the net or off the net) or six-on-three (on the net or off the net). A coach keeps score using a blackboard. One team must win the serve and the toss to stay in the game. Quick score. Rounds are played for five-minute intervals. (The whole drill will take from 45 minutes to more than one hour, because it takes time to tally scores and get drinks.) However, if your team plays a subset of all the possible combinations, the drill will take less time.

1		147	**258 (1)**	369
2	Outsides	**247 (3)**	358	169
3		347	158	**269 (2)**
4		148	259	**367 (1)**
5	Middles	248	**359 (3)**	167
6		**348 (2)**	159	267
7		**149 (1)**	257	368
8	Opposites	249	357	**168 (3)**
9		349	**157 (2)**	268

Bold type indicates a subset or a shorter combination to decrease drill time.

In-a-Row

The object of the in-a-row drill is just that: to score points in a row. For example, two scores in a row equals one little point, two little points equals one big point, or three scores in a row equals one big point.

   Begin the drill by forming three teams of four. One team serves, and when the first rally is over, the coach tosses a ball to the team that lost the rally. When the second rally is over, the coach tosses another ball to the team that lost the second rally. At this point, one of three things will have happened: (1) neither team will have won twice in a row, (2) one team will have won twice in a row, or (3) one team will have won three in a row. If a team won two in a row, they score a little point (remember the scoring above), another serve occurs, and the game continues. If a team won three in a row, they have one big point, the team that lost leaves the court, and the next team has five seconds to get on the court and serve. The game can be played to 15 big points.

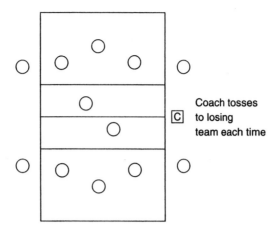

Coach tosses
to losing
team each time

Spiking Drills

Interval Hitting

Using interval hitting, the coach throws balls to the setter (or, if desired, serves balls to a passer or passers). Players (usually in groups of three) singly approach and spike the ball against one blocker, then immediately run around a chair or marker on their way back to the hitting line. Play for a certain period of time. Blockers should not be allowed to run around anything because they may start going under the net and the drill may become too dangerous.

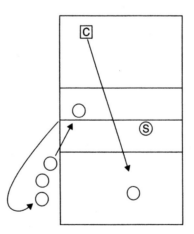

Transition versus Boxes

In the transition drill, three coaches or players stand on boxes at the net. Six defensive players are positioned on the other side of the net. Three players dig balls on the same side of the net as the coaches. One of the coaches hits a ball, and the blockers on the defense try to block it. The players transition and try to kill it (put the ball down on opponent's side). If the players on the same side of the net as the coaches dig it, the ball remains in play. The players must hit the ball from the back row. Keep track of the number of wins each group of three achieves.

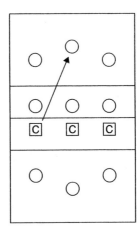

Plus-Minus Five versus Two to Six Defenders

At least three versions of this type of drill are possible. In one version, one hitter at a time plays. The hitter opposes a certain number of defenders. The hitter spikes continuously with virtually no rest between sets until he or she reaches a score of plus five or minus five. Then another hitter has a turn. Keep track of hitting efficiency or time to break the ties that will result. If this drill is set up properly, it can be very demanding for the hitters. It is possible to use outsides, middles, or opposites as the hitters.

In another version of the plus-minus drill, there are two hitters playing against each other. The hitters compete until one of them reaches a five-point advantage over the other or until a certain amount of time elapses. Athletes can play complete tournaments with this format so that every hitter plays against every other hitter. The tournament could be an outside tournament, a middle tournament, or an opposite tournament.

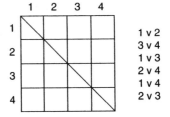

In the third version of the plus-minus drill, there are teams of two or three hitters, some hitting on the net and others hitting off the net. Use a middle and an outside on the net and an opposite hitting off the net. The tournament format is usually similar to the two-hitter format.

Setting

Texas Pepper

Three players form a triangle in the Texas pepper drill. One player is the setter, and two others alternate being passer and spiker. The setter begins with an overhead pass to the spiker (1), who hits the ball to the passer (2), who in turn digs it back to the setter (3). The setter then sets the ball back to the passer (4), who spikes it to the first spiker, who continues this pattern. After a certain time limit elapses, or a specified number of points are scored in a row, another player can become the setter.

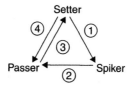

Up and Back 10 Times

Two players join as partners. One stands on the endline and the other at the net. The player at the net tosses the ball, which the partner on the endline passes back. The endline player runs to the spiking line, where the net partner quickly tosses the ball to the spiking line. They repeat the play up and back. The key is to get to the ball with the right foot forward and on a good base. Once the players have good control, eliminate the toss and start passing back and forth with the same routine. Repeat the play shuffling side to side.

50 Bounces

In 50 bounces, the coach stands near the desired target and bounces a ball that the setter sets back to the coach, who then bounces that same ball. Repeat the maneuvers until at least 50 sets have been made.

One-on-One

Three players participate in one-on-one: Two are on the court on opposite sides of the net, and one is the server on the sideline. The server serves underhand to one of the players, who overhand passes the ball over the net, trying to hit it so the other player cannot return it. The other player does the same. Play to three points. The winner stays, and the nonwinner becomes the server.

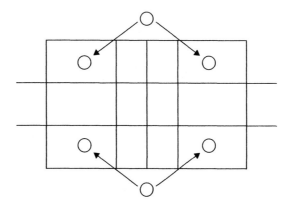

Blocking

Trips (5-3-3, 5-2-2, 3-3-3, 3-2-2, Q3-3-3, Q3-2-2)

These are the different blocking steps taught in Chapter 9. Each person has a partner opposite them on the net mirroring their steps. The partners change direction with each number; for instance, the 5 is to the left, the 3 is to the right, the next 3 is to the left, and so on.

Six Trips versus a Table
This drill is used sparingly in the goal phase of learning. The coach stands on a table and hits at blockers as they make their trips.

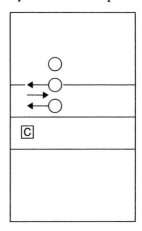

Ball, Setter, Ball, Hitter
This drill works specifically in directing the blockers' focus away from watching the whole flight of the ball and instead looking ahead to the intended target's actions. Six players in their defensive positions are lined up on one side of the court. On the opposite court are two to three hitting lines with a setter and a coach. The coach tosses a ball to the setter, who over- or underhand passes it back to the coach. The coach repeats the pass to the setter, who then sets the ball to one of the attackers. The offense loses a point for every hitting error or if the defense successfully converts the ball. The offense continues to hit until they lose 15 points. Then three hitters wave through (move over to the defense side of the net to block) and the three back-row players move over to the hitting or offense side and the entire sequence repeats until the offense loses 15 points again. The coach should watch blockers' eyes to make sure they are following the "ball, setter, ball, hitter" regime.

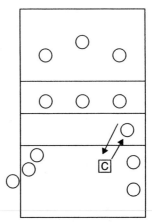

Two Coaches with Table
Two coaches position themselves on tables at opposite endlines. Three blockers are positioned on the opposite side of the net. Players line up behind the middle blocker. Each coach has a bucket of balls and two or three shaggers. The coach on

the left slaps the ball, and the middle hitter moves to block on that side. The coach tosses and hits. After the middle blocker moves, the coach at the right side repeats the maneuver. The outside blocker gets back in line after his or her turn. This drill enhances feet movement, sealing the net, and hand position. It should be used only at the beginning of the season.

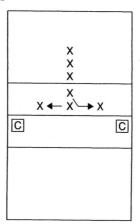

INDIVIDUAL DEFENSE

1. **Texas Pepper** (3 way) (see setting drills in this chapter)

2. **Positional Dig Lines** (see Chapter 8)

3. **First Time** (see Chapter 8)

4. **No Blockers.**   In a no blockers defense, three defensive players begin at their home position on the court. Three lines of spikers stand on the opposite side of the court with a setter. The goal of the defensive players can be either individual or collective. They dig three up in a row to get out (the digs must be playable). The play can be modified in several ways. If the defensive players touch the ball, they are allowed to keep their points and do not have to start over. If there are no touches, they go back to zero. As soon as an individual scores three points, another defensive player takes a turn. In order to keep spikers sending tough balls and not hitting in the net or sending balls out of bounds, there are two rules: (1) If spikers spike in the net or out of bounds, they receive a penalty of two approach jumps before they can spike again; and (2) if the ball is dug by the defense, there is a penalty of one approach jump (encourage attackers to hit in the seams or away from the defense).

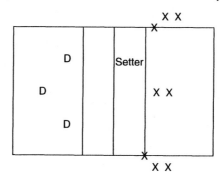

5. Exchange, Four-in-a-Row.   Using four teams of three, two teams are on the court and two are off. When a team player hits the ball over the net, his or her team exchanges with the team off the court. Every time the ball goes over the net, one-in-a-row has been scored. The goal is to get as many in a row as possible (40 is a great score). Accomplished teams will try to pass, set, and spike. Less accomplished teams will simply try to hit some combination of forearm passes and overhead passes. Keep score for both sides of the court. Every time the ball goes over, one point is scored.

For variety, you could implement a rule that a deep court attack must be from behind the spiking line. If it is not, but it is successful going over the net and being dug, it will not count as a point. In this case, the team can keep scoring points in a row. When a team misses a play, the coach can toss a ball similar to the one that caused the problem, and they have to get it over the net before they can leave the court. Play for 10 minutes, and keep track of the highest scores each week.

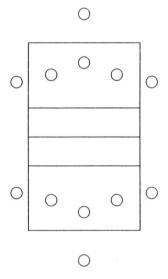

6. Exchange, Two of Three for Six Trips.   In another routine, players exchange as described earlier, but the object is to kill the ball. The coach throws the ball to the player who made the error. Quick score. The best 2 of 3 to 15 wins.

7. Neville's Pepper.   Bill Neville developed this technique. In it, the coach hits free balls to two groups of three that are exchanging. Allow five minutes per bout. The team on the defense can score a point by digging a ball or winning a rally. They lose a point for a hitting error (the teams that are exchanging do not score points).

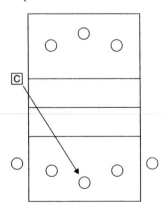

SUMMARY

The keys to using drills that work are

1. Make drills competitive.
2. Each drill should have consequences.
3. Drills should be measurable.
4. Use only gamelike drills.

Coaches need to limit their involvement in drills so that they can give their athletes individual feedback immediately. One or two positive cues are most effective if they are sprinkled liberally with praise and encouragement when skills are performed correctly.

CHAPTER 15

Games and Consequences

Practices should be as gamelike as possible. But how can your team improve if they spend most of their practice time simply playing games? We know from the principle of specificity discussed in Chapter 3 that if you allow players to play games during practice, 100 percent of the skills learned and 100 percent of the muscles conditioned will be transferred to the match. Because of that principle, we have included several choices of games to get you going.

If your team needs to work hard on defense, you can still play games, but you must emphasize defense. How do you do that? Simple. Make a rule that any ball that hits the floor without a touch from any of your players is either minus five points for them or plus five points for their opponents. Add a simple consequence for the loser of the game, like two-minute ball rubs, and just sit back and watch what happens. It will seem as if the ball rubs are a life and death matter! You will notice lots of go calling, diving, and scrambling for the ball, and you will realize that you are not ranting and raving. Is your defense improving? You bet.

But what about consequences? Where do they fit in the scheme of things? Have you ever lost a state or national championship? For some reason they hurt a lot more than losing out at third or fourth or not even getting to the playoffs. Why? Perhaps because the higher you climb, the further you can fall. Maybe because you have invested more, or come closer to taking it all. No matter what the reason, it is true, and it hurts. That is a consequence. Losing is a negative consequence no matter how you try to sugar coat it. This is a large part of what motivates us: not to lose. So, motivate your team. In order to do this, every game should have

1. A goal (competition against self, coach, part of the team, time, or for points)
2. A winner
3. A consequence

ADDING EMPHASIS TO GAMES

There is one more thing you need to add to your games: emphasis. Because you want to use them to improve your team, you need to pick a few points to stress, such as serving, passing, blocking, spiking, or digging. There are several ways of changing a game's focus to drive players to strive harder in different areas. Doing this will eliminate the need for you to yell at them to go for balls, look for holes in the court, and so on because they will be punished or rewarded for doing so simply by their actions. Following are a few examples:

1. Try to decrease passing aces and increase serving aces. In queen's court, triples, or any game, give double or triple points for aces and no penalty for missed serves; players simply lose the serve. The serving team will be working hard to capitalize on this, whereas the receiving team won't want to let them get too many points on one serve. This increases teamwork, because everyone will be helping to ensure aces don't happen by go calling and encouragement.

2. For blocking, you could double points for stuff blocks.

3. In order to increase a team's tendency to go for loose balls on defense (hustling or scrambling), you might try the following:

- Eliminate all points players have accumulated to a certain point if no one touches the ball before it drops to their side of the court.
- Minus five points each time there is a no touch.
- Give the other team five points every time there is a no touch (players will start looking for holes to put the ball down on the opponent's court without a touch).
- Make all six players on a team do two rolls or sprawls on a "no-touch" (this emphasizes teamwork).
- Stop the game at a dead ball, and hit the same type of ball the player did not attempt to get (or touch). They must get a specified number (10 or so) of playable ups (in the court and higher than the net) to go on with the drill.

4. You could penalize missed hits (those served in the net or out of bounds) with two approach jumps with full arm swings, which helps make the approach a habit.

5. You might try subtracting points for serve-receive passes or defensive digs over the net; for example, if the goal is 15 in a butterfly drill with passing serves, every time the ball is passed over the net, the team at fault loses one or two points.

CONSEQUENCES

Adding emphasis goes hand in hand with consequences. Try to have natural consequences (two approach jumps for missing a spike, for example). Some keys to good consequences include the following:

- Keep them short (one to two minutes), but not exhausting.
- They should be immediate; the quicker the better.
- They should not be humiliating.
- They should not be painful or dangerous.
- Keep teams balanced (give handicaps to better teams); don't allow the same players always to lose.
- Try to set consequences before a game begins so players know what they are working toward (which may also serve to decreases complaints).
- Use variety.
- Encourage winners to cheer on losers (this helps develop team unity).

There are as many different consequences as a coach's imagination can dream up. Here are some to get you going:

1. Implement ball rubs. Winners lie on the floor on their stomachs while losers roll a ball over the backsides of their bodies. This is a great massage technique and can be performed for one, two, or more minutes. Use it at the end of practice to warm down.

2. Subtract a set amount of points, such as one, two, or five. Or eliminate all of a team's points and go back to zero.
3. Give points, such as double for aces.
4. Make players do two sit-ups, push-ups, rolls, high-knee jumps, or approach jumps.
5. Allow winners to take the first water break while other team members finish playing.
6. Have losers gather the balls (shag).
7. Have losers set up for the next day's match.
8. Have losers sweep the floor before a practice.
9. Have losers be responsible for the equipment (balls, first aid kit, camera) on the next match day.
10. Give winners first choice of popsicle flavor (everyone gets them though).
11. Have players perform the good job routine: Losers lie on their stomachs at the endline, winners stand at the other endline with their hands outstretched. The coach calls "Go"; losers jump up and run around the court to the winner's side while the coach counts out loud to 10. Losers must slap winners' hands, saying "good job" to each one, and be back where they started by the time coach reaches 10. If not, they perform the routine again.
12. Ladders, long and short (last one in does five push-ups). Players line up at one end of the gym. When the coach yells, "Go!" the players sprint to touch the next line, then return to the starting line, after which they run to the second line, and so on. Use either the short or long side of the gym.
13. Roll or dive ladder. Like the ladder, except that instead of touching the line, each player rolls or dives at every line.
14. Give the winning team one minute to come up with a consequence that will take only one minute. (Remind them it should be reasonable, because there are always paybacks.)
15. Send losers off the court.
16. If a ball is dropped with no touches, the coach might hit the same type of missed ball to the person responsible until he or she has 10 playable ups.
17. If one side makes errors, the coach might toss a ball similar to the missed ball at the person who made the mistake until he or she successfully gets it over the net.
18. Have players do five cartwheels (they are good body stretches, but don't force a player to do them who cannot; give another option, such as two laps or 20 push-ups).
19. Allow losers or winners to lead warm-ups or warm-downs.
20. Allow winners to move up and losers to move down in ladders.

These are enough consequences to get you going. Let your imagination go, and watch your team become competitive and aggressive.

GAMES

You only need a repertoire of 6 to 10 games. If you try to introduce a new game every week, players may become confused. Also, it takes a lot of time to teach the team new games. Choose a few for your team to learn, and then modify the games by adding emphasis or changing a rule or two.

During the second half of the season, the majority of your practices should be spent playing games. Make sure some are as long as regular matches so your players get used to maintaining intensity and focus for that length of time. Another way to help your team develop concentration is by using wash games. Former national team coach Bill Neville introduced the concept of a "wash" game to the world. (Description follows.)

Games should have easy-to-remember names to further facilitate their recognition and implementation. Be imaginative. Here are our favorite games for your use and enjoyment. The particular emphasis of each game is given in parentheses following the game's title.

Wash Games (Concentration on One Specific Skill)

Wash games are designed to help teams develop concentration and work on one specific skill, such as transitioning or siding-out. Each rally win equals a little point, and a certain amount of little points (usually two or three) equals one big point. For example, if the goal of the drill is to practice side-outs, then the team who is receiving the serve can earn a little point by getting a side-out. If they earn two consecutive side-outs, they have a total of two little points, which convert into one big point. The term *wash* means if the receiving team earns one little point, but loses the second, the score remains zero, or a wash (because the two teams split).

The wash table game's emphasis is to evaluate each rotation and its effectiveness siding-out. It is discussed in Chapter 18, Statistics and Scouting.

Bounce (Transition and Conditioning)

Bounce is a two-way, six-on-six volleyball game. A team serves and a rally ensues. When the rally terminates, a coach on the side that lost the rally bounces a ball into the court. The bounce-ball is considered a dig, so there are only two contacts remaining, and the players should try to set and spike the ball. The coaches keep bouncing balls to the team that lost the rally until either team wins three rallies in a row. Three in a row is a point, and the team that scored the point rotates or flip-flops. Flip-flopping is switching the front and back rows. Play to six points. This drill encourages lots of activity, and it is possible to become absorbed in simply bouncing the ball. Coaches have to make certain that they are attending to the transition footwork that is occurring and give appropriate instruction.

Bingo, Bango, Bongo (Maintaining Focus and Intensity Siding-Out)

Bingo, bango, bongo is a two-way, six-on-six game. Begin with a serve and keep throwing balls to alternate sides of the net (throw to the serving team first) until a team wins three in a row (1 = bingo, 2 = bango, 3 = bongo). The team that wins three in a row gets a chance to serve for a point. If the serve is successful, they score a point and flip-flop (a team must score to flip-flop). If they don't score, then the other team serves and both teams try again to get three in a row. Play game one in rotations 1 and 4, game two in rotations 2 and 5, and game three in rotations 3 and 6. Less experience teams can be required to win only two scores in a row (bingo, bango). The team wins that has the most points in all three games.

In another version of bongo, the emphasis is on the players' ability to keep intense and focused attention on crucial plays and serves. It stresses the critical urgency that the players perform well. Each game will be six-on-six, using rally scoring, while rotating servers and teams. When one team wins three in a row, they go for a bongo point. In order to achieve this, they must win a point serving at each rotation in order, one through six. After they win a bongo point at service rotation number one, they must go back to the rotation they were at when they won the three in a row and start again from zero. The first team to reach six points (or achieve bongo at each rotation) wins.

Last Ball (Maintaining Focus and Intensity Siding-Out)

Start with a serve and a rally. When the rally terminates, give a free ball to the losing team, who must hit it over the net (this is their last ball). The team that gets the last ball from the losing team is now on offense, and they must win the last ball and three (or, if the teams are less experienced, maybe one or two) more free balls. If the offense cannot convert the last ball or the free balls, they get the last ball, and the team that was on defense goes on offense. Keep throwing last balls or free balls until someone scores. Both teams rotate when a point is scored. Play the game until all six rotations have been completed. Play the rotations in this order: three, six, four, one, five, two. If there is a 3–3 tie, each team picks a rotation and one more point is played.

Scramble (Reaction Time; Defensive Skills; Quick Decision Making; Concentration)

Scramble is an excellent conditioning drill. Play at least once a week. It can be easily adapted for all ages.

Equipment and personnel include: a timer or scorekeeper, two free-ball tossers, several shaggers, a stopwatch, a flip chart, chalk, an eraser, and a whistle.

Playing six-on-six, the A side serves (they are the scrambling side for two minutes). Immediately after every dead ball, a person out of bounds on the defensive side (B) under- or overhand hits a ball over the net to the scramble side. (They should target places you have trouble with, like seams or setter's right side.) If the B-side person hits the ball in the net or out of bounds, the scrambling side scores an automatic point. Only the scrambling side can score points with every successful play. If the A side does not go for or touch the ball any time during the two minutes of scrambling, they lose every point they have earned in that two-minute scramble up to that time. If they have, say, 30 seconds left and get three more points after they lost their points, they keep the three points at the end of the two minutes.

The defensive side, B, cannot gain points during A's scramble, but they can lose them. If they do not go for a ball or touch it, they lose five points each time that happens. During the scramble B players try to prevent A from getting points.

After A scrambles for two minutes, B scrambles. Then A moves to the next rotation and scrambles two minutes. Continue to flip-flop sides until each team has completed all six rotations. The highest score wins. It is very important to have people to keep the balls off of the court for safety reasons.

Some hints and variations include the following:

- If you have 12 players on a team and another less skilled team to compete against, in order to get subs in and have people to run the game, try the following. After the first minute of scrambling, allow subs to play. The subs have 10 seconds to get into the game before the scramble continues. Every two minutes all subs will return to the game. Following this format, each player gets two minutes; one minute playing offense and one minute playing defense. The players who are not playing should keep time, keep score, throw free balls, and shag. They stay involved in the game, because it is their team winning or losing also. No one is out more than two minutes. It is a very competitive game.

- To ensure the teams have the same chance of winning, you might give double points to the less skilled team during the scramble. You could also increase minus points for defense.

- If players do not go for a ball, try stopping the game after the dead ball and hitting balls to them similar to the one they missed. They should get 5 to 10 playable ups (depending on time and other factors) before continuing.

- Later in the season, you could emphasize a certain aspect of the game by giving extra points. For example, in blocking, give double points for a stuff; or give double points for an ace.

- Stand on the endline to see the court better and coach.

120 Serves (Working on New Serve-Receive Lineups and Plays)

One server serves 10 in a row, rally scoring. After 10 serves, the other side serves 10. Go through all six rotations on both sides. You can add emphasis on serve receive by doubling or tripling points for aces. (The serving side will serve smarter and harder and the serve-receive side will work together not to get aced.) It takes about an hour to play this game, but time could be cut in half by playing 60 serves.

Wash Table (Rotations' Capabilities to Side-Out; Revealing Strongest and Weakest Rotations)

This can be played as a one-way or a two-way six-on-six volleyball game. You can serve all the serves at once on one side, or you can alternate sides. There is a serve and then a toss to the receiving team. If the receiving team wins the serve and the toss, they score an offensive point. If the offense and defense both win, then there is a wash (no score). If the defense wins both, the defense scores a point. The best way to score this is with "golf scoring," with an opportunity to press. Depending on how much time you have, you will need to decide how many serves you want each server to have. It takes approximately thirty seconds per point.

In the diagram below, O indicates offense, W is a wash, and D is defense.

O	W	D		D	W	O

Serve-Toss (Side-Out)

Serve-toss can be a one-way or two-way six-on-six game. You can use little points to keep score. The team on offense must win the serve to get a toss, and they must win the serve and the toss to get a point. The team on defense has to win the serve to score a point. If the team on defense loses the serve but wins the toss, it is a wash. Both teams rotate on big points. The first team through all six rotations wins.

Serve-Toss-Toss (Side-Out)

The offense (serve receive) must win all three serves and tosses to score. The defense (serving team) can win the serve, the first toss, or the second toss to score.

Plus Three (Changing Momentum)

For a certain period of time, teams alternate serving. When one of the teams wins two of the rallies, they achieve a plus 1. However, if one team reaches plus 1 and the other team scores a point, the original point is eliminated, and the score reverts to 0–0 again. The game proceeds until one team reaches plus 3. To reach plus 3, a team must win either two serves or a serve receive, or two serve receives and a serve in a row. The losing team lines up on the end line and sprints back and forth touching six lines. A second aspect of the drill focuses on a certain area of play. Require one hitter (the middle, for example) to hit the first ball (anyone can hit on transition). When the team plays the drill again, you might require the right-side attacker to hit the first ball. In high school, most of the time probably would be spent on the outside hitters. Rotate through the servers (four minutes at a time) with only the featured hitters hitting, and then change the focus and repeat.

Baseball (Intensity)

Baseball is most beneficial as a two-way, six-on-six game, where each server is allowed three outs. A player from team A serves. If team B wins the rally, it is considered an out for the server on team A, who is allowed three outs before the serve goes to side B. If team A wins the rally, the coach throws free balls to team A until team B wins the rally. The score is determined by the number of runs (serve plus free balls that team A obtained). Repeat the drill until three outs are reached. Then a player from team B serves until three outs are obtained. Rotate and repeat the drill for six innings (rotations).

Opposite Volleyball (Side-Out; Offensive and Defensive Maneuvers)

Opposite volleyball is a two-way, six-on-six volleyball game. In this game, the offense is the team that can score; it is called opposite because usually only the serving team (defense) can score points. Team A serves. If the receiving team (the offense, team B) wins the rally, they get a toss (if the receiving team doesn't win the rally, they don't get a toss). If the offense (team B) wins the serve and the toss, they score a point, they rotate (the serving team doesn't), and they receive serve again. If the receiving team loses either the serve or the toss, they become the serving team, and team A goes on the offense and has a chance to score. In this game not too many points are usually scored; the teams keep switching from offense to defense to offense to defense. Thus, it is a good drill to teach teams new offensive and defensive lineups.

Challenge (Working on Team Plays)

Challenge is a 6-on-6, two-way game. The coach writes the teams' play sets on both sides of a chalkboard. Each team tries to complete their sets before the other. The coach erases a set when a team kills it. The offensive plays can be achieved in any order. The first team finished wins. The coach begins the drill with a toss and alternates the toss to each side. If you have particular plays to work on, this is an excellent drill to accomplish this task. You may write down the same sets more than once. If the setters are in the front row, put dumps on the board to allow them the opportunity to work on the offense. Then flip-flop the front and back rows and repeat the drill.

14 versus 12 (Tenacity)

In this 6-on-6 game, one side starts with a score of 14 and the other side starts with 12; they play to 15, when one team wins. The best three out of five or better wins. After each game, it is a good idea to review the teams' choices and ask them to reconsider what might have been better choices the next time. This game is designed to help your team learn to persevere. The game can start at any score you choose and also can be rally scored.

SUMMARY

Playing these games rewards your team with 100 percent transfer of skill and conditioning. This increases your team's proficiency during practice, allowing them to progress further in a shorter amount of time. Also, setting consequences before each game will motivate players to exert more effort. Rewarding certain actions during the games puts emphasis on areas of skill your team needs to improve. Using these suggestion will greatly improve your team's attitude and chances of success. Your players' motivation will become internal rather than originating from you. Isn't that our ultimate goal anyway?

CHAPTER 16

Tryouts

One of the most difficult tasks a coach faces is cutting athletes from a team. These players often have given much of their money and time, not to mention their heart, into playing volleyball. They may be players with whom you have developed close relationships and don't want to hurt.

Cutting players is a difficult decision, but what are the alternatives? Players sitting on the bench match after match, unable to contribute, will feel more and more inadequate and useless as people. Wouldn't they be better off involved in an activity in which they can excel and succeed? They and their parents are often upset and angry about your decision, but are the parents going to be any less upset if you keep their child on the bench rather than allowing them to play?

What about the team that has 40 players and 1 coach (Figure 16.1)? How much individual feedback can these players get? They may become mediocre athletes with very little quality coaching or playing time (like in an intramural program). If you want the team and the program to succeed, you need to determine the appropriate number of players for your team that have a role to fill.

AN OVERLOADED BENCH

FIGURE 16.1 Players who do not feel they contribute to the team usually detract from it.

Whenever you hold tryouts, look for future potential, and try to identify players that have the qualities needed to play in upper divisions. If they don't, don't keep them around even for one season. You will only be prolonging the agony and encouraging them to invest time, money, and effort into something that will not prove worthwhile for them. The athletes will not perceive it as a favor at the time, but that is exactly what it is.

Coaches of beginning programs in volleyball have an extremely hard time cutting players. One strategy that helps coaches evaluate players is a training program. Even with a training program in place, cuts are difficult because coaches will wonder if they are unknowingly preventing a late bloomer from what would have been a promising career. One method of reducing doubt uses multiple cuts. The first cut quickly removes the athletes you are sure are not suitable for your team. After a few more weeks of practice, you will have more confidence in evaluating players for the second cut. This strategy helps eliminate some of the doubt.

Training programs are important to the success of the athlete and of the upper division programs. It is imperative they begin early and emphasize appropriate coaching methods. Just as in gymnastics, skiing, golf, and so on, the earlier an individual gets started in a sport, the more proficient he or she will become. If athletes are taught the proper skills and how to use them, they will not have to spend time later fixing errors or bad habits. They will be able to move forward quickly in their athletic programs. Good feeder programs (elementary, junior high, club ball) are important to upper division teams' success. Enlightened administrators understand this and hire or encourage their staff to work together toward a common goal.

SUGGESTIONS FOR VOLLEYBALL STARTER PROGRAMS

Following are some suggestions for implementing or improving the volleyball program:

- Invite upper division players to demonstrate the game.
- Play intramurals in the younger grades. (Lower the net.)
- Always use a good ball, not a hard, rubber one that could hurt a player. Sometimes you can purchase usable older balls from upper division groups inexpensively.
- Ask upper division teams to put on a clinic for the younger group. If you try this strategy, you'll soon see improvements such as skill level rising with increased ball touches. Adolescents that went to camp will help those trying out who didn't go, which takes some pressure off of the coach. There are usually many players trying out, and only one coach. The inexperienced individuals will have the opportunity to see correct examples of plays. Your whole group will learn faster by observing.
- Teach the skills for a couple of weeks before having tryouts.
- Keep a few more players than an upper division team would.
- You might enlist a few player/managers who will get some practice time but won't expect any playing time. These athletes will have the opportunity to stay current with their group and, if they develop, might be able to make the team the following year.
- Ensure that coaches have the opportunity to attend coaches' clinics to stay abreast of current trends in volleyball.

- Provide discount tickets to upper division matches. Watching better, older teams play will inspire and give younger players ideas for improvement.

In the following sections, we consider some ideas to help complete this dreaded task of cutting players with the least possible detriment.

ANNOUNCE TRYOUTS

You've got to get the word out so everyone who is eligible and desires to play on your team will have the opportunity to try out. Here are some suggestions:

- Advertise in the local newspaper or on a local radio station.
- Distribute flyers.
- Announce upcoming tryouts at schools.

Make sure the information is complete and accurate, and distribute it early enough to allow all who are interested to make plans to attend. If there are permission forms for parents to sign before their child can participate, it is a good idea to have an informational meeting prior to the tryout date to hand out the forms and answer questions.

GENERAL TRYOUT CONSIDERATIONS

It is imperative that you are unbiased. Even though a potential player might be your neighbor, best friend's child, or a relative, your team's respect for your judgement can depend on these decisions. The tests or drills you run should be impartial and be administered as equally as possible.

Take notes that could be useful if you visit the people you cut. When a person puts a lot of effort into a sport, there are more repercussions if he or she does not make the team. Having concrete evidence to support your decisions if you are called on to do so goes a long way to nullify an angry confrontation. You should reveal results only to the individual at issue or his or her parents, no one else. Conversely, do not show that individual the rest of the tryout results. It is not their concern and an invasion of privacy.

Consider the positions that need to be filled on your team. Do you need a middle blocker, or do you have four of them already? Do you have two setters? What about quick defense players or passers? When you are finalizing who the last few team members will be, determining what positions you need to fill will help you make the final choices.

How many players do you want on your team? It is easier to play the games and practice drills in volleyball if you have multiples of three, such as 9, 12, or 15 players. You need to have backup players in case of injury for each position on your team. You also need to consider that you spend more time practicing than in actual matches, and the athletes who are competing with each other can achieve a higher or lower skill level, depending on the skill levels of those they practice with.

Don't retain players who are not performing at the level of the rest of the team. It is better to cut individuals at lower skill levels than to keep them to fill out the numbers on the team. Not only will they drag the rest down, but they detract from the better athletes' playing time. Also, the more athletes on your team, the less individual coaching attention each has. It is hard for them to keep an upbeat attitude on the bench and in practice if they are not contributing to the team.

Sometimes you will have a player you really want to keep that just doesn't have what it takes, but one that, nevertheless, has a great attitude, or one that is a real borderline choice. If you want to keep the individual, one technique that can work is to discuss options with him or her before you post the cuts; be very up front with the player about what you have in mind. Advise about how much playing time can be expected (probably very little) and ask the player to decide if he or she still wants to be part of the team. If so, it is very important that the parents understand and agree to the terms also. Some of those who decide to stay cannot only help your team perform better during practice but can be great attitude support on the bench. Following are items you need to consider when running tryouts.

Physical Ability or Attributes

The specific physical traits athletes need for volleyball are

- Quickness; speed and reflexes
- Vertical jump
- Lower body strength
- Abdominal strength
- Upper body strength
- Muscle endurance
- Coordination
- Height (helps)

Some tests for these physical attributes are

- For quickness, shuttle run, verticals (from 10-foot line to 10-foot line)
- For vertical jump, standing, block, and four-step-spike-approach vertical jumps
- For lower body strength, standing broad jumps (or three-in-a-row), max squats
- For abdominal strength, sit-ups
- For upper body strength, bench pressing, basketball soccer throw, push-ups
- For muscle endurance, 12-minute runs (six laps are excellent; five and a half, good; five, average; less than five, poor) or a seven-minute mile

Skill

The skill level you are looking for will, of course, depend on the level of volleyball your team plays. The following list begins with some of the simplest skills and progresses to more advanced ones.

Underhand pass

- Pass to self (count the number of passes for one minute; provide height requirement they pass to, such as above antennas or the net).
- Three passing positions: Toss the ball from in front of the endline over the net.
- Each person gets five tosses at each of the three serve receive spots.

- Have a target standing at the net rate passes (three is perfect; for two, the setter can still set; for one, another teammate besides the setter has to play, and 0).
- Partner, or three-in-a-line passing: The coach rates passing skill (platform, feet, angle of body, shuffle or other movement, and accuracy).
- Coach evaluation in a game situation.
- Serve-receive ladder evaluation (Chapter 14).

Overhead pass

- Set to self (same as pass to self).
- Set to target on a wall for one minute. Count the number of successful attempts.
- Coach evaluation of passing skill (base-feet, hand position, movement, accuracy of set) in a set drill or game situation.

Serve

- Serve 20 in a row.
- Serve five times in a row to six positions on the court. Count the number of successes in each.
- Serve-receive ladder.
- Coach evaluation of form in a drill or a game (toss, arm swing, accuracy, speed, type of serve).

Spike

- Coach evaluation in a game or a drill (approach, vertical jump, arm swing, control). Include different types of sets (shoots, shorts, slides, and so on).
- Divide the court in half. Count the number (out of ten attempts) players can hit into the opponent's court, cross-court, and down-line. Also, count deep court hits.

Game Skills

It is extremely important to include game play in tryouts. You might have an athlete who has top scores in all the static drills but can't relate or react to other players on the court. Most of your tryouts should be actual game play. It is wise to play games that offer each person multiple touches on the ball. Six-on-six does not always do this, because a more aggressive player will take the majority of the balls, and another player may not touch them at all in several serves. Some suggestions to circumvent this are

- Triples—Choose teams, and play for a limited amount of time (five minutes) then trade teams. Be sure to change the makeup of teams several times.
- Queen's court.
- Half-court doubles ladder (see Chapter 14)—This is a good drill, but be aware that if a player is not an all-around good player (good at all skills), he or she may be lower on the ladder. If you were to cut one of these players, realize that he or she might have been your defense specialist or your best blocker who plays only front row.

Take notes on the players, both positive and negative. Pit the ones you have concerns about against each other.

Other Considerations

There are other qualities to look for in players that greatly contribute to the success of your team. You need to be aware of these and watch for them during your tryouts. They are

- Coachability
- Team players who are willing to help others
- Positive attitudes
- Loyalty
- Hustlers
- Dedicated team members
- Hard workers
- Ability to handle mistakes
- Affable character

POSTING YOUR TEAM

There are lots of different ideas about how to handle this traumatic event. The most common way now is to post a list of the team or to announce the team at the end of tryouts. A less traumatic and more private method is to give each person an envelope (Figure 16.2). You can hand them out or have them in a pick-up spot at a designated time. In the envelope is a letter thanking them for their participation

FIGURE 16.2   Tryout Letter

in your tryouts and notifying them whether they made your team. For the ones who did, you might include a schedule of matches, team rules, and a list of future practice session. Here is a sample letter. (One is included in the masters appendix at the back of the book.)

[School Letterhead]

Dear _____,

We would like to thank you for taking your time and energy to try out for the _____ High volleyball team. You have made a definite contribution by participating and making it possible to hold a tryout.

It is a difficult time, the most difficult in all aspects of our coaching, we feel, to make the decision to keep some and to let others go. We always try to make our decision unbiased and based on fact. Be assured, whether you make the team or not, our main consideration was whether you could some-day be a contributor to the varsity program. This is difficult to measure and is something over which we agonize. We do not want to waste your time or have you sit on the bench and feel as if you are not helping our program.

This year you have/have not been chosen to be on the team. If you would like to review the reasons for this decision, please feel free to fill out the enclosed form for an appointment and give it to the office or one of the coaches.

Thank you for contributing to the quality of _____ High's volleyball program. Your participation has pushed all to higher excellence.

Sincerely,

_____ High School Volleyball Coaching Staff

There is quite a debate whether you should offer an opportunity to the ones that you cut to talk to you about your decision. Most coaches are quite busy, and this kind of meeting can be confrontational and emotional. However, the athletes have spent quite a bit of time and effort to try out, and they deserve an opportunity to find out why they failed. Many times they assume it is because the coach didn't like them, which can be dispelled easily with the facts. Also, talking to them will get that awkward first-time, face-to-face meeting out of the way. Giving them an opportunity to make an appointment to talk to you, or putting a slip of paper in their envelope with the time, would be appropriate.

Anyway you choose, try to keep the person and how they feel in mind. Rejection is difficult for anyone to bear. Not being good enough to make the team can not only be momentarily traumatic, but it can stay with a person quite a long time.

The situation needs to be handled quickly with tact. It is a necessary but painful situation for all concerned, including coaches. Good luck.

SUMMARY

To review our suggestions for running successful tryouts:

- The younger the athletes, the longer the tryouts, lasting several days of instruction.
- Note concrete observations on skill evaluations, both positive and negative.
- Keep information confidential.
- Include actual playing time in matches to observe each athlete's skill in team play and court and ball sense.
- Do not keep athletes that you do not think have potential to play a starting position.

And last, consider how much time and effort each athlete has spent preparing and trying out for the team. Please be tactful when posting cuts. Successfully selecting your team is the first step on your road to a championship.

CHAPTER 17

Designing Effective Practice Sessions

What makes some practices great and others a waste of time? Why do some teams evolve so far during the season? How do you keep your athletes excited to come each day to the gym and work as hard as they can? Why do some players scramble after every ball with perseverance, whereas others can't seem to make the effort to bend over and pick it up?

It's all in the way you run your practices. So, what does it take to put a productive practice together? How do you use the time, the talent, and the gym space to get the best product for your money? There is no magic formula, but there are some really important ingredients that have to be present. They are

- A season flow chart
- Practice equipment
- Basic facts to consider when planning practices
- Practice goals
- General practice outline
- Designing the best practices possible
- A sample practice

To begin with, there is an order of thought processing coaches go through before planning a practice session. Before planning your practices, consider what part of the volleyball season is involved in the practice. Is it the beginning, the middle, or the end? Where we are dictates what our emphasis is. This chapter begins with an outline of the goals for the season.

SEASON FLOW CHART

Early in the Season

The following issues should be covered in the beginning of the season.

- Teaching and reviewing basic skills (50 percent of the time).
- Team play (scrimmage, games) (40 percent); emphasize conditioning 10 percent to 20 percent of this time.
- Tactics, or scouting reports (10 percent).
- Stress serve receive and serving.
- Develop the starting lineups.
- Define players' roles.

Midseason

At midseason, you should turn your attention to the following issues.

- Skills (35 percent).
- Team play (50 percent); including conditioning (10 percent to 20 percent).
- Tactics (15 percent)
- Solidify individuals' positions and lineups.

Late Season and Play-offs

During the later part of the season and play-offs, consider the following items most important.

- Skills (15 percent).
- Team play (60 percent); including conditioning (5 percent to 10 percent).
- Tactics (25 percent).

Post- and Preseason

At postseason and preseason, you should stress the following.

- Weight training and conditioning (see Chapter 21).
- Playing sand volleyball, doubles, triples, club ball, or open gym.
- Mentally learning more by watching films, including the best team plays, and reading books.

The season flow percentages are explained as follows: More emphasis is placed at the beginning of the season on skills that solidify the basics. Extra time is needed for conditioning, to build muscle tone, and to enhance endurance.

Notice that, as the season progresses, more time is spent in team play. Because that is the most productive way to transfer skills to matches, you need to emphasize those drills as soon as the players have a solid base of skills. That doesn't mean you ignore skills; simply use specific cues (feedback) to keep your players improving.

Good planning gives you more time to increase the focus on scouting and finding and capitalizing on opponents' weaknesses. Also, during play-offs, less emphasis will be placed on conditioning. The athletes aren't building at that time, just maintaining. Shorter practices will enable your athletes to rest, allowing tired, torn muscle fibers to repair and rejuvenate. The speed and clarity of thought processes also improve with rest. More emphasis can be placed on improving your poorest rotations in defense and offense (which you've learned during your season from stating in your scorebook; see Chapter 18).

PRACTICE EQUIPMENT

In order to use the drills and games recommended in this book, certain equipment is needed. Because balls are so expensive, instead of getting cheaper ones, buy only a few of the best every year and rotate out the oldest ones. If you can't afford ball carts, use large garbage cans on wheels. Besides courts and nets, the following equipment is essential.

- Twenty to thirty good balls.

- Ball carts (baskets or buckets)—two per court are preferred—that hold at least 20 balls.
- A flip chart with three different scores, one for each team and a middle score to indicate the game number. A flip chart with a middlescore that goes to five is preferred (to use with wash games or a scramble).
- A stop watch.
- A whistle (plastic is preferable).
- Antennas that are quick and easy to move (two extra per court).
- Chalkboard, chalk, and eraser.
- Two to four cones or markers.
- Towels.
- Dust mops, dustpan, and broom.
- Elastic cords or small weights.

Now that you have what you need to play the game and know what to emphasize during the season, what facts dictate the content of practices? There are nine major considerations to take into account that will influence the drills you plan to use.

BASIC FACTS TO CONSIDER WHEN PLANNING PRACTICES

- Time of season and emphasis.
- Number of players; multiples of three are best (9, 12, 15). If any players are missing for a day because of illness, injury, or an excuse, the players who are at practice will many times determine what drills you can run (a setter, middle blocker, and so on).
- Physical state of players (perhaps exhausted from away matches or a big tournament).
- Mental state of players (homecoming, finals).
- Court and gym time availability.
- Availability of JV or other in-house teams for scrimmage.
- Talent.
- Match schedule (do we have a match tomorrow or was there one yesterday?).
- Is your practice court the same as the home match court? (The amount of room to play, serve, and so on, along with the athletes' perception, changes with the placement of the net in the gym.)

Now that you have the facts essential to planning a practice, what do you hope to accomplish in these practices? Unless you want the players to wander around trying to hit everything and getting nowhere quickly, you need a set of goals. Goals provide points to be heading toward, with markers along the way, telling you you're on the right road. With a set of goals in mind, you're more apt to reach your destination. The following section describes three major objectives that will help you reach your goals.

PRACTICE GOALS

I. Develop an outline.
  A. Emphasize the big picture and try to realize it in each practice.

       1. Prepare your team for every situation.

       2. Mold the group of individuals into a unified team.

       3. Provide experiences whereby individuals and the whole team can discover their maximum human potential.

       4. Provide an atmosphere in which players feel safe to take risks and gain greater heights.

    B. Develop seasonal, weekly, and daily outlines.

       1. Focus and decide on where you want to be on a daily, weekly, and seasonal basis.

       2. Set goals.

  II. Follow clear, understood, and respected rules.

Try to limit rules to a few enforceable ones, such as penalties for missing or arriving late for practices. All athletes should know that if they miss a practice they are behind.

 III. Provide gamelike practices.

    A. Players should practice like you want them to play in a match.

       1. Emphasize pressure, intensity, and hustle.

       2. Provide consequences, rewards, and penalties.

       3. Try to ensure lots of successes.

       4. Practice randomly. Do not do one skill repetitively, such as serving only. Instead, serve, then pass, then set and hit.

    B. Allow players to run drills 90 percent of the time. As the coach, coach, which increases opportunities for instant player feedback.

GENERAL PRACTICE OUTLINE

The first goal was to develop an outline. Once you have your outline, you can start building skills in drills and games. A brief example follows.

Early Season

Activity	Approximate Time
A. Prepractice activities (See Figure 17.1)	10 min.
1. List individual activities on the chalkboard for the team to accomplish before practice begins.	
2. As the coach, use this time to prepare for practice.	
B. Corner up/line up	1 min.
1. All balls shagged in buckets.	
2. Give instructions for warm-up.	
C. Warm-up	10–15 min.
1. Start with a low-keyed game and consequence.	
2. Gather balls, break for water.	
D. Stretch	5 min.
1. Led by the captain, a designated person, or a randomly assigned team member.	
2. Coach makes announcements and outlines practice goals.	

FIGURE 17.1   Prepractice on Blackboard

E. New skill, ballhandling/review skills (two- to three-   30 min.
   person drills)
   1. Demonstrate.
   2. Practice.
   3. Give feedback.
F. Individual combination drills   30 min.
   1. The skill focus is the whole team, such as defense,
      blocking, or passing.
   2. Pass, set, hit.
   3. Serve and pass.
   4. Dig, set, hit.
G. Scrimmage/competition drills/conditioning   50–60 min.
   1. Offense/defense.
   2. Transition.
   3. Match preparation.
H. Cool-down/ice   10 min.
   1. Stretch and ice sore muscles.
   2. Summarize practice; review stat chart kept during
      practice.
   3. Remind players about rest.
   4. Provide mental image homework.

DESIGNING THE BEST PRACTICES

It's time for the heart of the practice. The following suggestions, if put to use, will bring success not only in volleyball but also in life. Many of the ideas presented are ingredients for success in the business world as well.

FIGURE 17.2 Allow sufficient time after classes for athletes to dress, tape, and complete their preliminary warm-ups (so that they don't leave class early or are not late to practice).

1. Time. Allow sufficient time after classes for athletes to dress, tape, and complete their preliminary warm-ups (see Figure 17.2). Your goal is to use the time you have to the best advantage. At starting time be precise and don't be late. Don't accept excuses; don't give them. If any member of your team is late, he or she should get immediate, appropriate consequences. Quick implementation makes profound impressions on the rest of the team. They know you aren't bluffing.

- If a player has a problem, he or she should talk to you before, not after, a late arrival.
- Be ready with the balls, a swept floor, and other equipment needed for practice (flip chart, stopwatch, and so on).
- Write on the chalkboard early so all can follow preliminary instructions (prepractice drills).

2. Prepractice drills. Before practice begins, list a number of prepractice items on the chalkboard you want your athletes to accomplish before practice starts. These will include strategies to help with certain aspects of a drill, such as muscle group conditioning, footwork techniques, or skills that can be performed independently without any coaching. When you repeat an action enough times, it becomes a habit, enabling the athlete to perform it without conscious thought, so he or she can focus on other things, like opponents. Prepractice drills increase the number of repetitions athletes perform in one day, creating a habit sooner. Some of the recommended activities are (no more than 10 minutes total)

- Sit-ups at least three times a week (see Chapter 21).
- Push-ups at least three times a week.
- Elastic cord spikes (or two-pound weights) at least three times a week (see Chapter 21).

Choose from the following and alternate until athletes' habits are formed. Teammates should coach each other during practice. (If they see a pumping action in their partner during the pass, they should tell them).

- Blocking steps (dance) along net (5-3-3, 5-2-2, 3-3-3, 3-2-2, Q3-3-3, Q3-2-2; see Chapters 9 and 12).
- Tomahawk with two or three players, keep total maximum in a row (see Chapter 8).
- Overhead and underhand passing sequence (See Chapters 4 and 5).
- Partners 20, three's in-a-line 10 repetitions (middle count), triangle 45 right/ left (see Chapters 4 and 5).
- Up and back (10 underhand and 10 overhand passes (see Chapters 4 and 5)).

3. Be prepared. Plan the next day's practice at the end of every practice. The skills your team should improve will be fresh in your mind.

4. Teach new concepts. It is most beneficial to teach new skills, plays, and so on at the beginning of the week and early on in the practice. Practice passing and serve reception in the first half of practice, when athletes have more energy, their minds are clearer, and their retention is better.

5. Warm-ups. Play games or drills to warm up. The following points present the positive results of this type of warm-up:

- Increases athletes' skill level. The more times they touch the ball correctly, the more control they have.
- Makes them work harder. Competition pushes them instead of you.
- Improves athletes' attitude. They would much rather play a game than run around the gym doing the grapevine.
- Provides mental practice; they have to figure out a way to win with the ever-changing set of rules given for the game. They concentrate harder. They begin to look for ways of capitalizing on their opponent's weaknesses, for example, by serving to the worst passer or trying to take the best hitter out of the attack by serving at the hitter.
- Improves teamwork. All are punished if the ball hits the ground without a touch, just as the whole team is punished when poor play causes a game loss. These game warm-ups encourage teamwork among players to achieve success.
- Encourages team sportsmanship. Players get used to playing with everyone. Do not always let them choose their own team members. It can be very discouraging for the less talented players or junior-level players. Your team needs to fraternize with each other and eliminate cliques on the court. Some suggestions for integrating your team include drawing names out of a hat, lining the players up and counting off, lining up tall to short, or putting together specific positions.

So, what kind of games will work as warm-ups? Simply downgrade those you already use to slowly warm up without risking injury. Queen's court is one example of an adaptation. (Many more games that can be used for warm-ups can be found in Chapters 14 and 15). Review the rules for a regular queen's court game in Chapter 14. Start the game with an overhand throw from behind the 10-foot line; continue serving that way until one team has five points. Then go to regular serving from behind the endline. Players' serving arms should be warmed up soon. Following are some adapted rules for warming up (it's is up to the coach's discretion how many to use). Three hits on a side are required, unless the ball is blocked. Have players perform the following progressions for two minutes each before going on to the next set:

1. Three overhand passes.
2. Three underhand passes.
3. Two underpasses, one overpass, in any order.
4. Back-row hit (must jump).
5. Tip (must jump).
6. Front-row spike.
7. Anything goes (one to three hits is acceptable).

Following are additional rules to make the drill competitive or place emphasis on a certain skills:

- If the ball hits the floor without an attempt, or without being touched, all three on the losing team must have a consequence, such as losing all their points; two push-ups, sit-ups, high knee jumps; or one sprawl, roll, or dive, as soon as they leave the floor. Emphasize whatever the team needs to work on. (Blocks count as a touch.)
- Emphasize passing by giving two points for an ace or eliminating all points if a player passes over the net.
- Emphasize serving by giving the other team two points for every missed serve. Or if competitors serve to number six (middle-back position on the court), their team is immediately sent off the court. (This discourages easy serves to the best passer, who is usually in the number six position. (Use this technique later in the season when players have developed more control.)
- Emphasize blocking by doubling points for a stuff.

6. Stretch muscles.   All athletes should stretch only after they are warmed up. Start in the standing position, and stretch a whole muscle group at a time. After an intense drill that works one particular set of muscles, say the gastrocnemius (calf) muscle in jumping, stretch against the wall or on the stairs. Also, stretch during the cool-down period. This preventive measure helps with muscle soreness and possible strains and pulls. It also provides quiet time to talk to your team, additionally using your practice time wisely.

7. Use rifles, not shotguns.   If one player is problematic, don't punish the whole team. Chances are the one you are trying to reach with the scattered approach won't have a clue that he or she is the target, and the rest of the team either knows who the criticism is intended for or is upset because they don't know what the problem is and are wondering who caused it. The shotgun approach causes resentment among players because it seems unfair, and rightly so. Be direct; unless several players are problematic, direct your criticism to the appropriate player.

8. Make everything competitive with consequences.   Drills especially can be competitive. The following examples can be competitive and create a hustle atmosphere on your team.

- Cornering or lining up: the last one in does two sit-ups.
- Running ladders: the last one in does five push-ups.
- When shagging balls, the team to get the fewest in the bucket does five high knee jumps. Or, everyone does five high knee jumps, except for the three players who got the most (reward). If there are ties, try rock, paper, and scissors to break them. Make sure you vary the consequences.

These tactics serve a variety of purposes for your practices.

- They prepare players for the stressful game atmosphere where there are immediate consequences for their actions.
- They increase focus and intensity.
- The competition pushes them, so you don't have to.
- They creates an "I hate to lose" attitude, developing an athlete who will work hard not to lose.
- They help you use every minute efficiently because all are hustling.
- They improve the condition of the athlete.

9. Improving on drills.   Use gamelike drills with consequences. Always reveal the consequence before beginning the game. Consequences should be quick and immediate (approximately one minute). For example, in a warm-up drill, tell players before they start that the teams who lose will do as many push-ups as is the difference between their score and the winning team's score. If the winning team scores 25 and another team's score is 17, the losers will do eight sit-ups. If your players know that, they will work harder to keep the point differential small.

Drills should always have a specific goal to reach, such as 25 consecutive hits in deep court, or being the first team to reach 15 points, or an individual defense of 10 good passes in a row. Players get satisfaction by achieving and will strive hard to reach the goal.

- Don't bluff, follow through, but be reasonable.
- Use drills and games with a small number of players on the team, such as two, three, or four. This will increase the number of ball touches per person.
- Limit the variety of games you use to six to eight, such as baseball, bongo, and so on. To keep players interested, you can change goals or emphasis. Using too many games takes too much time to teach, and your players will not remember all the strategies and rules. Six to eight are plenty.
- It is a good idea to run some of your scrimmages the same length as your games will run—from 20 to 40 minutes on the average. This gives your team practice keeping their focus and intensity for an extended period of time.
- Demonstrate all drills or games. Walk players through them.
- When hitting, always come off the net with a transition, or in from a pass. Gamelike!
- Instead of tossing the ball to your setter, set it or pass it. (Why practice tossing if you don't do it in a game.)
- Practice random drills. Don't use drills in which the same person stands and serves 10 balls. In the game of volleyball players don't do that. They serve, run in a play awhile, then go back and serve, if they are fortunate. Their minds need to get used to random play.
- Use player-centered drills 90 percent of the time; this allows the coach to observe and instruct.

- Let competition, not you, drive your players. Do not yell at them; instead set up a competitive atmosphere whereby if they do not hustle or work hard, they lose. You don't make them lose, they lose by their actions and the rules of the game.
- Chart some individual and team drill results (see Chapter 18). This drives players to improve the score the next time, and it is a source of satisfaction when they do. It also reveals where improvements have taken place and can be an eye opener to the coach on which players are successful in certain situations.

10. Vince Lombardi once said, "If you cheat in a practice, you will cheat in a game, and if you cheat in a game, you will cheat in life, and I will not have it." Trust is imperative between a coach, team, and teammates. Coaches must trust athletes to be honest in reporting scores, honest with their teammates, honest in doing the required number of repetitions, and so on. If someone is dishonest, count the reps he or she reports every now and then, and confront him or her about potential dishonesty. You are not doing anyone a favor by allowing dishonesty to continue.

11. Be aware of your athletes' physical and emotional condition.

- Make sure they notify you first if they are sick or injured (not a trainer or a friend).
- Allow frequent natural water breaks, such as at the conclusion of a game or drill, or when an individual has reached a goal, or when they sub out. These should be short, one-minute breaks from which they return quickly. Each player should have his or her own water container. Check that they do frequently, and reward them when they do. Be aware of hot weather and the dehydration it causes. Hydration decreases injury and muscle fatigue (see Chapter 19) and helps the mind to function better.
- Give strategic, short rests. Encourage hard work, then provide a reward. Vary between long or intense drills. If you run a drill that works the setter and middle blocker more, for example, make sure you give them extra rests and water breaks.
- Sometimes a no-practice day is better than a practice. After a tough week (two trimatches and a two-day away tournament, for example,) a day off to relieve tired, sore muscles and to catch up on homework, or some personal time, might just be enough to rejuvenate a player and prevent an injury or improve an attitude.
- Be aware of things that cause stress in your players' lives, such as a tough class load, finals, family problems, or health problems.

12. Set your players up to succeed.   Improved self-esteem allows your players to venture out from their comfort zone and try new things.

13. Every ball is playable as long as the player and the ball are alive.   Encourage team members to play the ball off of the wall, the ceiling, the bleachers, everything but the floor. Try to create instant reactions; encourage players to go for anything gettable. If they automatically think everything is playable, they will be likely to try for it, whereas others will be looking and wondering if they could possibly get it.

14. Play by the rules.   If a player hits the net during a spike, or steps on an end line during a serve, penalize it. Don't allow it. You should be practicing like you are planning to play, with everything as gamelike as possible.

15. Teach players how to run drills and shag. This will help you accomplish more and run drills efficiently, while decreasing distraction and possible injury.

- Encourage team members to practice courtesy (respect others). Do not allow players to interfere with a teammate to shag a ball that has rolled their way.
- Encourage players to hustle when shagging.
- Make subs keep balls off the court during scrimmages, wash drills, and so on.
- Do not throw balls under the net when players are spiking.
- Be explicit about where you want the ball put (in your hand, waste high, in the bucket, and so on).
- If you run out of balls or a game or drill has to be stopped because there are no balls available (such as the butterfly), there are consequences for the team(s) responsible.
- Do not allow anyone to sit and just watch drills. They could be shagging, calling, scoring, mentally shadowing players in their position, or looking for holes (weaknesses on the other team) to help teammates.
- Urge players to run everywhere. No deposit, no return.

16. Videotape. Review individuals' skills in practice, such as spiking, blocking, passing, or serving. A picture is worth a thousand words. It is very informational to show a player what his or her hands and arms are doing in a blocking situation. Showing your players where they are on defense or what they are doing during transition is a reality check. There can be no denials when you have concrete proof. Sometimes, under stressful conditions, players don't realize what they are doing.

17. Be positive.

- Acknowledge every player positively every day. Look for things to praise. Write them down during practices and matches. Highlight players, trying to get as many good examples as possible.
- Laugh. Use humor to handle difficult situations. Remember, after everything is over, this is just a game.
- End practice on a positive note, such as a good play. Surprise them sometimes and let them go a few minutes early as a reward.

There might be more guidelines for successful practices, but if you follow these, they will prove sufficient. There is always more you can do. You have to decide when enough is enough. Included is a sample practice, which gives you an example of how to put the information provided together.

A SAMPLE PRACTICE

Date _____

Time	Purpose and Drill	Goal or Consequence
10 min.	**Prepractice** 20 sit-ups and push-ups; 35 elastic cords; block-5-3-3, 5-2-2, 3-3-3, 3-2-2, Q3-3-3, Q3-2-2; underhand pass, 45 each way; tomahawk with three triangles	Difference between top score of tomahawk; 5 high knee jumps

Time	Purpose and Drill	Goal or Consequence
12 min.	**Warm-up** North Pole, South Pole (three min. each), four sets Set only, bump only, back row hit, front row attack	Bottom two in charge of balls and first aid next match
5 min.	**Stretch** Captains lead; review today's schedule and goals	Improve team passing and serve receive
42 min.	**Skills Drills** Review underhand pass	
(2)	Cues: face ball, feet to ball, angle arms, simple Up and back with partner; move feet quickly; arrive ahead of ball; 10 each from 10 feet to endline	When finished, get a drink
(10)	Teach hitting line	
(15)	Demonstrate closing shoulders, timing, ball placement Two lines, two setters, start at net and transition Coach sits in chair on line or use bucket or chair as a target; first to hit is president of the bucket or chair club, second is vice president, and so on	Club members rest as others shag balls
(15)	Review blocking Rapid-fire drill (three trips up and down the net); one point for a touch; two points for a block, three points for a stuff	Push-ups, difference between scores
15 min.	**Individual Combination Drills** Butterfly; compete with JV; goal is 15 passes to target; JV gets two points each	Short ladder (under net)
	Five passes from each of three different serve-receive positions	
	Pass over the net gets minus two from score	
	Don't touch serve (ace), go back to 0	
60 min.	**Scrimmage** 120 serves with JV; two points each for JV Double points for aces (four for JV, two for V) Subs in after five serves (they stay for 10 serves, allowing half time on defense and offense)	Two-min. ball massage for winners
5 min.	**Cool Down** As they stretch out, tell them: Bus leaves at 2:30 tomorrow Blue uniforms Remind who is in charge of the equipment (loser of game) Team cheer (Hustle!)	
	Notes Things coach needs to do tomorrow Players to talk to Who did a great job	

SUMMARY

Now if you take all the x's and o's that we've given you to run a practice and leave out the following critical elements, your practices won't be nearly as effective as they could be. Try these following suggestions in your practices:

1. You need to focus on the here and now as much as you want your players to.
2. Have fun! You love this game and want your players to love it too.
3. Humor is wonderful in almost every situation. Use it.
4. Praise, praise, praise.
5. Don't overdo it. At the end of practice your players should leave wanting more.
6. Last, but most important, say only one-half of what you want to. Let them play!

CHAPTER 18

Team Statistics and Scouting

How do you know who is winning if you don't keep score? How can you tell who is helping or hurting your team if you don't keep track? Guesswork? How accurate is that in determining who won the match? Coaches need to have a factual way to measure athletes' input and progress just as they do for determining who won the game. Athletes also want to know if they are measuring up and improving. In order to know where they stand, scores or statistics need to be calculated.

When teams play opponents, they must take advantage of their opponents' weaknesses and be prepared for their strengths. This is where scouting comes into play. Do you know what to scout for and how to use the information gleaned to your advantage?

This chapter answers these questions and also shows how to use statistics in practices to improve your team. Examples of each chart are located in the masters appendix at the end of the book.

STATING YOUR TEAM IN MATCHES AND PRACTICES

How can you use statistics to help your team? Following are a few ideas:

- If you know who your most consistent passer is, you can place him or her in the number six passing position, which receives the majority of serves during all six rotations. This will improve your team's serve reception and offense.
- You want your best servers to be your first three servers (because your best attack is at the front left position and you would like them to stay in the front row as long as possible). Because of this, you need to know who has the best serving and ace percentage.
- Which of your rotations is the poorest siding-out? Which is the least effective defensively? Offensively? Which is the best? If you know this information, you can work harder on the rotations that are the least successful or make changes to improve them.
- Who are your best defensive players? Where do your opponents hit most of their attacks? It is a good idea to coordinate these two statistics (for example, put your best defensive player in the position opponents hit to the most).
- Find out who your best offensive players are. Have them compete against each other and determine who gets the most kills with the fewest errors.

There are many more reasons to "stat" your practices and matches; the preceding discussion mentions only a few. Stating your own team and your opponents can prove revealing. Many times, what coaches think is happening, and what really is happening, are two different things. Athletes also need a standard or goal to work toward and some way to measure their progress. Taking statistics at practices and matches is your answer.

One key to stating and scouting is personnel. It is hard to find people who know enough about the game to keep correct statistics, have the time to attend matches, and want to do it without getting paid. If you can't find people to help, you can take statistics from match videos (if you can find someone to tape your matches). These can produce the most accurate statistics, because you can slow down or rewind the videos so you don't miss any of the action. This takes quite a bit of time, and the results usually aren't available the day after a match (unless you get home in time). That is a problem, because the quicker the feedback, the more useful it is to the athlete and the coach (see Figure 18.1).

If you can find the personnel to help, you need to train them to take accurate statistics. Included in the masters appendix is a guide that can be handed out when instructing new personnel on how to score the following basic statistics.

This chapter discusses some simple stats that can be beneficial in making changes during matches and more complex ones that need to be analyzed in match videos and that can be used later in practices.

FIGURE 18.1   Keeping Stats

RECOMMENDED BASIC MATCH STATISTICS

Serves

It is beneficial to know the serve percentage (how many times serves are successful), which player has the highest ace percentage, and who are the toughest servers. Your team should be using the serve as an attack, preventing your opponents from mounting their best offense to side-out. Because of this, coaches need to know who produces the most difficult serve to pass. In order to determine this, start with the following basic scoring of your players' serves:

> 4 = Ace (not a playable up)
> 3 = Up, but not settable by setter (they could bump it, or others could set it)
> 2 = The setter can set to two places but is unable to run a quick attack
> 1 = Perfect pass, the setter could run a quick attack or all options
> 0 = Missed serve (in the net, out of bounds, player stepped over the line)

To determine the difficulty of serves, total the score and divide by the number of attempts (the goal is better than 2.5 or another number of your choosing).

To determine the total successful service attempts, subtract the number of misses from the total number of serves taken and divide that number by the total number of attempts (90 percent or better is preferable).

To calculate the ace percentage, total all aces, subtract the number of missed serves from that, and divide the total of all the service attempts into that.

Kill Percentage

The kill percentage tells which player averages the most kills and is the most accurate, because negative hits are subtracted from the number of kills. It applies to all attacks, whether they are spikes, tips, or back-row attacks. They can be recorded in the following manner.

> K = Kill, a hit that is not dug into a playable ball (this is not a free ball pass)
>
> 0 = This attack is hit in the court, but the opponents are able to make a playable dig on it
>
> – = This hit is out of bounds, in the net, blocked for a stuff, or the attacker is in the net. If it is blocked but dug up for a playable hit, record a zero. Some coaches like to keep track of how many attacks are tips or dumps, and this can be accomplished by circling the hit if it is tipped.

In order to score the kill percentage correctly, subtract the minuses from kills and divide that figure by the total number of attacks (25 percent or better from your outside hitters is desirable).

Many high school coaches tally the kill percentage incorrectly because they do not subtract the missed hits from the kills—they simply divide the total attacks into the kills. This gives an exaggerated kill percentage, which is not an accurate account of the effectiveness of the attacker and gives a mistaken impression to college recruiters and the press.

One more sophisticated way to record attacks is to differentiate between an error (E) and a blocked hit (B). Coaches would much rather have a ball that is blocked and in the court than a spike hit out of bounds or in the net. Both options of statistics are included in the masters appendix.

Serve Receive

Because the effectiveness of your players' attack depends on the passers accuracy in delivering the served ball to the setter and your team's ability to side-out hinges on their attacking capabilities, their ability to pass well is the most critical factor for success. You need to know who your best passers are, and then use them exclusively. Stating passing in practice gives you an indication as to who to use as primary passers in serve reception, but it is important to score passing in matches as well, because the difference in stress often changes the accuracy of the passing. Because each athlete handles match pressure differently, you will often find that the best passer in practice is not necessarily the best one in matches. It is to your benefit to place your most accurate passer in the middle (number six) position, because surveys have shown that 60 to 80 percent of serves (depending on the skill levels of the teams) are taken by the middle passer. The following stats give you an accurate account of each player's passing abilities.

0 = Opponent's ace (not a playable up)

1 = Up, but not settable to a front-row player by the setter (they could possibly dig it up, or other players could step in and set it)

2 = The setter can set but cannot run a quick attack (could set it front or back to two places)

3 = Perfect pass, the setter can run a quick attack or all options

The total score divided by the number of passing attempts equals the serve reception percentage. (A score of 2.25 to 2.5+ is preferable.)

Kill Assists

The kill assist statistic is similar to a passing assist stat in basketball. The set that leads to a kill is scored as a kill assist. It is a very simple skill to record and helps the setters gauge their progress. This is also a valuable tool to measure which setters are effective.

1 = Good set

K = Set hit for a kill (add a K to the 1)

– = Overset, setter in net, over center line, illegal set, miss set, out of bounds, or any unhittable set

Subtract minus sets from kills, and divide that number by the total number of attempts, which equals the kill assists percentage.

Digs

Players must dig (create) in order to kill (convert), and they must convert to win. So digging the ball from an opponent's attack is essential for success. If you want your players to improve defensively, follow the adage, "What gets attention will be pursued." Scoring the number of digs and rewarding the best with attention and year-end awards provides an opportunity for the defensive specialist to shine. It is a simple skill to tally.

+ or 1 = Playable dig off an attack (not a free ball pass)

Total the number of digs.

Blocks

It is hard to measure the effect or success of blocks, because good blocks force the hitter to go around them, over them, or into them. Good blocks funnel the hit into the areas covered by your defense and away from areas that are open. If you put up a wall of blockers at the net, it causes frustration and trepidation on your opponent's part, which can result in hits in the net and out of bounds (see Figure 18.2). Your opponents will be forced to go to a quick attack, which takes more skill and timing to be successful. How do you measure all that? You can't. But you can measure your players' blocks and stuff blocks, and they are what set up the opponent's respect for your block. Measure and reward successful players. You have alternatives in this stat; you can simply measure the number of good blocks, or you can record minus blocks and subtract them from the playable blocks.

S = Stuff block (no return)

O = Blocked, but opponents were able to play it up

– = The blocker is in the net, the block is out of bounds, or the ball is caught between the net and the player, and the players are unable to keep it in play

There are several ways to calculate these scores. You could total the number of stuff blocks and playable blocks separate or together. Or you could subtract the minus blocks from the playable blocks and then total all blocks, or keep the playable and stuff blocks separate.

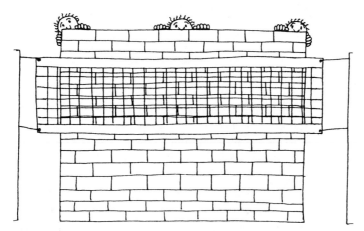

FIGURE 18.2   If you put up a "wall" at the net with your blockers, it causes frustration and trepidation on your opponents' part.

Plus/Minus Charts

Beyond these basic statistics are some others that have proven beneficial if you have personnel to take them during matches. The plus/minus chart is very simple and very effective. It shows which players are hurting or helping your team the most. All you score is the last hit by your team. If it was a kill, ace, or stuff block it is a plus (+). Any hit by your player that results in a point or side-out for your opponent is a minus (–), such as a missed serve, out-of-bounds attack, net, and so on. At the end of the match you will have several pluses and minuses by each player's name. Total them. It will look similar to this:

+10/–4	Jill	+ + + + + + – + – + – – – + +
+5/–8	Jerry	– – + – – + – +– – – + +

Players with several more minuses than pluses are hurting your team. The goal should be to have more pluses than minuses. There are some exceptions you need to be aware of though. Defense specialists and setters do not have as many opportunities to attack and create pluses as the attackers do (depending on how much your setter attacks and your defensive specialist spikes from the back row). Because of this, they usually will have more minuses than pluses. We have found three minuses to be an acceptable number for them (you need to adapt this for your team). The plus/minus chart provides good stats to share with your players after every match. It charts consistency and reveals who on your team is creating the most points for or against you.

RELEASING TEAM STATISTICS

Releasing team statistics is a controversial issue. Should you share all the statistics with your players? Do you make the stats available after every match to every player? Should the players see everyone's statistics or just their own? Should you only give out the leader's scores in each category, or the totals at the end of the year?

Some coaches think reality check is great, whereas others think that the statistics are primarily for their own use. How much you share depends on the skill level and confidence of your athletes. At the beginning of the year, sharing each player's statistics gives them a reference point, but if the stats are given for every match, some struggling players could become depressed. Also, if all players are privy to every other player's statistics, some athletes might question your decisions to use certain players over others based on higher stats. Some might forget that there is more to the game of volleyball, like playing defense, causing a coach unnecessarily to have to defend his or her position. Depending on the emotional stability and skill level of a team, here are some suggestions for dealing with this issue that seem to work well.

- Give each player his or her plus/minus totals after every match.
- Distribute personal statistics to each player.
- Highlight the leaders of each category in each match for the team and the media.

Remember this important principle: The things you want to get done need to be rewarded.

GOALS

It is better to shoot for the sun and only get to the moon—at least you went somewhere higher than where you started. Have your team set statistical team goals and personal goals to achieve for each match. Some ideas are

- Try for equal amount of aces and missed serves.
- No more than (set a number as a goal) missed serves.
- Allow no more than (set a number as a goal) aces to opponents on serve receive.
- Serve-receive 2.25 as a team and 2.5 as an individual.
- Attack .25.
- Keep track of team blocks in a match and try to improve in each game.
- Achieve more pluses than minuses on the plus/minus chart.

IMPROVING ROTATIONS WITH STATISTICS

On which rotations does your team score the most points? The least? Which rotations are your team's best defensively? Their worst? Use this knowledge to improve poor rotations in practice. How do you find this information? You already have it in your scorebook.

It is very easy to tabulate this information. From your scorebook, add up the points scored in each rotation for your team and your opponents for each match. Here is an example for two games in a match:

Rotation	Your Team	Opponents
1	3 + 4 = 7 (best offense)	5 + 4 = 9 (worst defense)
2	3 + 3 = 6 (second best offense)	1 + 3 = 4 (third best defense)
3	0 + 0 = 0 (worst offense)	5 + 3 = 8 (second worst defense)
4	2 + 0 = 2 (third worst offense)	0 + 2 = 2 (best defense)
5	1 + 4 = 5 (third best offense)	2 + 1 = 3 (second best defense)
6	1 + 0 = 1 (second worst offense)	2 + 2 = 4 (third best defense)
TOTAL	**10 + 11 = 21**	**15 + 15 = 30**

It is a good idea to total the final points to make sure you have added correctly. These scores indicate that in rotations 3, 4, and 6 of your team score your team is generating very few points. The problem could be with the server or your team's ability to create or convert (your defense, transition, and attack). Working or changing the server, plays, or blockers in these rotations will improve your team's ability to generate points.

Under the opponent's scores, your rotations 1 and 3 are giving up the most points. This indicates your siding-out capabilities on those rotations needs to be improved. This could entail a number of things. Maybe you need to change or work with your passers on serve receive or where the setter is coming from. The problem might be with your attackers. If they are part of your serve receive and have difficulty passing and then immediately attacking, you could either take them out of the serve-receive pattern or work on their ability to transition more quickly. You might want to change your offense options.

Keeping Statistics for Side-Outs

Do you want to find out what your siding-out percentage is? We have found that, to be successful, you should have 66 percent. How do you know what you have? You already have the information you need. Once again, it is in your scorebook. Look at your opponent's rotations. Add all the points and side-outs (that was a serve too) for each rotation separately. Those are total service attempts. Put this number on the bottom. Then add the number of times you sided them out on that rotation. Put that number on the top. If it is 3/6, you have a 50 percent side-out percentage, and it isn't good enough (66 percent is the desired percentage). Do this for all six rotations. This will show you which rotations you are good or bad at siding-out and which need more practice or some adjustment. Add all the top numbers together and all the bottom numbers and divide for your total percentage, which should be 66 percent. Here is an example:

Server

#8	/so	1	2	/so	8	/so		3/6 = 50%
#5	3	/so	/so	9	/so			3/5 = 60%
#2	4	5	6	/so	10	/so	/so	3/7 = 42%
#7	/so	/so	11	/so				3/4 = 75%
#1	/so	/so						2/2 = 100%
#9	7	/so	/so					2/3 = 66%

The two poorest siding-out rotations were 1 and 3 (servers 8 and 2).	Total 16/27 = 59%

Golf is an excellent game to play in practice to pinpoint which rotations are not as successful as others. Playing golf once a week and monitoring players' progress will not only reveal the least effective rotations, but it will also show any improvement. The game is explained later in this chapter.

Diagnosing the problem area is at the heart of fixing it. Pinpointing where problems lie and working specifically with the least effective rotations on either offense or defense in your practice facilitates using your practice time efficiently. Once you know this, the battle is half won.

USING STATISTICS IN PRACTICE

Using scouting reports of your own team provides you with a tangible goal to work toward in practice. Following are examples.

1. The first obvious statistics you use in your practice are your match results. If they show poor serving or passing, your players have to work on those areas to show improvement for the next match.

2. Serve-receive passes and hitting percentages are very important stats you need to gather to put your lineup together. You can find these stats using the following methods:

- Serve-receive passes. Using the practice chart (in the masters appendix), list all passers' names. Have three players pass at a time until all have passed 20 balls. Have them trade passing positions one-third of the way through the practice. Score each pass as a 1, 2, or 3 (3 being perfect). The highest total score indicates the best passer. Performing this drill a number of times at the beginning of the season gives you a good idea who your better passers are.
- Hitting percentages. Split your team into six-on-six. Position the two dueling hitters as front-row outside attackers on each team. For a set amount of time (two minutes) play a game alternating serves with every set going to the hitters. Keep track of the hitting percentages. Every two minutes, the following trades take place in order: (1) trade the front row with the back row, (2) switch hitters to opposite teams, and (3) trade the front and back rows. Each hitter gets eight minutes of hitting with equal ability of passers and setters. You can do this with middles and right-side hitters too.

3. Golf is an excellent drill to measure your team's siding-out percentage and to determine what rotations need work. Remember, you are shooting for 66 percent. You need to run this drill at least once a week in the first half of the season and then periodically to check how players are doing. Use six-on-six. One side can serve 10 in a row, or you can alternate sides, depending on what you are working on (for a new lineup, use 5 in a row; or if you want to make the drill more game-like, alternate).

Rotation	SR	W	S	%
1	II	I	II	5/10
2	II	II	I	6/10
3	I	III	I	5/10
4		II	III	0/10
5	III	II		6/10
6	III	I	I	7/10

After each serve, toss a ball over to the side that received the serve. If the serve-receive side won both, they get one big point (SR column). If they split, a point goes in the wash column (W), and if the serving side won both, one point goes in the S column. Using the first option (serving 10 in a row to one side), total the points for that side. Big points count as two each (they represent attempts), and a wash is one point (for each team). In the first rotation, the SR team won 5 attempts out of 10 (5 serves and 5 tosses). That is 50 percent and not quite good enough. Rotation 4 really needs work siding out.

Now for the golf part of the game: Another chart is used when the teams switch roles of serve and serve receive. The other six get to receive their 5 serves and 5 tosses (with the same scoring system). Whoever wins the rotation (has more points on the top of the equation) is one up. In match play, it would be the player with the most points or rotations (holes) won.

These are only a few suggestions on how to use statistics in your practices, but, hopefully, they are enough to show you that statistics are useful.

SCOUTING

When you watch your opponents play, what specific knowledge should you glean for your team's benefit? A lot of that will depend on how much time you have to scout them and how many people are helping you. Scouting from videos is the most accurate, but that is often not an option. When you are at tournaments, you can have your statistics people help or give scouting sheets to your team and have them assist you. This is a good mechanism for developing sympathy for the statisticians (and understanding from players when statisticians don't record every hit). A most beneficial aspect of having your team help scout is that it will magnify their abilities to search for weak spots on the other side of the court. Here are five techniques to use when scouting opponents.

1. Strike chart. A copy of the strike chart is available in the masters appendix for your use. To mark the strike chart, all you need to do is draw a line from the ball's point of contact at the time of the attack to the point of impact with the digger or floor. The attacker's number needs to be noted so you know who is hitting from what position on the net and where he or she is hitting. Either each attacker could have a separate court diagram, or you could diagram each rotation with all hitters. This depends on what level of play your team is at and how many hits are taken in a game. You could also add how the ball ended or how it was hit using a T for tipped, K for a kill, – for error, and so on. The accompanying diagram shows a decided tendency to hit on an angle. Noting the hitting (striking) tendencies of each attacker can help prepare your team's defense. Some of these are as follows:

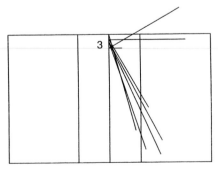

- Types of attacks: quicks, backcourt, high outside, backsets, and so on.
- Patterns or preferences: Examples might include the following: player 7 hits only angle on slides; 5 hits the line 50 percent of the time; 8 is left-handed; 10 has a slow swing and hits long; 4 comes in for 1s but never hits them (fakes) during a tandem play (8 always attacks the second hit off the option); the setter seldom attacks (only when a pass is tight).
- Where players hit from and to: 2 hits backcourt sets to 1 every time from B; 9 always hits left outside, deep angle; MB hits only two sets and slides, which go deep in the court and usually to 1.

All this information, and much more, can be used to prepare your team's defense. If an opponent never hits the line, your team can block angle and pull up a line defensive player to cover tips. If the opponent's setter attacks certain passes, your blockers need to cover him or her.

2. Serve-receive positions. Using a diagram with six volleyball courts (included in masters appendix), chart (using the players' numbers) the players' positions when they are waiting to receive the serve. Circle each passer who is in the front row, and indicate the setter's position. You could even show where each attacker goes after passing.

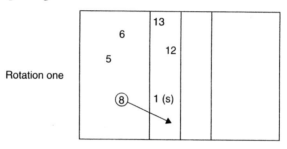

You should keep the same serve-receive stats on your opponents as you do on your own team (3 is perfect, 2 is medium, 1 is poor, 0 is aced). This information can be used to improve your team's service attack, and it may interfere with the opponent's ability to generate a good offensive assault, thus decreasing their ability to side-out. There are several things to learn from these diagrams and stats.

- Your opponent's poorest passer (you can target him or her).
- Which attackers serve receive. The younger or less skilled the players are, the harder it is for them pass a ball and then immediately spike. Passing also tends to distract many players, especially a poor pass, because it changes their focus as their minds are occupied with the poor performance. Also, if you serve the attacker/passer deep or extremely short, it is very difficult for them to shift gears and transition to hit.
- The setter's location. If the setter is transitioning to the net from the back row or the left side of the court, you can serve in his or her way or serve to passers they move in front of (and block their vision). Also, you could serve to the number 1 position on the court, which makes a short pass, allowing less time for the setter to get there, especially if he or she is coming from the left side.
- Serve-receive positions that "give" certain areas of the court. This means they leave more area free that is not covered. This changes with each rotation, because players worry about overlapping. Court position numbers 1 and 5 are two that are "given" the most. Charting your opponent's serve-receive positions shows you which areas are not covered on each rotation.

Another tendency to scout for is the passer's ability to move up and back. Some players have difficulty with depth perception and do not move to the ball well. As you watch, see if they consistently take the ball too high on their arms on a deep serve. That will cause the angle of the pass to be incorrect. Take advantage of that too.

3. Defensive positions.   Chart all six positions of your opponent's defense. Teams cannot cover the whole court. Each team gives certain areas of the court. Record their basic defense depending on where the ball is.

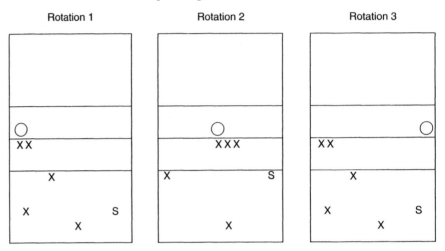

Rotation 1   Rotation 2   Rotation 3

Once you chart the basic defense in each of your opponent's major hitting areas, you can take notes on their defense anomalies and individual tendencies. Some of these include the following:

- Players who are slow getting to their defensive positions.
- Hitters who forget to play defense and transition to attack prematurely.
- Setters who cheat to get to their setting position quickly (leaving their defensive spot open).
- A team of poor overhead passers who are unable to set the ball well if the setter is taken out when they are in the back row (hit to the setter on defense).
- Slow playing tips.
- Blockers who are slow getting outside.
- A three-man block with the back-right and -left defenders too deep to dig angle tips.
- Only one blocker up in the middle, or, if they put two blockers up, which side of the court they come from (right or left) and whether they leave that side open for tips.
- How they defend quicks.
- Who is the best or worst defense player, back row, and blocker.
- Where the setter is coming from, back row or front.
- If the setter is in the back row and if they took the attack, was the opposite (right-front attacker) able to set the ball, for a quick attack?
- Be aware of defenders who do not go back to their defensive home position when the ball goes over the net. During rallies, these players will creep closer to the net, leaving the back third to half of the court open.
- Watch for blockers who jump with the setter every time and are easy to fake, or who do not set tight blocks.

- Look for opponents' poor individual skill execution and take advantage of it.
- Several other poor defense techniques to watch for are covered in Chapter 22.

4. Serve difficulty.   Score your opponents' serves just like you do your own, giving them a 4 (ace), 3 (poor pass), 2 (medium pass), or 1 (perfect pass). Keep track of what type of serves each has a tendency to use, such as floaters, jump serves, hard, or deep. Being prepared takes the surprise element out and lessens their advantage.

5. Use the same statistics for opponents that you take on your own team. These will show your opponents' weak and strong players in all six categories. You will see who gets the most and least sets, blocks, and digs. These scores tell you who are their best and worst servers and passers.

6. Plus, zero, minus.   This is a very easy stat to measure. Write each opponent's name or number down on each line, then score the following for each hit: + = perfect; 0 = could be better; and – = bad. Total them and you will see very quickly who their best and worst players are. That tells you who to defend the most and who not to hit the ball to. It also reveals who not to worry about and where to attack. Perform this measure on your own team, and you will know in one game who to set to or not very quickly by their totals.

TIPS

Following are a few tips that will make your job easier.

- Type or write your team members' names and numbers on a master statistics sheet, and make enough copies for the whole season. Do the same for official lineups you need to hand in before each match. Then all you have to do is insert each game's lineup numbers. This is a great time saver.
- Don't watch the flight of the ball; look ahead (ball, setter, ball, hitter). When looking for defensive positions, just before the attacker hits the ball, look at the defensive side's setup.
- Scout during warm-ups. Write down the setter's number, who is left-handed, the type of sets each attacker hits best, and any other personal quirks you might notice.
- Give copies of your scouting report to your team to study before your matches.

SUMMARY

Preparing and being forewarned can mean the difference between winning and losing. How well you exploit your team's strengths and attack an opponent's weaknesses can aid less talented teams in triumphing over tougher opponents. Looking to get the edge on your opponents? Statistics and scouting are two of the necessities in any championship program.

CHAPTER 19

Hydration, Nutrition, and Rest

What and when your players eat and drink has a huge impact on how they play. Did you know that lack of sleep creates body reactions very similar to being intoxicated? Eating, drinking, and sleeping have a tremendous impact on injury and sickness rates. Therefore, it is imperative for coaches who want to succeed to teach their players the correct principles of maintaining good health and to convince athletes to adhere to the principles.

Do you know what fluids absorb quickest in the body to assist with rehydration, or the fastest way to reenergize athletes? What are the most beneficial snacks players could munch on before a match? Many games are won only by a few points. Getting the edge on your opponent may be only a cup of water or a banana away. Following is the latest information on hydration, nutrition, and rest for you to give your athletes to use for maximum energy output.

HYDRATION

One of the biggest culprits of fatigue, injury, and illness is lack of water. Water makes up 72 percent of body mass. Water loss of only 2 percent of body weight affects performance. In other words, if you weigh 150 pounds, 3 pounds of fluids is 2 percent. Some people lose as much as 3 to 4 pounds of fluid while sleeping, which is equivalent to half a gallon. Imagine how much is lost during a long practice session. A half-gallon a day for most athletes is not enough for optimal performance and well being.

Dehydration Causes Several Negative Reactions in the Body

- Muscles tire or become fatigued earlier.
- Lack of water is a major cause of headaches.
- Muscles become more prone to injury and cramping.
- Dehydration causes a lack of coordination.
- It increases the risk of heat illness, stroke, and death.

Preventing Dehydration

One way of preventing dehydration is for athletes to weigh themselves before and after exercising; they should replace every pound lost with two cups of water. It is a good idea to do this a couple of times a year to get an idea of individual water loss. Athletes' water use in the body varies widely; some sweat profusely and others hardly at all.

Do not rely on thirst for dehydration; it is a poor indicator. It takes a water loss of 2 percent in the body before the hypothalamus, which regulates the body's water level, triggers a thirst reflex. However, there is a 20-minute lag time between the detection of water loss in the hypothalamus and the thirst reflex actually starting. So, by the time the athlete starts feeling thirsty, their performance has already been compromised for at least 20 minutes. Another reason athletes shouldn't rely on thirst as a guide is because it only puts back about half of what they need. Studies have measured the amount of water athletes drink and the amount of water they lose. The findings are universal: When people are given the opportunity to drink all they want, they usually only drink about 50 to 60 percent of what they lost.

Drinking lots of water within an hour of practice will not hydrate the body. The overload will end up in the kidneys and will need to be eliminated quickly.

So, how do your athletes get enough water in their bodies, and how can they tell if they do?

Tips for Hydrating Properly

Players should drink all day long, whether they are thirsty or not.

- They should have a drink every time they pass a water fountain.
- They should carry a water bottle and sip from it periodically.
- They should drink ice water during practice when the body is heated. Ice water is absorbed quickly into the muscles and helps cool the body.
- During practices and matches, they should take advantage of every break to drink water or sports drinks (even if they are not thirsty).

FIGURE 19.1 Hydration of Players

Now, how can athletes tell if they are getting adequate amounts of fluids? Very simply, if the fluid is at its optimum level, urine will be clear or pale yellow. If players are dehydrated, it will be a dark yellow.

Caffeine and alcohol are major culprits in fluid loss. Caffeine is a double offender when it is in the form of chocolate or carbonated drinks because of the sugar. Caffeine acts as a diuretic, which draws fluid from the body by stimulating the intestinal tract to greater activity, which in turn sends food through the body too fast for the water to be absorbed adequately in the large intestine. The sugars that accompany, say, a carbonated drink, are too high in glucose for the muscles to accept (about 12 percent), so the body has to dilute them to a 6 percent solution to be useable as an energy source. In order to do that, it has to draw water from the muscle tissue.

Alcohol is a worse culprit than caffeine. It is deceptive, because the color of urine after drinking alcohol often will be very pale, but the muscles will be extremely dehydrated. It also acts as a diuretic, draining water from the muscles in the body. After a night of drinking, cotton mouth, or a very dehydrated body, is the result.

What fluids could your athletes drink for a quick energy source? Suppose, your team is playing in the final tournament of the year and they possibly could play four to five matches in one day with only half an hour between matches, depending on their win/loss status. This competition includes only the best teams, so the matches are long and physically exhausting. How can your athletes recharge themselves? If you think orange or apple juice will work, you are wrong. These juices contribute to dehydrating your athletes, because they take too long to help them. To understand that, you have to understand how muscles use glycogen as their energy source.

Muscles can only use glycogen at a 6 percent level, as indicated earlier. Orange or apple juice is usually at a 10 percent glucose level. This glucose will stay in the body until more fluid dilutes it to a 6 percent solution. If none does, the body will take fluids from the muscles, thus dehydrating the exact things you are trying to hydrate.

If the activity for which you need to recharge your team is within one hour, recommend sports drinks, which are at the 6 percent solution. They are manufactured with this information in mind and are made specifically for these conditions. It is very important, though, for the athletes who use sports drinks, that they do so in workouts too. If not, they are more prone to stomachaches. If used only during competition, which is a much more stressful situation anyway, introducing a new product into the body may bring about a negative reaction.

It is also a very good idea to accompany any carbohydrate (food source) with lots of water for maximum efficiency and speed in digestion.

One question that arises quite often when discussing hydration is whether sodium intake should be limited. Surely an excess amount has been found to be detrimental, but the elimination of it has some very negative results, also. Salt has its uses, because it is essential for intestinal water absorption, improves taste, maintains the body's drive to drink, maintains fluid balance, and is essential in the nervous system.

Hydration and Your Team

Following are suggestions to improve hydration with your team.

1. Require water bottles at all practices.
   - It helps eliminate missed time from practice for water breaks.

- It is easier to take frequent quick individual water breaks when players are out of a drill and will result in better hydration.
- It decreases the spread of germs among team members.

2. Give frequent water breaks, especially in hot weather. At least one every 15 to 20 minutes is recommended.
3. Make ice available to your athletes and encourage them to use it in their water bottles.
4. Make sure players hydrate during matches (even if they don't think they are thirsty).
5. Encourage them to drink all day long, for example, whenever they pass a water fountain, or take a water bottle with them and use it.
6. Encourage them to stay away from caffeine and alcohol.
7. The following suggestions indicate how much water athletes should drink and when:
   - 8 to 24 ounces more than an hour before practice.
   - 4 to 8 ounces just before the activity begins.
   - 4 to 8 ounces every 15 to 20 minutes during a workout.
   - The minimum amount of water intake should be 64 ounces, or about eight 8-ounce glasses per day.

NUTRITION

When I contemplate what food I ate during my competition years as a setter for BYU (hot chocolate and toast for breakfast, an apple and red licorice for lunch, and a taco or burrito for supper), I shudder and wonder how much better our team might have been if we had known about and eaten the right foods. Maybe that national championship match might have had a better outcome than second place. Knowing now what nutritional experts have discovered about athletes and their nutritional requirements makes me wonder how we did as well as we did on what we ate and drank.

Because they understand the tremendous impact nutrition has on performance, most college coaches now require a daily intake journal and monitor closely their athletes' hydration. Just like using a high-octane gas to get better and more efficient performance from your car, the same holds true for your athletes. The care each person takes of his or her body, such as getting the proper food, rest, and exercise, will equate to better productivity with fewer problems like sickness and injury.

There are several points to be taken into consideration for proper nutrition for the athlete that will be covered here. They are

1. Best choices of food.
2. Glycogen recovery in muscles.
3. Pregame meals.
4. Eating on the road.
5. Weight loss or gain.

Best Choices of Food for the Athlete

Sound general human nutrition is sound nutrition for athletes. Most nutritional experts recommend that a balanced diet contain 10 to 20 percent protein, 25 to 35 percent fat, and 50 to 65 percent carbohydrates. Konstantin N. Pavlou and George H. Blackburn (1984), research associate and director, respectively, of the Nutrition Metabolism Laboratory of New England Deacons Hospital of Boston (of Harvard Medical School), recommend the following:

- The first 2,100 kilocalories for females and 2,700 kilocalories for males should be 15 percent protein, 20 to 25 percent fat, and 60 to 65 percent carbohydrates.
- Any additional calories should come mostly from complex carbohydrates (vegetables and grains).
- Consume calories at three main meals and two smaller snacks.

The following foods are recommended for athletes:

- Grains: cereals, popcorn, breads, rice, some crackers, pasta.
- Legumes: beans, peas, lentils.
- Vegetables: carrots, potatoes, spinach, corn, dark green leafy varieties, tomatoes, squash, cabbage, turnips, and so on.
- Fruits: bananas, apples, oranges, peaches, grapes, tangerines, melons, prunes, and so on.
- Tuna fish (in water), most filets, cod, halibut, catfish. Most fish is great if not battered and fried.
- Poultry (not fried), with skin removed, in small portions (3 to 6 ounces).
- Beef and pork are usually so high in fat that they should be consumed in moderation only.
- Milk products: skimmed or 2 percent milk, yogurt, and so on.

Recommendations to complement these foods include the following:

- Eat before becoming hungry.
- Drink generous amounts of fluids with each meal.
- Eat with as much variety as you can.
- Eat four to five meals per day.
- Follow this sports nutrition motto: All foods fit in moderation. Be smart about when to choose which foods.
- The megavitamin concept is not supported by scientific evidence. Use of moderate supplemental amounts of vitamins and iron are plenty, and if proper variety in the diet is maintained, often vitamins are unnecessary.

Carbohydrates are the preferred source of energy. They are found mainly in fruits, grains, vegetables, and milk. Complex carbohydrates, those loaded with starch or fiber, are some of the best for lasting energy. Those are found mainly in grains and vegetable products.

Glycogen Recovery in Muscles

Glycogen is the energy source for the muscles. As the athlete works out, the energy stores are used up in the muscle resulting in fatigue. It takes at least 24 hours to completely make all the glycogen the athlete needs to replace what was used the day before at practice, if eaten properly. Studies show that muscles are most receptive to glycogen replacement within the first two hours after exercise. After the two-hour period, glycogen is still produced, but at a slower rate.

The consumption of carbohydrates immediately after a hard practice enhances glycogen synthesis. Athletes who need to recover within 24 hours before another practice or match should consume at least 1.5 grams of carbohydrates per kilogram of body weight within 30 minutes after completing an exercise. This is critical in order for the food to move through the system within the two-hour window of optimum glycogen replacement.

If athletes don't replace spent glycogen, their energy levels will gradually deplete with each daily practice, until they are dragging at the end of the week. This will decrease their effectiveness at matches and also the amount of skill and mental learning going on in practices. Recovery is an important challenge for the athlete to attain; if they follow these guidelines of optimum glycogen replacement, they could have higher energy levels and better quality practices.

To maximize glycogen replenishments, have your athlete follow these guidelines:

1. Consume high-carbohydrate meals or snacks within 30 minutes of completion of practice. Fruit drinks or sports supplements are excellent. Include a piece of fruit or slice of bread for a replenishing dose of carbohydrates. Continue eating carbohydrates for the next two to four hours.
2. Small, frequent meals help the athlete achieve high-carbohydrate intake with less stomach upset.
3. High-fat foods and excessive amounts of protein should not be consumed at the expense of carbohydrates.
4. The athlete needs lots of antioxidants, which are found in fruits and vegetables (carrots, bananas, strawberries, and so on).
5. During tournaments, within the 30 minute window following the activity, the body can load up to 100 grams of carbohydrates back into the muscle. Some good choices to eat at this time are bagels, bananas, yogurt, chocolate milk, power bars, sports drinks, and fat-free Fig Newton bars.

Precompetition Meals

What is the meal that will have the most impact on your team's match? Believe it or not, most experts agree it is three days before the match. But, if you want your players to give their best performance, they need to eat well all seven days. The U.S. Olympic Committee (USOC, n.d.) provides the following information: "Scientists have researched both the timing and the content of the precompetition meal and found that there really is no one menu that everyone should follow." Additionally, "a nutritionally sound precompetition meal will not compensate for an inadequate training diet." "Performance depends more on the foods and beverages you consume for days, even weeks, before an event."

So, how important is the precompetition meal? It is important, but it is not as important as an adequate diet throughout the whole season. It may mean, though, the difference between a sluggish or peak performance. It takes the body two to three hours to rid the stomach of the meal ingested, and longer if lots of fat and protein are consumed. Also, the increased stress and tension that athletes experience prior to a match slows blood flow to the stomach and small intestine, decreasing absorption. This causes digestion to slow even more.

The recommendations for precompetition meals include the following:

■ Avoid gastrointestinal stress; athletes should eat familiar foods, especially when they are on the road.

■ If they eat three to five hours before a match, they should have a large meal such as spaghetti, rice, potatoes, vegetables, lean meats, chicken, or fish.

■ Avoid fried or high-fat foods on game day (they digest too slowly).

■ Two to three hours prior to the game, have a light (400 to 1,000 calories), high–complex carbohydrate meal, with moderate protein, low fat, and very low fiber, accompanied by 24 ounces of fluids. Larger meals interfere with respiration and place excessive stress on the circulatory system.

■ Some athletes feel better if they have something light in their stomach for a match. If so, from 30 minutes to 2 hours before game time, they can choose light snacks, such as yogurt, a banana, toast, a bagel, fruit, juice, a power or energy bar, chocolate milk, and a bowl of oatmeal, and lots of fluids. They should stay away from carbonated drinks.

■ If eating a meal before exercise doesn't fit in with your schedule or you lack the appetite, have 8 to 16 ounces of a sports drink 30 minutes to an hour before you exercise for an energizing dose of carbohydrate.

Eating affects individuals differently, and it may also be influenced by their stress levels. A general principle to remember is that eating lightly two to three hours before a match generally benefits performance. In most cases, athletes desire empty stomachs for a performance. In some cases, eating lightly (especially simple carbohydrates several minutes before a performance) has shown improvements in performance over no food at all.

Eating on the Road

Most all teams have to travel, and the majority of tournaments will be away from home. Eating on the road is inherent in playing sports, and after a while experience will teach athletes what is the best and the worst way to handle this situation. Do you want to wait until your athletes have experienced the worst to tell them what is best for them and what is not? Hopefully not. Here are some great suggestions they won't have to experience firsthand to find out. Have your athletes eat what their bodies are used to. This will decrease the risk of stomach upset. Take into consideration that there is no refrigeration on busses or vans. Keep the following suggestions in mind:

1. Try packing a cooler with fruits (strawberries, bananas, apples, oranges, peaches, plums, and so on), vegetables (carrots, celery, tomato juice).
2. Try dried fruits, such as apricots, banana chips, raisins, dates, dried apple, or pineapple (remember, they should drink lots of water).
3. Try canned fruit, such as peaches, pears, applesauce, pineapple, or V-8 juice.
4. Try grains, such as bagels, pretzels, popcorn (no butter), crackers (saltines, Ritz, graham), vanilla wafers, rice cakes, animal crackers, granola bars, taco chips, muffins, breads, Pop-tarts, dried cereal (Frosted Mini-Wheats).
5. Other suggestions include cheese sticks, yogurt, chocolate milk, pop-top cans of tuna, peanut butter sandwiches, Fig Newtons, peanuts or other nuts, packets of cheese and crackers.

Meal Alternatives

When you and your team are traveling, inevitably you will all be eating in restaurants, fast-food places, and from grocery stores. Again, eat familiar foods. Skip high-fat, fried foods. When athletes travel, their match is usually imminent, and many times they are playing back to back on consecutive days, so they need to understand the importance of eating complex carbohydrates and glycogen replacement. For specific meals, the following foods are recommended:

■ For breakfast choose pancakes, cereals, waffles, French toast, bagels, muffins, toast, fruit, juices, nonfat yogurt, and low-fat or fat-free milk. Skip high-fat breakfast foods like bacon, eggs, sausage, whole milk, and cheese.

■ For lunch and dinner choose sandwiches, salads, juices, pasta, salads, bananas, baked potatoes, lean meats (grilled chicken, turkey, lean beef), soup, chili, skim milk, and yogurt. Skip high-fat foods such as cheese, french fries, milk shakes, candy bars, potato chips, ham, bacon, fried meats like chicken nuggets, or fried fish or chicken sandwiches.

Some tips that will help when eating at fast-food restaurants are

1. Hold the cheese and mayo. Avoid mayo-based salads, like potato salad.
2. Of Mexican food, choose soft shell, not hard, or bean burritos, and go easy on the cheese. Use salsa instead of sour cream and guacamole. Rice is great, or plain tortillas, not chips.
3. For pizza, thick or double crust has increased carbohydrates. Don't order extra cheese. Limit the amount of pepperoni and sausage eaten. Canadian bacon is lower in fat. Choose vegetable or low-fat pizza, and have a salad with oil dressing.

Eat healthy on the road and stay away from fat or fried foods. Another alternative is to take your players to grocery stores. Many of the larger chains have deli counters with a variety of foods from which to choose, in addition to the wide choices in the grocery aisles and bakery. Many players would rather stop at a market and get fruits, cereal, and so on, than go to a restaurant. The most important things for your athletes to keep in their minds is to eat what they are used to, drink lots of fluids, and not to overdo it.

Weight Loss or Gain

Athletes who are not at least close to their ideal playing weight will not be able to play as well, period. So what happens when they show up to play at the beginning of the season and they are under or over where their weight should be? It would be a lot better for them if they took care of their weight problem before or after the season, but sometimes that just doesn't happen. Before we give you a sound basis for weight control, we need to make sure you understand that for some, especially females, it can be a touchy subject. Do not humiliate or nag them, especially in public. For very intense, in-control perfectionists, this can lead to anorexia or bulimia. So, what are the options?

Very simply, weight is a matter of balance between caloric intake and caloric expenditure. To lose weight, caloric intake must be less than caloric expenditure. In other words, to lose weight you must eat less or exercise more, or both. To gain weight, the reverse is true.

Dr. Jacqueline Berning, Ph.D., R.D., professor at the University of Colorado, and the nutrition consultant for the U.S. swim team, the Denver Broncos, the Denver Nuggets, and the Cleveland Indians minor league baseball teams, gives some excellent directions for weight control. From her handout, *Through Thick and Thin: Weight Control for Athletes*, we have gleaned the following information. For the average person to lose one pound, he or she would have to run about 35 miles or eat 3,500 fewer calories. Either would be difficult to do in one day. But if you put it into perspective, it is much simpler. 3,500 calories ÷ 7 days per week = 500 calories per day. Eat 500 calories less, work 500 calories harder, or eat 250 calories less and work off 250 calories every day, and one pound of weight is gone in one week. Reverse this formula if you want to gain. This is the healthiest and most balanced way of losing or gaining weight. It has been found that weight gain or loss is most successful if diet and exercise are combined. A safe weight loss or gain for an athlete is no more than two to three pounds per week. If you lose more, it is usually water or lean muscle mass, neither of which your athlete can do without.

Weight Loss

Many athletes, faced with the dilemma of losing weight, will look for the quickest way to get the job done. They've taken the whole off-season to put the weight on, but they now want it off in a few weeks. Fad, or crash, diets look very appealing, but in reality they are trouble. Some of the problems that arise from using them are

- The weight lost is mostly from lean muscles, water, and stored energy, not loss of excess body fat. Consequently, most athletes become tired and lose stamina.

- A lower calorie intake is usually associated with a lower intake of vitamins, minerals, and protein. That can cause several problems. Low calcium intake contributes to stress fractures and osteoporosis. Low iron stores increase the risk of anemia and impaired performance. A lack of vitamin C decreases iron absorption.

- Protein diets are high in protein and can create dehydration if water excreted with the nitrogen compounds is not replaced. These diets also lack a variety of foods, causing the vitamin deficiency problems noted previously. Protein diets decrease physical performance because they displace needed carbohydrates from the diet. They also result in high calcium losses through the urine.

- Fasting causes dehydration, lost lean muscle mass, fatigue, and impaired athletic performance.

- Warning: Watch for sweating, shaking, anxiety, hunger, weakness, nausea, racing heart, tingling, dizziness, headache, blurred vision, confusion, and irritability. These are all signs of hypoglycemia. Some athletes deplete their supply of glycogen in the body to such a point as to cause this. If this happens, boost their blood glucose level quickly with sugar.

Weight Gain

Being consistent is the key to gain weight. Athletes must eat three meals a day with snacks in between. They need to eat enough to satisfy their needs and then a little more. They should snack several times a day on high-calorie foods. They should not eat high-fiber foods because these fill up the person too quickly. For each pound gained as muscle, the athlete needs to consume about 500 to 1,000 additional calories each day. They still should continue to consume a wide variety of foods.

REST

As stated in the introductory paragraph, it has been shown that sleep deprivation can induce a state similar to intoxication. Poor sleeping behaviors result in a confused state of mind and muscle fatigue, which can lead to injury and sickness. As a general rule, athletes should get a minimum of eight hours of sleep each night. Some need more, and each person needs to discover for him- or herself what it takes to feel rested.

Because volleyball is a team sport, it is a good idea to impose curfews to help emphasize the importance of rest to the whole team. Also, when choosing motels for overnight stays, if your budget allows, each player should have his or her own bed (though most don't have that luxury). Select a motel away from noisy places. Make sure you specify nonsmoking rooms, because your players will sleep better with less irritation to their nasal passages. Try to block the rooms so your team is sandwiched in between your room and your manager or bus driver, so other unruly guests do not disturb them. Choose the second floor in most two-floor motels. This helps eliminate noise overhead, cars pulling in late with their lights on, and foot traffic. A good night's sleep is often critical to peak performance.

SUMMARY

You don't want to leave anything to chance. Your players have practiced long and hard. You have put immeasurable hours and energy into your team. Why have the outcome spoiled by a sleepless night or a stomachache? Planning ahead and using every single angle to your advantage is what elevates the good teams. To briefly sum all this up, here are our recommendations for your players:

1. Eat a balanced diet with adequate intake of carbohydrates and fluids seven days a week.
2. Avoid foods high in fat on the day of competition.
3. Ingest only a light meal two to three hours before competition.
4. In between back-to-back matches, use sports drinks or a 6 percent glucose solution.
5. Drink every time you think about it, and even when you don't.
6. Eat the foods you are used to.
7. Refuel immediately after practice.
8. Get a good night's rest.

CHAPTER 20

Prevention and Treatment
of Injury

There aren't many things that are more devastating to teams or bring a sicker feeling to volleyball coaches' stomachs than to see crucial players on their teams crumble to the floor after landing on an opponent's foot under the net. Every team has to deal with injuries and rehabilitation. Are there ways of preventing injuries or speeding up the time spent in recovery? Yes, there are several things that can be done that will contribute to the well being of your players and help them stay healthier all season long. Let's see what we can do to prevent injuries before we talk about how to treat them.

INJURY PREVENTION

Hydration

One of the major causes of injury is lack of water. Dehydration is the underlying cause of most muscle cramps and pulls. The muscle is not as flexible and is more likely to tear if fluids are low. Coordination is negatively effected, causing increased risk of accidents. (For proper hydration, see Chapter 19).

Proper Nutrition

A lack of energy from inadequate nutrition is another major culprit that causes injury. Muscle fatigue, which is brought on more quickly by lack of glycogen and water, creates inept movement, which invites disaster. Food for people is like gas in a car, and athletes only perform as well as the fuel they use.

The brain runs on food and oxygen. When food is inadequate, the brain does not run as efficiently. Because the brain runs not only the muscles but also the rest of the body's functions, inadequate food consumption has a domino effect. Chapter 19 discusses proper nutrition for your athletes.

Rest

Chapter 19 discusses sleep deprivation and how it mimics the actions of an intoxicated individual. Reactions become slowed and clumsy. The brain is not functioning clearly. Quick thinking is a thing of the past. At least eight hours (minimum) of sleep per night is recommended.

Many coaches are so driven to practice hard and push their athletes to do their best that some push too hard. Just as important as working hard is resting adequately. The muscles cannot strengthen without the rest that goes in between. Sometimes a day off of practice will do more good than practicing. The body must be allowed to recuperate in order to function properly. To provide for this, shorten practices the day before a match and toward the end of the season. Do fewer drills and play more games. Give some Fridays off for a long weekend to speed recuperation. Spend more of practice watching films and plotting strategy.

Pay attention to other things that are going on in your players' lives. For example, during test week or homecoming, players are stressed out more, which results in increased fatigue. Home or personal problems take their toll also. If coaches stay in tune to their players, they can sense when enough is enough and when it is time to retreat. Encouraging and providing adequate rest for your players can not only prevent illness and injury but many times will result in a step up to the next competitive level of performance.

Weights

A good year-round weight-conditioning program is an excellent preventive measure for injuries. Besides strengthening muscles, it strengthens bones, ligaments, and tendons, which decreases stress fractures.

Flexibility should be a part of every weight program, and the extra range of motion it provides the athlete gives more latitude of movement before an injury occurs. Chapter 21 covers what to do in weight training and conditioning for the volleyball player.

Warm-Ups

Increasing the temperature of the muscles before stretching facilitates flexibility. Play some mild volleyball (toned down), 10 to 15 minutes, until the muscles are warm, then stretch out. Do the first one or two stretches standing before sitting down. Stretch each major part of the body.

Prevent Muscle Pulls during Practice

It is a good idea to stretch after a drill that targets a group of muscles repetitively. After an intense workout, some muscle groups will contract and tighten if overused, which can cause muscle pulls or tears. Stopping and immediately stretching the affected muscles can circumvent this. For example, if a player has been doing lots of spiking approaches one after the other, following the drill have him or her stand on toes on the edge of steps and let the heel drop slowly, or exercise against a wall with a hamstring stretch. After an intense and lengthy bout of serving, have the player stretch the back. This not only helps prevent injury but also tends to alleviate soreness.

Three of the most prevalent injuries in volleyball are to the back, shoulder, and ankle. Stretching during practice goes a long way to avert muscle problems in the back and shoulder.

Cool-Down

It is so easy to forget to stretch after a workout is over, but it is as important as stretching at the beginning. As your team stretches, you could review key points in your practice, talk about tomorrow, remind them about hydration or eating as soon as possible, or provide positive imagery. During cool-down, the few minutes spent stretching muscles that tend to tighten after heavy use can go a long way toward prevention of soreness and pulled muscles, especially the back, groin, or thigh. Remember to start stretches standing, and work up the body.

The number one injury in volleyball is probably sprained ankles (See Figures 20.1 and 20.2). So much of the game is played on the net that the possibility of coming down on a foot under the net during the season for any front-row player is not only a likelihood but almost a given. If you realize that part of a foot can be

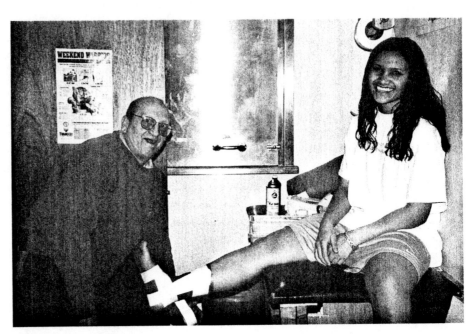

FIGURE 20.1   Taping an Injury

FIGURE 20.2   Active Ankle

over the centerline legally anyway and that that foot could very well be a size 12, you'd better expect it to happen and plan accordingly. Being forewarned can be a blessing if you prepare. The following true story (sadly) illustrates the point.

That year my team was one of the top two teams in the state. We had won the state championship before and were hungry and ready to do so again. During the last match of our district championship, our middle blocker sprained her ankle when landing on an opponent's foot coming under the net. We won the championship and the right to play at the state championship, but our middle blocker had a bilateral third-degree sprain. We had no one talented enough to take her place. She was leading in blocks and second in kills for the season. A week later she played, kind of, at the state tournament, but without the ability to move quickly or jump much. We lost the state championship match 16–18. There is no doubt in my mind what the outcome would have been if she had been healthy. That sprain cost us dearly.

Since that time we have made some specific requests of our team and have not had another repeat performance of that type. While watching some of the best college teams, we noticed their players wore rigid braces (active ankle) that prevent the ankle from rolling. At that time our players had been wearing a lace-up brace (if they had prior problems with their ankles) or were being taped, but we still had some major sprains. So, we required all front-row players to wear the rigid brace. For many years now, although our players have had sprains, none have been serious, and no one has been out longer than a couple of days.

The braces cost quite a bit, but they are not nearly as costly as X rays for a broken ankle or sitting out two to three weeks of a season until the ankle is healed (and then still having a weak ankle) or a state championship. The braces can last two to four years, with the purchase of a replacement kit for the padding and Velcro tabs every so often. Using them also decreases the costs in athletic tape.

A few people have argued that wearing the rigid braces (active ankle) causes weak ankles, but that would be similar to saying that wearing a helmet causes a weak neck. Using them in practices and matches is very similar to wearing a helmet while driving a motorcycle or a seatbelt in a car. It is there in case you ever need it, and when that happens, boy are you ever glad you had it on. This has been one of the best preventive measures in which we have ever invested.

Shoulder Problems

One of the biggest causes of shoulder problems is being "goofy footed." If your player is right handed and approaches for an on-hand spike, left, right, left, right, the player is being goofy footed. It is the incorrect approach, because it turns the body away from the ball instead of opening to it. The individual has to overcompensate by twisting the body around (which causes back problems too) and contorting the arm to hit the ball. Repetitively putting that much unnatural rotation on the shoulder joint can damage the cartilage in the rotator cuff. It is all a matter of jumping off the wrong foot. You need to make sure your players are executing the basic approach correctly. Especially pay attention to athletes who have injured an ankle or knee, because (unconsciously) they might try to compensate for the pain or protect the injured part by jumping incorrectly.

Sit-ups, Push-ups, and Using the Flex Cord on Arm Swings

It has been recommended in this book, as part of the warm-ups, to incorporate these items. You can also use sit-ups and push-ups after drills or games as consequences.

Sit-ups strengthen not only the stomach but (if done properly) the back also. Serving and spiking the ball has a twisting motion, which can cause back problems. Strengthening these muscles decreases the occurrence of back injury.

Push-ups help prevent shoulder, neck, and upper back problems. The arm swings using the flex cord mimic the actual motion used in spiking and serving, creating a resistance factor. Using both of these prior to practices will warm up the muscle and strengthen bone, ligament, muscle, and tendon.

Flu Shots

It is recommended to prevent illness that your team be encouraged (not required) to get their flu shots. If players allow their health to get run down, they are more susceptible to all types of viruses. Because of the long hours traveling to and from matches and the stress associated with competition, athletes are very prone to viruses. It takes 7 to 10 days for the flu virus to run its course. It usually takes longer than that for the athlete to get back to full strength. Because of this, damage to the athlete's skill growth or to your team's success depends on when the illness occurs. Most flus are prevalent in winter or early spring. If this holds true and your player catches a virus, it will be toward or at the end of your season, which is the most critical time. Unless your player has strong objections to it (because of allergies to eggs or a bad previous reaction, for example), having a flu shot is very similar to carrying insurance, just in case.

Blister Prevention

Friction causes heat, and heat on the skin causes blisters. Just as a good pair of gloves will help prevent blisters on the hands, a good pair or two of socks will prevent them on the feet. Make sure players wear a clean pair of socks every day. If they wear two pairs of socks, it is recommended that the inside pair be made of cotton, which is better at absorbing moisture.

New shoes sometimes rub the wrong way until they are broken in. Placing Band-Aids or pads in the sensitive spots can help prevent painful blisters. Foot powders also help absorb sweat. Do not buy new shoes for a tournament. Some shoes require a break-in period because of a change of fit from the previous shoe. A tournament is no time to break in new shoes.

Communication

Because coaches haven't yet gained the ability to communicate telepathically, their players still need to tell them if they are having physical problems. This is one of the most important ingredients of injury prevention, but it is like pulling teeth to get most athletes to comply. They want to play. They know every practice they miss makes them slide down the skill ladder and down the bench from the starters. They want to be indispensable to the team, and the reality that someone else is playing in their spot is very difficult for a competitive, driven individual.

They and their coaches need to understand some very important principles for injury prevention and treatment. With many types of injuries, one of the principles is the quicker we treat it and rest, the slighter the injury and the faster the recovery. For instance, we know that the most important days for recuperation of a back injury are the first two after the injury occurs. If the player gets the proper treatment, and, most importantly, rest, the recovery is quick. If not, the injury lingers on for a long period of time, consequently doing more harm. So, if a player tells you immediately and treatment is begun quickly, the injury can be a short-lived one.

Coaches do not want to contribute to the injury of their players, especially permanent injury, but if players do not communicate, that can happen. It is expected in practices and games that athletes give 100 percent effort. Coaches will push them to achieve this, and players will try to comply. Many times there are ways of compensating or working things out with an athlete who has a lingering soreness, sickness, or injury to make the best of the situation. But there has to be communication for this to happen. Giving players a long weekend, taking them out of some drills, and resting them for a few weeks (especially in the first half of the season) are some of the ways a coach can help a player recuperate or prevent something worse from occurring. But this can only happen if coaches know there is something wrong.

Coaches are part of the problem of communication. They have to be approachable. Most coaches hate to hear that a player isn't feeling up to par. The "suck it up," "grit your teeth and bear it," "toughen up," "don't be a baby," "no whiners" sayings are legendary in sports. Because of this, many coaches do not take to physical complaints kindly. Players who are constantly moaning about every little pain, cut, and sore are difficult to contend with. But, they are few and far between, because most players are competitors and don't want to be benched. The majority of athletes by far fall into the "tough it out" category. Coaches should encourage players to sift out the regular sorenesses and report the potentially serious ones. If the athlete isn't sure, he or she should report it anyway to the coach, trainer, or physician, who is more qualified to make a diagnosis. Because we are discussing injury treatment already, let's jump into it in the next section.

INJURY TREATMENT

Diagnosing Injuries

Coaches need to be extremely careful when diagnosing an injury, and if there is any question as to the extent of an injury, the player should see a doctor. Sometimes a break is not as painful as a sprain, but permanent damage can occur if it is not diagnosed properly.

Only a physician should treat dislocations. If they are replaced improperly, permanent nerve damage can occur. Eye, back, and head injuries are three other injuries that fall into this category. Because of the seriousness of the injuries, and the lasting damage that could occur, coaches should abdicate the treatment of their players to health-care professionals immediately.

Athletic Trainers

If you are fortunate enough to have an athletic trainer, and especially a good one, consider yourself blessed. They provide a great partnership in keeping your players healthy and on the court playing. You need to work closely with them, respect them, and heed their advice.

Trainers want to work within the parameters of your program, and in order to help them do so, you have to communicate with them. If you clue them into your expectations and listen to their expertise, your players will be the beneficiaries. Be aware that if your players repeatedly have the same types of injuries, your trainer can help you devise preventive measures. It only makes sense to use the people who are experts in their own fields to your advantage.

RICE

RICE is an acronym for the correct treatment for minor sports injuries: Rest, Ice, Compression, Elevation.

R is for rest. That means stop exercising. A small injury can become a major one if the body isn't given the chance to heal. This is critical. Most players and some coaches want a return to play sooner than they should. This can cause permanent problems, such as weak ankles, as they don't heal properly, or cause lingering ankle problems all season.

I is for ice. When applied to the injured part, ice should be either wrapped in towels, placed in a plastic bag, put in a bucket of water, or kept moving on the body. Ice deadens pain and reduces bleeding by causing the blood vessels to contract, which lessens swelling and inflammation. The quicker it is applied, the better. Start out at 20 minutes, and then apply for 45 to 60 minutes every few hours for up to 72 hours. After that, alternating hot and cold is best. (Do not use scalding temperatures, but as warm as the person can tolerate comfortably.)

C is for compression. Wrap the injured part, if possible. This helps reduce swelling. Also, keeping it wrapped when using it will help prevent it from being injured even worse while it is healing. In many joint injuries, ligaments have been compromised and stretched, making the joint looser until it heals. If the athlete were to, say, twist an ankle again before it was healed, even more damage could occur without the support of a wrap.

E is for elevation. Raising the injured part slightly higher than horizontal allows gravity to drain the excess fluid away from it. This decreases pain and allows circulation to continue normally. When circulation is restored without the pressure of swelling, healing will occur faster.

Pain Relievers

It has been proven that the absence of pain with an injury allows the body to heal faster. Without pain to deal with, the body can apply all of its resources to healing the injured part. Ibuprofen has been found not only to aid in relieving pain but also to act as an anti-inflammatory. It is suggested for use three times a day with meals (taken alone it can irritate the stomach) for not longer than 5 to 10 days after the injury, or as recommended.

Muscle Soreness

To treat muscle soreness, and prevent it from developing into anything worse, right after exercise have your athlete either apply ice to the sore part or put the sore part in a cold whirlpool. This greatly alleviates the amount and duration of the soreness. Ice and whirlpool treatments are very beneficial, especially at the beginning of the season, when typically most of the soreness occurs.

Cold versus Hot Treatment

Ice is the recommended treatment for injuries for the first 72 hours. After that it has been found that an alternating cold and hot treatment speeds healing. In other words, after the 72 hours of icing as recommended previously, start alternating the ice treatments with soaking the body part in as warm water as the athlete can comfortably tolerate. Epsom salts have also been known to aid in the healing process. They are reported to help lessen swelling. It has been recommended that they be used in the water in an amount that is thick enough to stir.

Pulled Muscles

If possible, the RICE treatment is the best to start with for pulled or torn muscles. One of the most common of these types of injuries is to the muscles in the thigh or groin area. Practices that have been found to decrease further injury and heal the area quickly include keeping it wrapped or wearing compression shorts all day (but wrap it if practicing). After they are healed, if players have a tendency to pull muscles, have them wear compression shorts all the time, during practices and games. The extra support keeps the muscles warm, keeps fluids inside, and encourages blood circulation flow to the area, which decreases the possibility of a repeat injury to the area.

Back Injuries

Back injuries are serious, depending on the extent of the damage. If they are more than soreness or mild irritation, or if they are chronic, they should be seen by a physician, chiropractor, or massage therapist. For mild back problems, immediate rest is one of the best measures. Also, lots of back stretching before, during, and after use is advised. Anti-inflammatory medicine and pain relievers such as Ibuprofen are also recommended. As with all sore muscles, use the RICE followed by the hot/cold treatment.

It is very important that after the body part heals, players spend more time stretching and warming up the injured body part. Because of the previous injury, it is more prone to being reinjured.

Massage Therapists and Chiropractors

Many college teams have their own massage therapists and team chiropractors. We have found their use to be a personal preference for each coach or player. Use what works. Both have been found to be productive in certain circumstances. Because many of the injuries that occur to volleyball athletes are muscle related, massage therapists have been having a remarkable positive effect on them.

Air Casts

When you can't do without injured athletes because they are crucial to your team's success and doctors have determined that using them won't do permanent damage, air casts are a possible solution. The best choice would be, of course, to let their injury heal before letting them back into action, but there are circumstances when that isn't the best alternative. Make sure at those times that the players and their parents (or people responsible for them) concur with your decision. Play them as little as possible and take every opportunity to allow them to recuperate, because the best possible scenario is playing a healthy athlete.

SUMMARY

All coaches must deal with the specter of injury during the season, but if correct precautions are implemented, it need not be as devastating as it could be. Now that you know what preventive and treatment measures are available, injuries should occur less often, and recuperation time should be faster, which will result in your season proceeding smoothly with many successes. After all is said, good luck.

CHAPTER 21

Conditioning and Weight Training

How much conditioning does your team need? How much practice time does it take up? What conditioning is best for volleyball? How will it improve your team? Ever ask these questions?

In Chapter 3, research explains about specificity of exercise and skill. Following that dogma, we will answer the preceding questions and provide suggestions for how to condition your team during your regular season and the preseason and postseason.

CONDITIONING

Conditioning strengthens bone, muscle, tendons, and ligaments, which helps prevent injury, increases vertical jump and quickness, and improves endurance. It prolongs skill effectiveness and lessens mental and physical fatigue. Conditioning increases mental toughness and reliability and builds cohesiveness.

CONDITIONING FOR VOLLEYBALL

There are two major types of conditioning: specific and auxiliary. Specific conditioning involves performing the actual skill many times. In other words, in order to increase setting strength, set for 15 minutes straight. To increase endurance in volleyball matches, play longer, more intense games in practice. Auxiliary conditioning is training related to the skill, such as sprinting ladders to mimic quickness required on the court, or throwing a weighted ball overhead for the spiking or serving motion, or lifting weights.

There are many studies that show that the principles of specificity remain dominant in almost all facets of sport conditioning and training. In other words, the best conditioning for volleyball is playing volleyball (specific conditioning), not doing the grapevine or running two miles a day.

One such study by Sale and MacDougall (1981) indicates that for a cyclist, a small amount of improvement will be derived from endurance running, though the amount of transfer is marginal at best.

For example, the aerobic benefits that could be derived from 100 hours of endurance running might translate into the equivalent effect of 10 hours of endurance training for cycling. It would seem to be more expedient and economical to just train for 10 hours on a bicycle rather than perform 10 times as much running training to get an improvement in cycling. (p. 87)

That doesn't mean that if you do run there is no benefit; there is, but there would have been more if you had spent the time playing intense, running volleyball instead. Using gamelike drills that work the athlete hard for a continuous 30 to 60 minutes will benefit your players in many more ways than ladders or jumping up steps. The transfer to the athlete is 100 percent compared to the 1/10 percent in an auxiliary type exercise. If athletes want to improve their vertical jump for the spike approach, have them do lots of approach steps. Supporting arguments following are found in *Training for Sports and Fitness* by B. Rushall and F. Pike.

PRINCIPLES OF TRAINING

There are three principles of training.

1. There must be progressive overload.
2. There must be recovery. A failure to adapt training programs to each athlete's need for recovery represents poor coaching. The accommodation of recovery requirements is perhaps the single most important need for effective training. The avoidance of overtrained states is a paramount responsibility of an effective coach.
3. Training is specific. The maximum benefits of a training stimulus can only be obtained when it replicates the movements and energy systems involved in the activities of a sport. This principle may suggest that there is no better training than actually performing in the sport.

This text maintains that the principle of specificity is the single most pervading factor that influences the improvement of performance from a physiological perspective. Training effects are, in the main, so specific that even minor departures from movement forms, velocities, and intensities result in undesirable training effects. This means that incorrectly designed training activities will have no carry-over value for a particular movement form, and may even have the potential to negatively influence activities. (Rushall and Pike, n.d.)

So what does research say about strength/weight training's benefits to specific sports? Two theories were evaluated in light of the published literature (Sale and MacDougall, 1981).

1. Strength training exercises should simulate the sport movement as closely as possible in terms of movement pattern, movement velocity, type of contraction, and force of contraction.
2. It is only necessary to train muscle groups. Increases in strength can be reeducated into a sports action.

Movement Pattern

1. A large part of strength training involves skill acquisition.
2. Strength gained from eccentric/concentric contractions is only partially transferred to an isometric contraction.
3. Adaptation even may be purely specific to the joint angle at which training occurs.

Implication

There is little likelihood of carry-over value of strength training effects derived from simple activities to actual applied strength in complex activities.

Contraction Velocity

In summary, strength training should be as specific as possible. The movement pattern and contraction speed, type, and force should replicate the intended activity. Any departure from one of these factors will result in inappropriate adaptations.

In light of this information, why even do auxiliary training? There are four circumstances where this type of training is beneficial.

1. Rehabilitation from injury is facilitated by general activities and specifically designed localized programs to promote particular tissue growth.
2. General resistance exercises and other forms of training can be used to prepare the body for unusual circumstances that can occur in competitions and, thus, serve as a method for reducing the likelihood of injury.
3. General endurance training has behavioral effects that are beneficial to target sports and sports where attention and decision making are crucial elements.
4. General activity training involving most capacities is beneficial if the fitness level of participants is particularly low. This is true of young performers or adults starting new activities. When the new performer is so low in general fitness characteristics, any improvement in them, whether or not they are specific, will be beneficial. However, those benefits are only displayed when the level of performance is very low. As performance improves in the sport, the value of any transfer of general or unrelated training effects diminishes rapidly.

To recap the application of these studies to volleyball, specific conditioning is the best conditioning possible. Not only will the conditioning have 100 percent transfer, but the player's skill level will improve too, killing two birds with one stone. So, find lots of conditioning drills that include ball-handling skills.

Is weight lifting or auxiliary training (jump and interval) worth the time and effort it takes? Yes, especially in injury prevention (not counting all the other benefits) and especially during the off-season. The best teams will do all it takes to tip the scales in their favor. And all of those little things add up to a championship. Information on weight training, jump training, and interval training follows.

Weight Training

What kind of weight program is recommended for volleyball players? Following are some suggestions for conducting a successful weight lifting program and for the type of weights to use (see Figures 21.1, 21.2, and 21.3.)

■ Coaches must stay involved with the athletes at all times. Your attention demonstrates to the athletes the importance you place on weight lifting in your program. It will increase the amount of effort athletes put into lifting.

When athletes are injured and going through rehabilitation, it is very important for the coach to stay in contact with them. They are already feeling isolated from the team and mentally down because of how the injury has interfered with

FIGURE 21.1   A qualified person supervises athletes in the weight room.

FIGURE 21.2   Supervisor with Athlete

FIGURE 21.3 Supervisor watches jump training.

their desires and goals. They still require direction and need to feel important. Coaches should keep in close and frequent contact to facilitate their athlete's complete recovery and return to the team.

- Athletes should always warm up before beginning a workout. They should stretch and raise the muscle temperature. It will decrease injuries.

- They should use free weights when possible. Free weights require more muscle strength to control and impact on a wide range of muscles and tendons.

- Jump training and weight training can be done the same day. If it is during the season, they should only be done after practice. Never let players condition on game days.

- Conditioning should be started at least two months before the first team workout. (Year-round conditioning is preferred.)

- In the off season, athletes should weight train three times a week. During the season two times a week is sufficient to maintain.

- Make sure you allow your athletes to rest in order to recuperate.

- **Crucial:** If athletes use a muscle group extensively, have them stretch it out immediately following the exercise. This is very important for injury prevention.

Weight Training and Adolescents

Studies have shown that weight training is not only safe for most youths, but it is also beneficial. According to the National Strength and Conditioning Association (1996), the following precautions should be strictly adhered to:

1. Close supervision by a qualified weight coach.

2. A conditioning program appropriate to the initial capacity of the adolescent.

3. Safe and properly sized equipment for the adolescent.

Suggested Weights

Choose a weight program to suit your athletes from the following selection: squats, lunges, butterflies, upright rows, plyometrics (dot drill and boxes), jumps rope, cleans, straight leg deadlifts, pullovers, sit-ups or ab crunches, back hyperextensions, arm curls, triceps extensions, toe raises, and hip extensions. If there is no access to a weight room, the following exercises are excellent:

Push-ups	3 sets of 50
Sit-ups	3 sets of 50
Inverted sit-ups	2 sets × 10 reps with at least 5-second holds
Pull-ups	3 sets of your max
Dips	3 sets of your max
1 leg bend	3 sets × 6 reps each leg
Squats (someone on back)	3 sets × 10 reps
Squeezing a tennis ball in each hand	3 sets × 20 reps or more
Toe raisers (someone on back)	3 sets of 20

Here is an example of BYU's men's volleyball weight lifting program (a sample also appears in the masters appendix to copy).

Brigham Young University

Men's Volleyball

Warm-up:

5 minutes on the exercise bike and stretching

R = Reps   W = Weight

Max's should be recorded on the back

Week sequence = L-M-H-L-(Max + L)-L-M-H-L

Name_____

Light (L) week = 3 × 12
Medium (M) week = 4 × 8
Heavy (H) week = 5 × 5

Cycles last for 1 week

L week

Exercise	R	W	R	W	R	W	R	W
Cleans (3 × 5—75%)								
Bench press—65%								
Squats—60%								
Straight leg deadlift								
Pullovers—65%								

Oblique-torso (15 each way)	30		30		30			
Ab crunches	30		30		30			
Back hyperextension	25		25		25			

M week

Exercise	R	W	R	W	R	W	R	W
Cleans (3 × 3—85%)								
Bench press—75%								
Squats—70%								
Straight leg deadlift								
Pullovers—75%								
Oblique-torso (15 each way)	30		30		30			
Ab crunches	30		30		30			
Back hyperextension	25		25		25			

H week

Exercise	R	W	R	W	R	W	R	W
Cleans (3 × 2—95%)								
Bench press—85%								
Squats—80%								
Straight leg deadlift								
Pullovers—85%								
Oblique-torso (15 each way)	30		30		30			
Ab crunches	30		30		30			
Back hyperextension	25		25		25			

Jump Training

Jump training should be practiced at least three times per week. The program consists of approach jumps plus one other variation. You may vary the other three jumping methods, but the approach jumps must be done at least three times each week. Start with 10 minutes a day, and work to 20 minutes per day.

Approach Jumps

Using a four-step approach like in practice, have players do three sets of one minute each to total three minutes. Hang several strings of different lengths from the basket rim and have athletes touch the highest one possible using a four-step approach.

Variations of Jump Training

There are hundreds of ways to jump train. Here are some ideas, or use your own imagination.

- Continuous jumping: One minute using both legs, 45 seconds for one leg, 45 seconds for the other leg, one minute using both legs again, 30 seconds for one leg, and 30 seconds for the other leg.

- Block jumps: 4 sets for 40 seconds (allow a 30-second rest in between sets). Have them do each of the following continuously: 5-3-3, 5-2-2, 3-3-3, 3-2-2, Q3-3-3, Q3-2-2. Do not allow stops between jumps. Have them come down on the outside foot so they can push off that foot for the next step.

- Stairs: Have them use two feet at a time jumping as many steps as possible. Then have them use one foot, then the other, then run down the stairs.

- Continuous standing broad jumps: Players should jump off of both feet with no steps in between and no stopping. They can jump three to five in a row, walk back or forward the same distance, and go again. Start with three sets and progress to five.

- Tuck jumps: Standing in place with arms raised, athletes jump up and bring their knees in front of the chest. Start with a minimum of six sets of 30-second intervals. A variation would be to perform the same jump in a sandpit.

- Targets: At a backboard or other target athletes should use a four-step approach and touch a spot. Have them do three sets of 15 continuous jumps. Continuous means each approach is made during the set without stopping. They could jog around a basketball court, approaching and jumping at each backboard, net, or rim.

- Elastic: Buy elastic to sew together on one end and station your players in a zigzag pattern three to four feet apart with one leg in the elastic. If you have 12 on your team, have 9 players start with the elastic at knee level (that would give 8 opportunities to jump). Your three other players would be jumping off of two feet continuously (no hops or steps in between) over the elastic, one right after the other. Start out with three trips through, and raise the elastic higher after each trip.

- Tennis balls: Each player gets a tennis ball. They are to do a four-step approach, with a full swing, and throw the ball over the net. You can make rules, such as the ball has to land in the court, or in front of the 10-foot line to count. You can start out having them go for either two minutes or 25 successful approaches. They are to run the whole time (they have to chase their own balls). You could make this a competition based on successful approaches and swings in a certain amount of time, with consequences. You could make a stipulation that if you see someone make an incorrect approach, they lose all their points to that point (if they are hurrying to win, they aren't practicing bad habits).

Interval Training

Following is a suggested routine for an interval training program.

1.	4 sets × 4 reps for 220 yards	1 to 1 rest
		2 to 1 in between sets
2.	3 sets × 8 reps for 110 yards	2 to 1 rest
		2 to 1 in between sets
3.	5 sets × 10 reps for 55 yards	3 to 1 rest
		2 to 1 in between sets

Allow 20 minutes doing something with the ball and 5 minutes jogging to stretch out at the end. Start with 1, then 2, and then 3, then repeat 1, and so on. Give 70 percent effort for 1, 80 percent effort for 2, and 90 percent effort for 3.

We will show you how to put all this information into practice throughout the whole year by giving you our suggestions to optimize your conditioning program.

IN-SEASON CONDITIONING PROGRAM

Following are some suggestions for an in-season conditioning program:

- Your players should lift weight two times per week to maintain (but only after practice).

- Use sit-ups and push-ups as drill consequences (examples follow later).

- Prepractice and warm-up on board: Always include sit-ups, push-ups, full arm swings, blocking steps, and approach steps. Increase the number each week. Level off or lighten up the last half of the season.

- Six-on-six drills and games, such as wash or scramble, that are continuous for 30 to 60 minutes (equivalent to a match). Run these toward the end of practice.

- Two-on-two, three-on-three, or four-on-four games, such as doubles or triples or king's/queen's court. Use consequences in these games to incorporate conditioning, for example, in triples, if there are no touches on the ball before it hits the ground, they do two sit-ups or push-ups. Limit the amount to keep the game flowing. Also, to encourage competitiveness, you could use the sit-up/push-up consequences for the losers in the game. Have them do the same amount as or double, the total points their score was away from the first place team. For example, the first place team has 25, the other teams have 15 (resulting in 10 sit-ups for losers), 8 (17 sit-ups), and so on. This consequence encourages them to keep working hard, even if they are losing, to minimize the consequence.

- Butterfly: Emphasize no walking to spots. If you see anyone walking, the whole team runs a lap or a ladder.

- In blocking drills, to encourage the balls being spiked to be kept in the court so the blockers have something to block, require the attackers who have a minus attack (in the net or out of bounds) to do two approach jumps before they can hit again. Make sure the consequence is immediate so they can get back to spiking.

- Use conditioning longer and heavier in the first three-fourths of the season, and lighten it toward the end of your season. Drills and games should ease up and practices shorten to restore muscle response and mental clarity.

PRE-/POSTSEASON CONDITIONING

The following suggestions are activities that could be incorporated into a pre-/ postseason conditioning program depending on time allotment, commitment, equipment availability, and level of program (elementary, middle school, high school, college, club). A coach needs to sift through the choices and select what is best for the team at the current level of competition and time allotment.

- Encourage your players to play as much volleyball as possible, including doubles, triples, fours, six-on-six, coed, or sand volleyball.
- Suggest they run one to three miles each day, except Sunday (for recovery), or swim.
- Suggest weight training three times a week.
- Suggest jump training at least three times a week.
- Encourage interval training at least three times a week.

SUMMARY

These are the best ways we've found to use the time you have for optimum conditioning of your team. If you apply this information to your players, you will find they have the stamina they need to finish a match or tournament with intensity, develop less injuries, and have more control of the ball because you are spending more time on skills rather than simply conditioning. There are many more benefits, but these three should be enough to give anyone a reason to implement them if they want a successful team. Now take the edge and run.

CHAPTER 22

Competition Strategies

How do you prepare and focus a team? It takes timing and the right words said the right way. Experience is the best teacher, of course, but there are lots of strategies that you don't have to spend a lifetime learning to use. In this chapter you will discover how to give your team the best advantages available. Using proper game strategy can help teams win against opponents who may have more athletically talented players. "Winning is never accidental...I have seen teams short on talent win famous victories simply because they were better prepared, more focused than their opposition. They had clearly defined goals and consistent work habits. And they weren't afraid to make the sacrifices required to raise their play to another level" (Holtz, 1998, p. xi). But before you can make those sacrifices, you've got to have goals. And knowing and doing is what makes the difference in the win/loss column.

WINNING STRATEGIES

When you get right down to it, there are only two ways to win points: Either your player must hit a winner or your opponent must make an error. The following sections discuss strategies for increasing the chances of these events happening.

Playing Percentages

Volleyball matches are not won by a few great shots. They are won with many, many good shots. Like chopping down a tree, you win with the accumulated effect of many small efforts. At a casino on a single roll of the dice your chances of winning are nearly even. But over the course of 1,000 rolls, your chances of coming out ahead are virtually nil. Play consistent, high-percentage volleyball, and force your opponent to come up with great shots to beat you. Taking unnecessary risks costs matches. This doesn't mean you shouldn't take any risks; it means you should take only those risks that maximize your probability of winning the point.

Maximizing Strengths

Real competition requires intense and prolonged concentration. In order to win, your players must have more willpower and concentration than the opponent. All winners have great willpower and concentration. They can play every point at 100 percent efficiency for hours. An opponent may be better than them for 30 minutes, but that does not mean the opponent will be better than them after three hours. Everyone tires mentally if they are forced to concentrate long enough.

Matches have many temporary ebbs and flows. Successful players are not shaken by these. As a match nears its end, pressure mounts. Winning the last few points against a tough opponent is often a tough and unpleasant task.

Exploiting the Opponent's Weaknesses

Matches hinge on your ability to use your team's strengths and exploit your opponent's weaknesses. A weakness usually will get worse if it is played relentlessly. The more important the point, the more your team should play to the weakness. At the same time, try to hide your team's weaknesses and stay away from your opponent's strengths. Nobody is good at everything. You win by doing things your team is good at and lose by doing things they are not good at. You want to force your opponent to try difficult rather than easy shots.

As in a battle or a chess game, you and your team should always try to outguess your opponent's next move, set up your defense where you think the next offensive assault will take place, then counterattack where opponents are not prepared or expecting it. It is a gamble. You are gambling if you play one offense; or another blocking strategy with one, two, or three up on the middle block; or if you position your players on defense in a certain spot.

Much of this battle depends on the preparation and attitude or state of mind of the athletes as they approach it. If they believe they can succeed, odds are they will, and if they believe they can't, odds are they won't. It is up to you as the coach to set the stage for your team's bid for success. In order to do this, you need a plan. The components of the plan should be (1) How are we going to score points? and (2) How are we going to side-out?

General principles you need to take into consideration for this are

1. An understanding of one's own and one's opponent's strengths and weaknesses.
2. A general plan of how to score points: Are we better off with offense or defense?
3. Specifics on the general plan. This usually involves constant pressure on the opponent's weaknesses. Find an exchange where you have an advantage, and work on it over and over.

If you change your game plan, the change must be within your team's capabilities. It is rare that an original plan remains completely intact for an entire match.

All players choke sometimes. It is a normal human condition. Your opponents have problems as well. Do not let them see your problems. All teams make mistakes. Don't let them see that it influences you. Never change your walk, your demeanor, or your expression. Slow the match down when you are anxious.

Following are strategies broken up into the major divisions of competition, which are designed to give your team the advantage over their opponents.

PREGAME STRATEGIES

Preparation is the key. Teams feel much more comfortable playing an opponent if they know something about them. Run through the scouting report with them. During practice, have your players hit at the places your report shows will be the most advantageous against your opponent. Plan your serving strategy, and direct your team to practice serving to those court areas that your opponent does not cover well. Know your opponent's hitting tendencies. Getting your team ready mentally and physically will build confidence in their abilities. Watching videos of your opponents also helps your team know what to expect, and it takes away the fear of the unknown.

Each player is unique and has certain pregame rituals that help him or her to reach a peak performance state. Help your players define those. Some use music, relaxation techniques, mental practice or thoughts, or specific warm-ups to get them ready to play. If your players begin a match unprepared, the results are usually less than desirable. There are several approaches to being prepared.

Guidelines for Rituals

1. Rituals should be performed at a specific time before each match or tournament.
2. The goal of a ritual is to focus the energy of the player on preparation for the match.
3. Rituals train the player mentally and physically to focus and gear up for action.
4. Personal rituals have their own timelines depending on the competition, travel, tournament play, single matches, home games, and away games. The rituals may vary from 1 week to 24 hours, 6 hours, 2 hours, 1 hour, 30 minutes, or 5 minutes.
5. Sleep habits are important in rituals. They prepare the body for readiness. Players should wake at the same time before a competition as any other day.
6. When traveling to away matches, arrive at the site a specific amount of time before the match.
7. Let the players eat the food that is most comfortable for them, but have a specific time before each match to eat.
8. Provide a way for the players to dress, get taped, and warm up at a specific time before each match.
9. Before the match allow players time for their own personal rituals.
10. We highly emphasize performing mental imagery with each ritual. Mental imagery plays a very big role in personal rituals. Have athletes practice this skill frequently so it becomes a natural part of their ritual before a match.

Three ideas to use just prior to matches are

1. Pregame talk (reemphasize a few key points for this game found in the scouting report).
2. Use a relaxation tape (quiet nature music) and talk them through a muscle relaxing exercise with visual imagery.
3. Allow 10 to 15 minutes of silence so they can work on the mental part of their game. Some players like to put on a headset at this point with music that pumps them up.

Warm-ups

Warm-ups are part of pregame strategies. They should prepare a player physically and mentally for the match. Using a set procedure helps athletes feel more comfortable in a stressful situation. It lessens the confusion and creates order in the brain.

What kinds of warm-ups are recommended? You guessed it, gamelike ones. Make sure players talk and move their feet. They should warm up like they intend to play, with intensity. They should go after every ball, and pass angled balls, so two-person pepper (hitting back and forth) is out. It creates more problems than it solves and is a poor warm-up skill to use. Sometimes you see teams only spiking for warm-ups. If you can't pass or serve, you won't get many balls to spike at either.

It is also very important that a team get used to the court. They need to be familiar with playing under the lighting system, the ceiling height, court lines, reference points, and any impediments, such as basketball backboards and supports. Some suggestions on how to accomplish all this include the following:

- Three-man pepper (spiker, digger, setter—the digger passes to the setter, who sets it right back to the digger to spike. The setter remains the same, but the spiker and digger trade back and forth. After a specified number of hits, the setter changes places).
- Up-and-back over- and underhand passing (one player at the net, the other on the endline. The one at the net tosses to the 10-foot-line, and the partner on the endline runs to the 10-foot-line to dig it to the net player, who catches it and then tosses it back to the endline while their partner runs backward to pass it up to the one at the net. They do 10 each and trade. Make sure they go call and attempt to make each pass perfect. They should work on their foot placement and quiet arms).
- Butterfly serving and passing.
- Queen's/King's court.
- Six-man pepper.
- Triangle over- and underhand passing.
- Spiking off of transition or with the set coming from a pass.
- Serve, pass, and hit. This could be off a butterfly (half a net) or from a three-person serve receive. Whoever passes the ball goes in and hits. The server, if successful, goes over to pass.

COACHING RESPONSIBILITIES

There are many choices a coach makes before a match even begins that may influence the outcome. Here are some that will give your team optimum conditions.

- Who will you schedule matches against? "If you want to be the best, you have to compete against the best even if it means risking a loss. Why seek out weak competition? That's why we play such an exhausting, competitive schedule at Tennessee" (Summitt, 1998, p. 210).

- The most important role a coach can play in a game is to be a cheerleader and advocate for the players, no matter what they do (or aren't able to do) in the game. The reason it is so important for coaches to support their players in game situations is because the athletes are most vulnerable at those times. When a player is playing badly, it is essential for that player to know that the coach will still provide encouragement and support (there is no point in sinking the boat when you are in it).

- Have a game plan.

- Make sure that the players know that volleyball is supposed to be fun.

■ Make sure your team arrives at the game with time to prepare adequately. You don't want them to have to rush. Make the trip pleasant, stress free, and positive.

■ Your team should have uniforms that fit them and that are comfortable. Uniforms affect their attitude. Function is also important. Make sure uniforms allow the freedom to swing at the ball, are modest (so players aren't self-conscious), and are durable.

■ Delegate the responsibilities for the equipment, stats, and filming early so you won't be occupied with those issues rather than focusing on your team.

■ Make several copies of your lineup with the players' names and numbers for both sets of uniforms. Then all you have to do on game day is write in your six players for the starting lineup. (An example is provided in the masters chapter.)

■ During the pregame meeting with the officials, set a pleasant tone with them. You want them on your side, or at least impartial. There are some choices you need to make on the outcome of the coin toss that will be advantageous for your team. If you receive the choice of court, choose the side that has the best approach for outside hits. Also choose the one that has the least amount of traffic. Check out the conditions of the court, such as light from the windows and so forth. Don't automatically choose the one that you warmed up on. Also, head coaches will often send their assistants to handle the pregame meeting, allowing them to focus on more pressing matters.

■ If it is rally scoring, it is usually best to choose to receive, because this gives you the first opportunity to attack and side-out, which would result in a point. If you have an exceptionally strong server, you might want to choose serve. Be careful, though, if you choose side, and be aware that there are two choices left: to receive or to serve.

■ Make your court conditions the best for your team. If possible, move chairs or benches back to give your players more room to play the ball. Get water bottles, ball bags, and first aid kits out of the way. Have a shorter bench by having statisticians sit behind or up in the stand, or near the scorers, so the players can go after errant balls without any impedance. Check for water spills or possibly dangerous situations that could injure your players. Don't leave anything to chance. Take towels with you.

■ Make sure your team is comfortable with their lineup. They need to have practiced enough that they are used to the people playing beside them, and be sure they are aware of the possibility of overlapping situations. They need to know what the contingency plan is for when they need to "hide" passers legally who are shanking balls on serve receive. Prepare in practice.

■ It is a good idea to practice with the same type of ball you will be using in the matches. Different balls tend to serve differently. Setters will feel more comfortable with a ball they are used to touching. If you get a variety, practice with a variety.

■ Home matches should be to your advantage, but many times they are not because of the added distraction and pressure of a home crowd. Don't allow your team to be drawn into interaction with the fans during the match. They need to stay focused and intense.

■ Make sure your team has adequate fuel, water, and rest. The practice before the match should be intense, but not too long.

■ If possible, have a short practice the morning of an important match. It takes away the jitters, reinforces skills, and is relaxing for the players.

■ Where you sit should be most beneficial to your team. Try different places on the bench. Some coaches like to sit right in the middle so they have a pulse on the team's attitude. The end of the bench is a great place for seeing the court without having the standards in the way. This position also keeps you out of the officials' faces when you get a little carried away. You will be closer to make serving suggestions. It is also a quieter place to talk to individual players during the match as they sub in and out. Don't just sit in one place, try them all out and see which you prefer.

■ Toward the end of the season and playoffs, it is more important to rest the team than to continue to have long, hard practices. Your team needs to recuperate so they will be fresh and rested both mentally and physically, so shorten practices.

GAME STRATEGIES

Now, where to deploy the troops? For what to prepare them? How to outguess your opponents? Every team is different, but there are many aspects of their games that are similar. Following are strategies that are inherent in the game of volleyball.

Offense

■ Generally, players should attack, attack, attack. Even a free ball should be placed smartly and to your team's advantage. All hitters should approach as hard as they can every time. According to W. H. Danforth (1998),

> opportunities do not come to those who wait. They are captured by those who attack...I am daring you to think bigger, to act bigger and be bigger. And I am promising you a richer life and a more exciting life if you do. I am showing you a world teeming with opportunity. The rewards for daring were never so rich or so plentiful. Science, religion, business, education, all are looking for the man who dares to face life, to attack rather than defend. (p. 11)

■ Encourage your players to celebrate their great successes. Celebrating does several things; it pumps them up with adrenaline, unites them in a victory, and encourages them to take risks again. Also, the other team may be watching and getting depressed.

■ Never play it safe, play it sure. Many times, when one team is ahead, they stall out and the other team starts catching up. This is usually because the team has ceased to play to win and is just playing not to lose. This is a passive approach, and the more aggressive team will come back. A team needs always to play to win, and attack.

■ Have all front-row hitters calling for the ball. It lets your setter know who is available; it gets the hitters ready; and it helps confuse the defense, which many times will split blockers.

■ During an intense, quick rally where your team is out of position and getting ragged, it is a good idea to have your players put the ball deep into the opponent's court. This serves two purposes. First, most defenses tend to creep up in the court, not going home every time in a long rally. Second, if the ball goes deep, it will give your team more time to recover and return to their defensive positions.

- Try to only tip sets that they expect you to hit.

- Anytime they expect a tip (a tight set for instance), try to hit it sharp angle or push it to deep corners. Setters on tight passes should try to punch it up on your side for a hit. If the middle is awake, this is a good set to hit a quick on, because they are hard to power set outside or back.

- Don't tip anything off of the net, hit it. Tips are slower, and if it is off the net, the defense has more time to respond.

- When the ball is on your own players' side, they should track it all the time. Many players will take their eyes off of it when they transition or come in for hitter coverage. They get caught with shanks, miss-hits, or having it bounce off of beams.

- Try to match up your best blockers with the opponent's best hitters. Your opposite is blocking their best hitter.

- Have your players talk, talk, talk. They should be go-calling each ball hit by a teammate, calling the balls they intend to hit, and talking to each other. If setters communicate effectively with their hitters, they can increase the hitters' kill ratio (for example, by calling the numbers of blockers or the places to hit to or by reminding the hitter of a technique to improve on to be successful, such as swinging fast or jumping behind the ball). The rest of the team can be calling where the opponent's attack is originating; the blockers can call other blockers over to help, or to let back-row players know that tips, down balls, or free balls are coming. Players can audibly remind each other where the setter is and how many are hitting front row.

- When your opponents are serving, notice how quickly the server goes to their defensive position. If they move slowly, attack with quicks or setter dumps there.

- Make sure hitters get a set at which they can swing. On quick transitions, have your setters put the ball higher to give them more time to approach and swing.

- Anytime your players can attack on the first or second hit, have them do it. Anything not expected is to your advantage. A team gets into a routine of pass, set, hit. If you counterattack with something out of the routine (such as spiking on the second hit), it will take the defense by surprise.

- Use signs to communicate holes in the defense or hitting strategies to your hitters on the court without having to call time out.

- As a general rule, hit most free and down balls to the number 1 position on the court. Sometimes when the setter transitions to the front row to set, the middle back does not move over to cover the court. It is also harder to set a ball coming from behind, and a quick attack is much less likely.

- Use fakes to draw a block away or make them hesitate and be late. You can have a player come from the back row and fake hit one quick set or back slide as long as they don't hit the ball. It is especially effective if your opponents know they hit quicks well. Then use them in a fake in the rotation just before they come to the front.

Serving

■ Your team should have a variety of serving skills: spin serve, floaters, and short, deep, and jump serves.

■ When your team is winning points, it should get the ball to its server fast.

■ When struggling or losing points, your players need to slow the game down.

■ Don't have your players serve right at passers (that makes it easy for them); instead, make your opponents move to play the ball. It adds another element that can go wrong. It is even better if your servers "seam" players (go between them), which incorporates another person into decision making and can complicate things, or it might make them late or less sure when playing the ball.

■ Target whoever made the last mistake. Pick on them. It is natural for the opponents to be preoccupied thinking about their mistakes, decreasing their focus. Take advantage of that.

■ Target substitutes. They aren't into the rhythm of the game, are under more stress to perform, and many times are not ready to play.

■ If the setter is coming from the back row during serve receive, have your server serve at him or her, or in his or her path to the net. The setter will obstruct the view of the passer and confuse him or her, and sometimes the setter will be forced to take the serve.

■ Don't let your opponents get used to the same type of serve; keep them guessing (hard, soft, floater, deep, short?). Mix them up.

■ Use your team's natural screens to serve over legally. Many times a receiving team will screen their own players from seeing the ball. Say you have your middle front and your left front standing together at the net (with the prescribed distance between them), and their middle front is standing at the net and happens to be right between your two players. Your server has a nice three-man screen to serve over and the opponent's passers won't see the ball very quickly. Look for bunches like this to increase the effectiveness of your serve legally.

■ Serve to number one (their back-right side facing the net) a lot. A pass coming from behind the server's shoulder is difficult to set and not as effective to run quicks on because most setters turn slightly to take the ball. Also, a lot of teams will move closer to the net on that side and give more open court in the deep corner. It is a harder serve to pass in the direction of the setter than a number five or number six.

■ If a front-row hitter is passing, target that player to take the serve. It is often hard for the player to pass and then get outside to hit. You can slow down the action by serving deep or short so the hitter can't get an approach, or run quicks.

■ Hard serves create more aces. Players have to make decisions quickly, and the ball is more apt to be passed tight or over the net. If mishandled, it goes farther and is hard to retrieve. Passers have less time to move up or back. If you couple the hard serve with a floater or mix them up with a short soft serve when the opponent expects a hard deep one, you set up success.

■ Jump serves are mentally winners. Just the fact that you have a player that is aggressive and talented enough to attempt them adds a mental block to your opponents, even if the serve isn't great. Because of the downward spin of the serve, it is difficult to determine if it is in or out. Because it is so effective, postsecondary teams are leaning heavily in this direction.

■ Emphasize that the serve must be in the court in the following situations: after a time out (the opposing coach may call many to put pressure on your team to miss—don't let them win); on game point; after the player before missed the serve. Two missed serves in a row can really put a team in a mental slump. Volleyball is such a momentum game that two missed serves in a row can have quite a negative impact. Tell them, this must be a sure serve.

■ Is your server struggling? Here are some strategies that help in a game situation: Give the server a focus, a particular spot. Don't tell him or her to simply get it in. If you do, he or she will be very careful and usually toss too low or swing too slow and float the ball right out of the court. Tell him or her to be deliberate and take time with the toss. The toss is usually the key to a good serve. Tell him or her to keep the elbows up. Watch the hand hit the ball. If the player is missing it (many players get distracted), just refocus the player and have him or her watch the contact. Have the server follow through and put the hand on the target. Some servers will side-swipe the ball, and it will go out of bounds to the left or in the net. They need to transfer their power through the ball to the target. So just tell them to put their hand on the target. If the ball is going in the net, the toss is usually too far out in front of them. Just tell them to step under the ball. Tell the server to take a deep breath and let it out slowly. Tell servers to visualize the ball going over to the spot they are aiming for. You have to believe it to achieve it.

■ There is a real debate among coaches whether a coach should call where the player is to hit the serve. This same debate rages in football circles—of whether to let the quarterback call plays or the coach. It is an individual preference and a control issue. On the one hand, the coach is more knowledgeable about serving strategies, but on the other hand, this is your players' game; teach them and let them call the shots. They know which serves are their best and most successful. Giving them the control empowers them and demands of them to think. According to Summitt, (1998) "Real success is when they don't need you anymore" (pp. 246–247). Ultimately, the decision should be one with which the coach is most comfortable.

Setters

■ When the setter is in the back row, it is good strategy to hit at his or her position. Setters are, after all, the specialists in setting, and if you take them out by forcing them to dig the first ball, a less competent player will have to set, thus increasing the possibility of a less successful set (or overset) and consequently a poor attack. If a player other than the setter sets the ball for the attacker, this will usually prevent the attacker from running a quick attack, because a specialty set requires the proper timing the setter has developed. Also, many setters cheat (take off early from defense in order to get to their setting positions near the net), leaving their positions open to attack.

■ It is a good idea when players have to hit a free ball or down ball over to direct it to the setter's position on the court (number one). Setters release from their defensive positions on free balls, and many back-row players forget to split the back-court and cover their positions, thus leaving a hole on the right side of their court.

■ If your setter is struggling placing the ball, have him or her focus on one of these keys: Feet to the ball, square to the antennae, hands shaped and up early, extend and hold.

■ When your setter is in the front row, have him or her attack the second hit every now and then. It keeps the blockers honest (not leaving them to direct their blocks toward the other two hitters) and takes the team unawares.

■ The best setter dumps are the ones off of perfect passes with the hitters calling and coming in for quicks. The blockers have to be ready for the quick (if you have been successful with it), and their attention is diverted from the setter to the hitter. This play is totally unexpected, because the blockers are focused on the approaching hitter.

■ When your setters release from defense, have them go directly to the net. If the passes are tight, they will have a much better chance of setting them because they won't be jumping into the net.

Outside Hitters

The majority of sets should go to the outside hitters.

■ They should be your best, most consistent, and most experienced hitters.
■ They have more room to put the ball into the court.
■ If the balls are set on the sideline, it is harder for the blockers to set up a good two-person block, especially if it is a quick set (greater distance to travel).
■ Outside left is the best hitting position for right-handed players, because the ball comes to their right side (not across their body). They have more time to approach because it is a longer set from where the setter is located, and the attacker can gain more speed and height in the jump.
■ Have outside hitters hit from different places on the net. This is easy to do from a serve-receive position. They can also hit swings, tandems, or slides. Also, use them attacking from the back row.

Middle Hitters

■ Middle hitters have only half of the court to get the ball in.

■ Your setters will be more inclined to set the ball to the middle of the net because it is an easier set and doesn't take as much strength and accuracy. Keep track of the number of sets to this position. The majority should be going outside.

■ Middle hitters almost always will have at least one blocker up in the middle, so they should never hit straight on but always at angles. Have them hit mostly to the number one position on the court. Half the time the setter is there and will be forced to take it, and the other half they are in the front row, and it is a difficult pass for a setter to handle.

■ The most effective tips are the ones hit on good sets (the ones players want to kill). Have them tip toward the line, right or left, from wherever the blocker came. It is a difficult hit to pass without going over or under the net or out of bounds. Whenever the defense expects a hit, give them a tip, and vice versa.

■ Set up the defense for tips by first spiking one side deep, then coming back with a tip.

- Players can run screens, tandems, quicks, or slides to create problems for the blockers and create either a one-on-one blocking situation or a hole in the block.

- Middles can come in and call for quicks, even if they aren't going to hit. It can distract and cause even a slight hesitation in the blocker, making him or her late, and hopefully, provide a hole in the block to hit through.

Opposite Hitters

- Defense is not usually as good for opposite hits (right side), because the defense doesn't get as much practice as with on-hand hits.

- Middle blockers don't go left as well as they go right, so they tend to leave more gaps in the block or fail to seal the net adequately.

- An angle or power hit is directed to the opponent's setter half of the time, which prevents the setter from setting the ball.

- Because this set is right behind the setter, it is a shorter timed set, so the middle blocker doesn't have as much time to get there.

- Lots of setters don't set behind themselves because that is a blind set.

- If you have a left-handed player, the right side of the net is a great spot for him or her because the set ball will be on his or her on-hand side (the ball does not have to cross the body to the hitting side). Use left-handed players often; it is like having two on-hand hitters at one time.

- If your off-hand hitter is right-handed, cue him or her to line up with the ball. Because the ball is coming across the body, the player has a tendency to approach with the ball to his or her left. If this is the case, when the ball is hit, there will be a lower swing because the hand has to come across his or her body to hit it. There is no choice as to the direction, because the ball will have to be angle and will usually go into the net.

Defense

In general, the big key for defense is to look ahead of the ball. Use the ball, setter, ball, hitter technique (explained throughly in Chapter 12), in which the key for players is, after contact or pass, to look at the setter. If the setter is going to dump the ball, he or she will usually give it away. Right after the set leaves the setter's hands and your defense knows where it is going, they should look at the hitter. Watch the hitter's approach and shoulders and how tight or far back the ball is from the net. This is very important for a read defense.

Blockers

- Your blockers should own the net and patrol it like guard dogs.

- They should watch where the set goes (not further than the peak) and not be drawn into going with the hitter unless the ball goes there. Blockers should concentrate on where the setter sets the ball.

- Your blockers should jump and attempt to block any ball coming close to the net. This intimidates the opposing hitters and setters.

- Tight over-sets that are right on top of the net, should be blocked away from your opponents, who are usually gathered close to where the ball came over the net.

- Blockers should watch the hitter's approach, shoulders, and arm swing.

- If there are any tight sets, blockers should expect a tip but play for a spike.

- Blockers should be aware of where the opponent's setter is and what offense he or she is running (5-1, or 6-2, or 4-2, and so on). When the setter is in the front row, your defense can concentrate on blocking two hitters, but realize that the setter can attack. Many times the setter has the best attack percentage because the defense is not expecting the attack. When the setter is coming from the back row, your blockers need not worry about his or her attacking and can concentrate on the hitters. Many times a blocker will jump with the setter and be late getting to the set outside because of it. Paying attention to where the setter is coming from can eliminate that.

- Middle blockers should keep hands high for quicks.

- Outside blockers should turn hands in. Their outside foot should close perpendicular to the centerline. They should block to the center of the court.

- Players should seldom block hits off of the net. The timing will be off, and the blocker will hinder the vision of the back row from digging. Hitters are more apt to use blockers to deflect hits. If you do have a block up on a down ball, use a middle blocker. They can get the soft balls that dribble over, or even a direct hit.

- Don't allow blockers to automatically block everything. They should be there to read the approach and where the set goes.

- If the set is beyond the antennae, the only hit the attacker can make is sharp angle. The blockers and back-row defense should pull over to cover the angle and leave the downline open.

- Blockers should know hitters' tendencies. If some only hit angle, give the line (move in and block angle).

- If a team has one hitter they key on and that is hurting you, focus on him or her; put three blockers on that hitter if you can. Serve at that hitter and make him or her move back deep or up short to take it. Make it difficult for that player to get the set.

Back-Row Defense

- Encourage the back-row defense to go, go, go, they'll never know unless they go.

- They should dig balls to the 10-foot line. If they are going to err, it is better to err away from the net than over it.

- On quick returns, they should dig higher to allow time for the setter to get to the ball and the hitters to transition. If it is a free ball, because it is already slow and everyone has time to transition, they should pass it quick to speed up the attack.

- The back-row defense should watch the ball the whole time it is on your team's side, even during transition from defense to offense or to hitter coverage.

- They should go home to defensive spots quickly as soon as the ball goes over the net, but keep an eye on the ball.

- As soon as the ball is released from the opposing setter's hands, the defense should get to the defensive spot quickly, with arms out, and stop before the player hits it so the defensive player can move in the direction of the hit. If the player is moving, say, back when the attacker tips the ball, it is extremely hard to shift momentum and go forward. If the defensive player does read a tip, he or she can be on the move to get to the spot, though.

- Defensive players should always expect a tip and play for a hit. If they expect the front-row setter to tip the ball every time he or she touches it, the defense won't get caught.

- The defense should read the hitter coming in, the speed of the approach, the height of the jump, the speed of the swing, and the angle of the shoulders. A lot depends on the set—tight, move in, off the net, move back. Defense players must know the attackers' hitting tendencies.

- Communication is imperative on defense because of the need to call for the ball quickly. There are six people playing intensely in a small space. If people don't talk, there will be a lot of dropped balls or interference. The sooner the defense calls the ball, the quicker the decision will be made so the other players can back off and let the one who called it take the ball. If the ball goes between two players, they need to scissor (one goes short, and one goes deep) or both go.

- Players closest to the side and endlines should call the ball in or out. The player going for the ball often has lost court sense and can't tell if it is in or out, so it is crucial that a teammate help out.

Hitter Coverage

- Players should follow the hitter in, arms out and eye on blocker's arms, ahead of the spiked ball (they will see it quicker).
- Expect a blocked ball always.
- Dig it up, above the net, hopefully to the 10-foot line.
- This is such a quick dig, reaction has to be extremely fast. Because of this, being in position with arms ready is very important.

Time-outs

Time-outs should be called when

- Your opponent is making a run on your team. Don't let them get more than three to four points in a row. Call a time out, set up a play, and refocus your team.
- One server has your team flustered. If that player served two aces, it is time for a time-out. Use it as a momentum break or to put heat on the server (many times a server will miss right after a time-out because of the stress).
- You need to try to stop the momentum. Don't wait until 13 or 14, unless you are tied or it is a close game.
- Your team needs some direction, such as overlapping problems; or to redirect the attack or defense.

■ After the other team wins a long, intense rally. It is such a letdown for your team that it is a good idea to regroup and give them a breather. At the same time it might help slow the momentum the other team gained from the rally win.

What to Say or Do

Following are some suggestions for strategies during time-outs.

■ Be positive. Tell your team what you want to see, not what they are doing wrong, which will be their focus. Remember, you are trying to encourage them, not discourage them. You want them to go back on the court more determined, infused with confidence, knowledge, and determination to turn the game around. In short order, you want them to go back out to play in better shape than they came in.

■ Pull them together; do not fragment them.

■ Give only a few pointers. Too many coaches overload players with knowledge and then wonder why the team doesn't follow any of the directives they were given. Don't give them more than two or three things to work on.

■ Refocus them with points from the scouting reports for attack or defense, or give them new information gleaned from the match they are playing.

■ Build confidence. Remind them of their past successes. Let them know you believe in them.

■ Challenge them (see Chapter 24).

■ In long matches, allow the players to sit and get rehydrated.

■ Do not call a time-out and then not talk to them. Your players are not deliberately losing or trying to make you frustrated. Your job is to try to come up with something that can help them play the best game they can. Disgust, sarcasm, and rudeness on your part during time-outs shows a lack of character in you. Remember what your job is.

■ Know your team. Sometimes it is good to not call a time-out and let them struggle to see if they can pull it together. Do not abandon them, though. Have a sense of when they need your intervention.

SUBSTITUTIONS

Your bench is an integral part of your success and your happiness as a team. How you treat your substitutes and how important they feel can make or break a team. It is imperative that they know and feel comfortable with their role on the team. That doesn't mean they shouldn't try to improve their status, but they should understand your decision and what you have chosen for them to do. Also, they usually are going to be the backbone for your next year's team, so the growth and the experience they gain during matches is imperative. Here are some ideas to help you accomplish this juggling act.

■ Keep them in the game while they are sitting on the bench. Have them look for places to attack when they go in, blockers to hit over, when the setter is in the front or back row and can attack, and the opponent's hitting and serving tendencies.

■ Before they go in, they can stand, stretch out, and mentally prepare.

■ If a player they go in for has something that needs fixing, have the sidelined player help with go calls from the bench. They can help with such things as transitioning outside to hit, or arms out on defense, or going in for hitter coverage, or following through on a spike. This reinforces that behavior and really helps with the camaraderie on the team.

■ They need to understand there is no dead weight or sulking on the bench.

■ When players come out, they should treat their replacements well. Do not allow prima donnas or tantrums. They should not take out their frustrations on their substitutes. This is not an individual sport, it is a team sport, and individuals will not win without the whole team. Your players do not live in a vacuum, and all they do will influence and reflect on others. Each individual is responsible for that. Many times the players will be mad at themselves, but it may seem otherwise. Make sure they understand that pouting is not acceptable and why.

■ Subs should go in and spark the team. They need to have enthusiasm and ooze confidence and aggressiveness.

■ They need to understand that this is their chance to show what they can do; so they don't want to hold back and be careful. They need to attack and take risks. Nothing will be gained by not risking.

■ Allow players the opportunity to take risks without the fear of being pulled back out. They cannot go to the next level of play if they aren't allowed to take risks and make mistakes. Substitutes need to be granted the same latitude as starters. Too often, they are pulled out for fewer mistakes than the starters.

■ When players are taken out of the game, give them positive feedback first, not negative. They are more receptive and their confidence will not be as negatively affected. Tell them what you want to see, not what they are doing wrong. You want them to be an asset to your team, not a liability, and how you treat them will have a great effect on that outcome.

■ Quick, direct communication is usually best. If a player who is removed from a starting position on the team during a game sits down on the bench far away from the coach and stews about possible reasons of being removed, or wonders what his or her status is with the coach, it just breeds a negative atmosphere. It is usually best to talk immediately to the players and be direct.

OFFICIALS

Treat officials with respect, and make sure your team does too. You want them on your side. Yelling, berating, harassing, and trying to intimidate them does not endear you to them. There are many split decisions to be made, and if you have made their lives miserable, unconsciously they can hurt you.

■ If you constantly blame or plead with the officials, it takes your focus and your team's attention away from the game. Why not have your team focus on what they have control over—their own actions?

■ Be fair and honest both with your team, your opponents, and the officials. It always pays off.

■ When officials come to your gym to referee, treat them well. Have their checks ready, be prompt, and have your facility in tip-top condition. If there are multiple matches, provide soft drinks or water for them.

SUMMARY

Implementing these strategies can put your team on the winner's side of the war. And just like in a war, in the game of volleyball there will always be new attacks, better defenses, another way of looking at things, and something unique to try to counter. This is what keeps coaches on their toes—always trying to stay one step ahead. Anyone who is not learning and moving forward is stagnating. Strategies must change with every team encountered and with each team coached. Using the right strategies gives your team the edge to succeed.

CHAPTER 23

Teaching the Winning Attitude

Why do some teams seem to always win, even in their off years? How can they beat bigger, more talented teams? The keys are confidence and a winning attitude. So, how do you develop that in your players?

This triangle indicates the building blocks needed:

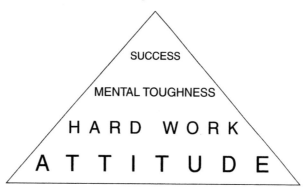

ATTITUDE

Scott Hamilton summarized the importance of this building block with the simple statement, "The only disability in life is a bad attitude." It is truly your attitude at the beginning of a task that will determine the outcome. You will find that winners say what they want to happen and losers say what they fear might happen. Developing the right attitude on your team is paramount to a successful sports program. One of the best quotes revealing the magnitude attitude has on your team is as follows:

> Attitude is more important than the past, than education, than money, than circumstances, than what other people think or say or do. It is more important than appearance, giftedness or skill. It will make or break a company, a church, a home, a team.
>
> The remarkable thing is, we have a choice every day regarding the attitude we will embrace for that day. We cannot change our past. We cannot change the fact that people will act in a certain way. We cannot change the inevitable. The only thing we can do is play on the one string we have and that is our attitude. (Swindoll, 2000)

No wonder attitude is the supporting block that holds up the whole structure of a winning team. What kind of attitude do you want your team to have? From the U.S. Olympic Training Center/U.S. Shooting Team Division comes the following guide that can help you create the winning attitude you are looking for.

Winning Attitudes

To develop the Winning Attitude you must:

Become excited, confident, and enthusiastic about your goals.

Give yourself permission to be a winner.

Winners have the ability to look inside themselves and find that special dream.

The winner always has a goal.

The winner stresses solutions, not problems.

Winners have plans to reach their goals.

Winners make total commitments to their goals.

Winners have positive attitudes in all elements of their lives. The more you think about, talk about, and write about a thing happening, the greater the certainty of that thing happening.

Winning is an inside job.

Self-discipline is the winner's creed. (Vande Zonde, n.d.)

How do we teach our players that the perception we have of an event is our choice? Lynn Peters describes our options:

> Happiness isn't about what happens to us—it's about how we perceive what happens to us. It's the knack of finding a positive for every negative, and viewing a set-back as a challenge. It's not wishing for what we don't have, but enjoying what we do possess. Choose your attitude. We can change the way we view the picture. (Peters, 1996)

There are many ways coaches can teach a positive attitude. The first is by portraying it. We know the number one way to learn is by having a good example before us. If coaches can say five positive things for every negative one, that would be a start. You might try asking your assistant coach to count the number of positive versus negative comments you make during a practice.

Tape record or videotape practices and matches and observe your behavior. Listen to what you say and how you say it. Ninety-three percent of communication is body language and voice tones; 7 percent is words. Look for the behavior you want to be repeated and verbally recognize it. Ignore the negative. The things that get rewarded get done.

Reward people who otherwise might go unnoticed, such as passers, setters, blockers, and defense specialists. Everyone wants to look good, feel important, and be needed. To maintain good attitudes on your team, your players need to fill a role on the team with which they agree. But, they don't necessarily have to accept it. If a team member is the seventh person on the bench, you don't want them to be satisfied to stay there—you want them to continue to strive to become a starter. But the players need to know where they stand and what contribution is expected of them.

Attitudes are all about making choices, for example, choosing to be upset, mad, or happy. Abraham Lincoln said, "Most folks are about as happy as they make up their minds to be." Sports are a fertile field in which to practice making choices of attitude. If coaches can demonstrate the positive way to deal with stress, mistakes, winning, and losing, their athletes will be more likely to model the desired behavior. Also, if coaches do not allow certain negative behaviors, such as swearing, yelling, towel throwing, kicking objects, or badmouthing officials and opponents, those behaviors will not be rewarded and will stop. You have two choices: to react negatively or positively. The following story illustrates this point.

Jerry was the kind of guy you love to hate. He was always in a good mood and always had something positive to say. When someone would ask him how he was doing, he would reply, "If I were any better, I would be twins!" He was a unique manager because he had several waiters who had followed him around from restaurant to restaurant. The reason the waiters followed Jerry was because of his attitude. He was a natural motivator. If an employee was having a bad day, Jerry was there telling the employee how to look on the positive side of the situation. Seeing this style really made me curious, so one day I said to Jerry, "I don't get it! You can't be a positive person all of the time. How do you do it?" Jerry replied, "Each morning I wake up and say to myself, 'Jerry, you have two choices today. You can choose to be in a good mood or you can choose to be in a bad mood.' I choose to be in a good mood. Each time something bad happens, I can choose to be a victim or I can choose to learn from it. I choose to learn from it. Every time someone comes to me to complain, I can choose to accept their complaining or I can point out the positive side of life. I choose the positive side of life." "Yeah, right, it's not that easy," I protested. "Yes it is," Jerry said. "Life is all about choices. When you cut away all the junk, every situation is a choice. You choose how you react to situations. You choose how people will affect your mood. You choose to be in a good or bad mood. The bottom line: It's your choice how you live life." I reflected on what Jerry said. Soon thereafter, I left the restaurant industry to start my own business. We lost touch, but I often thought about him when I made a positive choice about life instead of reacting negatively to it. Several years later, I heard that Jerry did something you are never supposed to do in the restaurant business: He left the back door open one morning and was held up at gunpoint by three armed robbers. While trying to open the safe, his hand, shaking from nervousness, slipped off the combination. The robbers panicked and shot him. Luckily, Jerry was found relatively quickly and rushed to the local trauma center. After 18 hours of surgery and weeks of intensive care, Jerry was released from the hospital with fragments of the bullets still in his body. I saw Jerry about six months after the accident. When I asked him how he was, he replied, "If I were any better, I'd be twins. Wanna see my scars?" I declined to see his wounds, but did ask him what had gone through his mind as the robbery took place. "The first thing that went through my mind was that I should have locked the back door," Jerry replied. "Then, as I lay on the floor, I remembered that I had two choices: I could choose to live, or I could choose to die. I chose to live." "Weren't you scared? Did you lose consciousness?" I asked. Jerry continued, "The paramedics were great. They kept telling me I was going to be fine. But when they wheeled me into the emergency room and I saw the expressions on the faces of the doctors and nurses, I got really scared. In their eyes, I read, 'He's a dead man,' I knew I needed to take action." "What did you do?" I asked. "Well, there was a big, burly nurse shouting questions at me," said Jerry. "She asked if I was allergic to anything. 'Yes,' I replied. The doctors and nurses stopped working as they waited for my reply.... I took a deep breath and yelled, 'Bullets!' Over their laughter, I told them, 'I am choosing to live. Operate on me as if I am alive, not dead.'" Jerry lived thanks to the skill of his doctors, but also because of his amazing attitude. I learned from him that every day we have the choice to live fully.

Attitude, after all, is everything. You have two choices.

More learning occurs if coaches can create a positive atmosphere in their practices. Victor Weisskopf (1990) explained this in the book *The Privilege of Being a Physicist*. "People cannot learn by having information pressed into their brains. Knowledge has to be sucked into the brain, not pushed in. First, one must create a state of mind that craves knowledge, interest and wonder. You can teach only by creating an urge to know" (p. 194). It is up to coaches to create this atmosphere at practice. With increased learning, all can win.

A common attitude problem most coaches will face occurs when their team is way ahead in a game and just stalls out, loses steam, and gets beat. One of the biggest culprits of this problem is the "playing not to lose" instead of "playing to win" syndrome. The first is a cautious, tentative, careful approach, whereas the second is an aggressive, attack one. Which one will carry the momentum? In volleyball, momentum is everything! And again, attitude is the source.

Coaching a positive attitude is reinforced when you give your players uplifting reminders or post them in the locker room. Here are a few thoughts that epitomize the attitudes most coaches want in a team:

- When you get kicked, make sure it is forward.
- Turn stumbling blocks into stepping stones.
- Birds need resistance to fly, and kites rise in the wind. Use adversity to soar!
- We can't change the direction of the wind, but we can adjust our sails.
- Light fires from which others can become warm; dig wells from which others can drink.
- Butterflies are okay as long as they are flying in formation.
- Don't take life so seriously—you're not getting out alive! (Bugs Bunny).
- Even if you are on the right road, you are apt to get run over if you are standing still.
- Believing is half the battle.
- Focus on what you want and you will move in that direction.
- It is your attitude toward others that determines their attitude toward you.
- How much you want out of volleyball correlates with the risks you are willing to take, the exploring you are willing to do. Dare to be great!
- If you always do what you've always done, you'll get what you've always gotten.
- More is lost from not trying than not succeeding.

Sports, like life, are not fair. So stop whining and get on with it!

When working with the youth of today and trying to create a positive atmosphere, it is important to remember "adolescence is like a house on moving day, a temporary mess." It is a volatile time period in their lives with lots of change, and change is the number one cause of stress. Because of this, it is essential to understand that it isn't your job to be liked, but to like. Kids know if you like and care for them.

Another invaluable key to understanding human nature is embodied in a quote by Malcolm S. Forbes, "Too many people overvalue what they are not and undervalue what they are" (1998, p. 73). People will almost always be much more demanding of themselves and have great difficulty ever being good enough. Because of that, a negative comment lasts a lot longer than five positive ones. Be stingy with the criticism and generous with the praise.

HARD WORK

You can be confident when you are competent. If you've covered all your bases, are strong in the basic skills, and are prepared for anything the other team may throw at you, you will be confident. This can only be accomplished with lots of hard work.

Hard work develops pride in yourself and your accomplishments; you deserve to win. You've earned it. Your players will develop a tenacious attitude. They've put too much commitment and energy into the team to go down easily. Working hard promotes a bulldog type of team personality.

Commitment is a big part of hard work. In order to give their all, your players need to buy into your/their program. One way of doing this is by having your athletes come up with personal and team goals. This will help them own a piece of the dream. Here is a suggestion on how to accomplish this: Each week have your team meet and write down their personal and team goals (without your input). If they post these goals somewhere visible (like on the outside of their lockers), they become a daily reminder and help develop commitment. The next week they should review the goals and make new ones. Doing this funnels your whole team in the same direction, working on the same goals, and they eventually will strive to get much further than with a more random method. Colin L. Powell (1998) summarizes this strategy with the following statement, "The best method of overcoming obstacles is the team method"(p. 73). A sample goal sheet is provided in the masters appendix.

Hard work doesn't have to be drudgery. If your team's conditioning and practices are competitive and gamelike, working hard can be fun. Not only that, but also your team will play harder and drive themselves further. You will find that if the athletes push themselves, their attitudes will be more positive than if you constantly yell at them. The atmosphere during your practices will be constructive.

A team that is in great condition because of hard work will still be going strong at the end of the day. Mental toughness develops when a team has to dig in and play hard right to the end of a two-hour match. You want players who can reach deep and block with just as much intensity in the final few minutes of a game as at the beginning. A team that practices hard and long gets used to maintaining their intensity, focus, and clarity of mind even when they are exhausted.

MENTAL TOUGHNESS

Mental toughness develops when teams are put in difficult situations repetitively. During practice, if a team loses, immediately have them review the cause and effect, and play again, giving them a chance to win.

Drills that make one team the underdog, forcing them to claw their way back, helps build confidence in their ability to do just that. When individuals have to figure their way out of problems, they will develop confidence in themselves. It is important that coaches not always give all the answers. Allow your athletes to develop the confidence to find the solutions on their own. A team needs to know they can rely on each other during the tough times.

Players have to maintain control of themselves before they can control their performance. Athletes who can let go mentally of their mistakes and focus on the next ball are much tougher opponents. "Mistakes are a fact of life. It is the response to the error that counts" (Giovanni, 2000).

Many players have a difficult time owning mistakes. For example, if they had a bad spike, it was a poor set. If they let a ball drop, it was because a teammate didn't go call them, or faked them out, making them think they were going for the ball. They are great at blaming others or making excuses for their actions. It is never their fault. John Wooden sums up this attitude eloquently, "A person may make mistakes, but he isn't a failure until he starts blaming someone else" (Wooden & Tobin, 1988, p. 120).

Advocating the "better the ball" policy helps eliminate this attitude, which destroys mental toughness. Teach your athletes that it is their responsibility to improve on anything they get. In other words, they must make the best choice with whatever chances they have to play the ball. There are no excuses. The results will tell the tale.

Likewise, if players are incensed with a teammate, opponent, coach, or official, or even themselves, their attention is diverted and so is the focus of their intensity. If their opponents realize this and capitalize on it by forcing them to handle the ball, the results could be disastrous and could lead to a steadily declining performance. This is an important strategy to remember and use on your opponents. The individual who will come through for you in a crisis situation will

1. When the game is on the line, *want* the ball.
2. Anticipate, not dread games.
3. Confront the negative.
4. Control emotions.
5. Be persistent (see the big picture).
6. Refocus quickly after failures.

One way to help athletes focus in a pressure situation is to redirect their attention to performing proper technique. If you can get them to remember specific cue words or basics techniques, rather than the score or the circumstances, their stress level will decrease and their performance will improve. Getting your players back in the comfort zone of basics helps them feel more competent. Peter T. McIntrye (2000) takes it a step further in this statement, "Confidence comes not from always being right but from not fearing to be wrong." Minimize the negativity that follows mistakes. Focus on learning from them and playing the next ball.

Do you allow your players to make mistakes without criticizing them or pulling them out of the game? Can they take risks without second-guessing your reaction? In order for your team to step up to the next level of play, they have to have the encouragement and confidence to try new things. Mistakes aren't the problem; it is what you do about them that is.

Players who can be totally absorbed in what they are doing at any given moment will have the focus for which all coaches strive. When they can do this, it won't matter how they look, who is watching, where they are, who is officiating or coaching, or what they just did. This is mental toughness.

One last point extremely important in developing a team that can stand up under pressure is the difficulty level of teams you play. If you are starting out with a young, inexperienced team, it is a good idea to set them up for success. Make sure they play some teams they will have a good chance of beating. If they experience too many losses, they may develop an apathetic attitude. Success breeds success.

Give them a taste of it, and they will want more. However, easy wins may help build confidence, but little else. Tough teams find your weak spots, easy teams don't. You can't fix something if you aren't aware it is broken. The better your opponent, the more fundamental problems will appear. To develop championship teams, playing a tough schedule is imperative.

SUCCESS

Handling success is easy, right? Wrong. There is a classy way to handle it and a poor way. Winners are at the top only for a moment, but the limelight is on, and a lot will be said by their actions. Remember, the team didn't get there by themselves. Even the teams they beat influenced the victory. Tough league competition can drive your team to great improvements in order to win. Administration, parents, community, and support staff (statisticians, trainers, managers, and so on) all had a hand in it. Following are some characteristics of a winning attitude.

- Graciousness.
- Enthusiasm.
- Sharing of widespread deserved credit.
- Appreciation of worthy opponents (or your win would be insignificant).
- Satisfaction at reaching a goal.
- After an adequate celebration, going on to the next goal. There are other mountains to conquer.

Be careful not to treat opponents badly, because what goes around comes around. All teams tend to have some years that are better than others. You want your team to be classy winners for others to emulate. They should be considerate and empathetic to the losing team, for if you stay in coaching long enough, that will be your team someday. If it wasn't for second place, your team wouldn't be first. Know that your team will mirror your behavior—sometimes for the rest of their lives.

Now that you've reached the top, guess what? You get to start all over, right at the bottom and build again. But you've got a great path to follow and some wonderful memories to sustain you until you reach the top again. Remember, the journey is more important than the destination.

SUMMARY

Paramount to becoming a successful coach is not just coaching physical skill but molding the proper attitude in your players. This will not be a temporary achievement either, as the right attitude will continue to benefit your athletes throughout their lives. Help your players understand attitude and their control over it. Teach the simple concept that mistakes happen to everyone; however, what counts is their action after the mistake. Do your players learn from their mistakes and step up to a new level, or do they continuously repeat them? Do they blame others, make excuses, or take responsibility for their mistakes? Have you inspired your athletes so that they are not afraid to err? If so, you have given them not only success in sports, but more likely success in life.

CHAPTER 24

The Challenge

We would like to propose a dimension to coaching rarely found in the literature, but one used by many of the best coaches: challenge feedback. Pat Summitt (1998b) states, "If you come to Tennessee we are going to challenge you" (p. 75). Lou Holtz believes, "Leaders must challenge and inspire." What is a challenge? How does a coach ignite the spark of the competitor? How does a coach get players to bite the bait? Do you know how to push the right buttons to get an athlete to perform well? Does it take a particular skill to challenge an athlete? How does a coach go about using this tool effectively?

WHAT IS THE CHALLENGE?

The challenge is an adventure and the discovery of self and those you lead. With each passing day, you change. The challenge talks about not only reaching one's potential but exceeding it. It's about risks, battles, expectations, and achievements greater than you thought yourself capable of. The challenge is about overcoming the fear of success or fear of failure.

To clarify what the challenge is, specific definitions are provided. The definitions are the heartbeat of the challenge. They widen the scope so that at any specific time you have choices from which to draw. Without these, one is ignorant of the tools that are available.

1. A good challenge is stimulating and thought provoking.
2. It is something that, by its nature or character, serves as a call to battle, contest, or competition.
3. It is words that incite or quicken actions, feelings, and thoughts.
4. It rouses to action or effort as by encouragement or pressure.
5. It is a call or summons to engage in any contest that takes skill, technique, strength, and so on.
6. It can be provocative or intriguing (a challenging smile; a shake of the head yes).
7. It stirs up, arouses, or calls forth feelings, desires, or activity.
8. It can annoy, aggravate, or infuriate.
9. It is a gauntlet. To take up the gauntlet is to accept a challenge to fight, to undertake the defense of a person. To throw down the gauntlet is to challenge, as to combat.
10. Daring is having the necessary courage or boldness for thoughts and actions. Daring challenges or provokes a person to make a show of courage.

FOUNDATIONS

There are basic characteristics that successful coaches, who use the challenge, exemplify (i.e., love, passion, respect, fervor, chemistry, dedication, loyalty, hard work, knowledge, details, practice, networking, and risk taking. We have discussed many of these traits throughout the book. If the coach has earned players' trust and respect, then he or she can move forward with this very effective tool.

WHY CHALLENGE?

You might ask yourself, why challenge my players. The answer is because the challenge can instill trust, build confidence, and create an "I can do this" attitude. Players want to meet challenges, to prove they can perform at a certain level and beyond. The coach has the responsibility to recognize a player's potential and expect nothing less of the player. Challenging the player at the right moment gets the maximum potential out of the player. Also, if the player accepts the challenge and is successful, the coach can take them to the next level.

The challenge can be used when you're having tryouts. You need to know if each athlete is coachable and competitive. Throw a challenge out and see how they respond. Do they become aggressive, attacking animals, or are they submissive, whipped puppies?

TIMING OF THE CHALLENGE

Because no two personalities are the same and individuals change from day to day, the challenge is enduring and ever-changing. As a result of these personalities and changes, the challenge always stretches the mind to seek new techniques that will lift one particular person to a higher level. The challenge becomes contagious and rewarding when a leader recognizes the ability of team members, and challenges them to reach beyond a preconceived potential, propelling them to succeed beyond their wildest dreams. A person must be willing to be challenged. Before you issue a challenge, you need to ask yourself a few questions.

1. What does this player need today?
2. Is it the right time to issue the challenge?
3. Are the setting and location appropriate?
4. What can I say or do to inspire each player today?
5. What do they need specifically today: a kick in the butt or a positive challenge?

The challenge is a judgement call and a risk, but the best know how to handle it. They are not always 100 percent effective. But they are aggressive and are not afraid to issue the challenge.

BALANCE OF THE CHALLENGE

Balance is critical when issuing the challenge. Too much positive or negative feedback, corrective action, or punishment will not be effective. A combination of these is better. The coach must always be thinking and brainstorming new challenges for each player. This is why offering the challenge is an art.

ISSUING THE CHALLENGE

Challenges are often given by a question (i.e., what, when, where, why, and how), declarative statement, exclamation, or direct command (see Figure 24.1). Most of the time the challenge is brief, to the point, disguised, and well thought out. Following are some examples of challenges.

1. **Deserve.**   Did you deserve to be a starter or to win the next game? Are you better than they are? Have you worked as hard?
2. **Direct Command.**   Serve the ball into the court. Try that dig again and see if you can do any better. Guard that net like a junkyard dog; be vicious. Are you a poodle or a Doberman? (To blockers: Be a wall—nothing gets through.)
3. **Show Me.**   Show me you can hit the ball through the block.
4. **Responsibility/Accountability.**   What do you think our team rules should be?
5. **Vision/Dream.**   If you play this hard and give this much effort, you will be at the state tournament. I wouldn't let height keep you from being the starting setter. You should start working today to improve your vertical jump. Just think what you could do with a few more inches on your vertical.
6. **Potential.**   Offensively you know what you are capable of doing; take care of that first.
7. **Question.**   Are you ready to play in front of 500 spectators? Is there anybody in this room who can get Cindy's spike? Are you going to let them ace you again?
8. **Self-Reflection.**   Is that server intimidating you? Can you block/dig him/her?
9. **Execution.**   Who wants the ball?

FIGURE 24.1   Issuing the Challenge

10. **Expectation.**   After you serve the ball in, play defense. I've told you where their holes in defense are; who is going to start hitting them?
11. **Reverse Psychology.**   I do not know if we can handle this altitude; just do your best. The server before you missed; are you going to?
12. **Preparation and Conditioning.**   I don't want to have to call the first time-out. Are you going to let them beat you in twice in a row?

Explore, study, and ponder these suggestions. Like any other skill, the challenge takes practice. If you want to learn more about the challenge, watch for the new book *The Glory of the Challenge* by Hilda Fronske.

BE WILLING TO BE CHALLENGED

From challenges come growth. There should be many obstacles in a person's path, because the easy road does not produce winners. Seek challenges personally. Be willing to be challenged yourself.

ACCEPTING THE CHALLENGE

In researching the challenge, this particular story came to my mind. I was visiting with my grandfather, who was 100 years old and a medical doctor. I shared with him my dream that I wanted to go back to college and get my doctorate degree, because I wanted to keep the distinction in the family. He said one word to me, "When?" I was stunned by his comment. I could feel a surge go through me. He died in April and I was enrolled in school in August. At the time I had no idea that he had challenged me. I just knew it stirred me to action, which has made a tremendous difference in the path my life took. Now, 15 years later, I am writing about the challenge.

A physiological change takes place in people when they accept, and from that moment on their lives are changed. Whose life are you going to change?

SUMMARY

Have we got you thinking about a new tool to use in coaching? This chapter was meant to arouse curiosity, stimulate awareness, stir emotions, and encourage coaches to investigate and experiment with the use of challenges.

Leaders who capture the vision and incorporate the principles of the challenge into their teaching style will find a new fervor for their work and love for people. The best coaches use it. Find your style.

CHAPTER 25

Dealing with Conflict

You don't even need two people in the same room to have conflict (inner conflict, like guilt). But the more people you put in a gym, the greater the likelihood that conflict will occur. Couple that with the competitive, high-stress atmosphere of team sports, and you have the perfect situation for confrontations.

This is a great opportunity to teach a skill that will be used the rest of the athlete's life. Conflict resolution using the *I* technique is a wonderful skill that everyone needs. The sports arena is one of the best places to learn it, because of the multiple opportunities that are available for practice.

There are some important points in the *I* conflict resolution technique that you need to teach your players. They learn best, though, by observing you. The *Glencoe Health Text* (Merki & Merki, 1989) outlines the steps for this skill as follows.

1. Start all of your statements with the word *I*.
2. Tell what has happened and how you feel.
3. Try not to use the word *you*. By using the word *I*, you are taking responsibility for how you feel rather than blaming someone else. Usually when people are blamed or accused of something, they try to defend themselves. When you use *I*, other people have no need to be defensive and are more likely to talk out the problem.
4. Tell the other person how your anger involves him or her.
5. List measures you think will reduce your anger and how the other person can help you. (p. 91)

Following these steps does not ensure that you will solve the problem. The other person may choose not to talk about the problem. You have no control over how the other person will respond or react. But you have expressed your feelings in a healthy, constructive manner, and you will feel better for doing it. Here is an example that may help you understand how to put this into practice:

> You have a player who is unhappy with the playing time she is getting in matches. You hear from your captains that she is grumbling after practice in the locker room to other players and is badmouthing you. Her attitude in practice is sullen.
>
> Ask her if you can visit with her before practice tomorrow in your classroom. Make sure you are alone and your privacy is assured (you don't want to be interrupted). Sit in a student seat, not at your desk.
>
> Tell her you wanted to talk directly to her, because you felt she would like to know what you have heard and have a chance to respond. Tell her what you were told. Do not implicate the people who told you. Before you ask for her response, tell her how you felt about hearing this. This part is really important. Do not reprimand her or tell her what she should have done.

Then ask for her response. Between the two of you, come up with measures that can help the situation. If you cannot, make sure she understands that her behavior is not acceptable on your team (whether she owns up to it or not) and you cannot allow it to continue, in the best interests of the team and for her. Tell her you appreciate her coming in to clear the air or correct a misunderstanding.

Even if she denies saying anything, you still have accomplished something. You have made her accountable for something she said, and she knows you are willing to confront her if it happens again. This is a great deterrent. It is like an electric fence with cows. It keeps them in the pasture, and when once in a while one will come try it, the incentive should still be there.

There are certain points that need to be emphasized in order to improve the success of your confrontation (See Figure 25.1).

- The place you talk to them is important. Make it private and nonthreatening. Meet in a neutral place (don't sit behind your authoritarian desk or in your office). Try an empty locker room or the bleachers. You don't want to be interrupted, distracted, or pressed for time.

- Talk to them when your emotions are in control.

- Take care of conflict quickly. The longer it goes on, the more intense it becomes and the more problems may increase. Also, between the time of the incident and the time you take action about it, most people will have been miserable dwelling on it. So take care of it, let it go, and get on with life.

- Explain the situation that is causing the conflict very carefully as you perceive it without saying "you did this." Many times, how we interpreted what was said or done is the problem and can be cleared up without going further. You might not know the whole story, and, once you discover all the information, the whole situation may change. Or you might have misunderstood the person's intentions. Clear communication is the key.

FIGURE 25.1   Classroom Setting for Conflict

■ It's a good idea to practice what you are going to say; either write it down or practice it with someone (for example, a member of your coaching staff). Practice speaking in such a way as not to make them feel defensive. Ask for input.

■ Say how you feel. Don't gang up on them saying "all of the coaches feel that way." Keep it one on one. You want them to take responsibility for what they did, and you need to take responsibility for how you feel. You are important yourself, and so are they.

■ Have them come up with a solution or ideas on how to resolve the problem, if the situation lends itself to a solution. If they have input into solving the problem, they are more apt to abide by it.

■ Often it is a good idea to give them an "out." When explaining the situation causing the conflict, you could start with "It probably wasn't intended in this way," or "Maybe you didn't know I would take it like that." It's okay to give them a loophole, even if you have them cold. You have accomplished what you intended by making them accountable for their actions and letting them know you are willing to confront them. This will allow them to redeem themselves and still usually stop them from repeating the behavior.

■ Keep the conflict "in house." Practice and teach that if "it" starts on the court, "it" stays there. The more people involved, the bigger the situation gets.

■ Don't bring past issues into the conversation. Deal with the current situation. Let the past go.

One way of circumventing conflict is prevention. If you have at least two to three private meetings a season with each of your players in which they feel they can discuss things that are bothering them without reprisals, you will prevent many problems.

Another excellent situation in which to talk to players is during long bus trips to matches. You can review their roles on the team and your expectations of them. One of the biggest causes of individual problems is lack of knowledge. If you don't let the players know where they stand in your mind, what you expect of them, and where they fit in the scheme of things, they have to guess. And most of them guess negatively. They will usually think the worst, and that breeds discontent.

CONFLICT INVOLVING THE WHOLE TEAM

Many of the best teams have some major conflict during the season that is like a festering sore and must be dealt with. If it involves the whole team, it is best to have the team deal with it as a whole. Talk to your captains, and ask for their input. Find out if they think a certain technique is warranted and would be beneficial. If you all feel something is needed, try the following strategy.

Before practice starts, have your team meet in a private, quiet classroom. Explain the problem you have noticed, or just tell them you know there is one. Set the ground rules for the meeting so it won't disintegrate into a griping session and so no one gets attacked.

■ Remind them to use the *I* conflict resolution technique.
■ Explain the situation, and tell them how you feel about it.

- Do not verbally attack anyone. We are trying to clear the air and find a solution.
- Everyone's feelings and opinions are of equal importance.
- Do not gang up on any one individual.
- Captains are ultimately in charge.

You could give them a volleyball and specify that only the one with the ball can speak (this helps prevent a free-for-all). Inform them that they are on their own, because you are leaving and will not interfere. It is very important that you leave. If you do not, they will be reluctant to air their grievances for fear of what you will think. Staying in the room would be a hindrance to the players being open with each other.

Tell them to find a solution, that it is as important as a practice, and that even if it takes a long time, it is worth it as long as they solve the problem. Expect it to take a long time, and understand that it is just a technique and may not always work, but the results will justify the gamble. The new openness, understanding, and comfort that they demonstrate being around each other outweighs the risk.

Getting everything out on the table and discussing their problems encourages all to take responsibility for their actions. Knowing where you stand and not guessing what others are thinking is also refreshing. Most times, problems are caused by innuendos and gossip that are far from the truth. Clearing the air can bring a troubled team back together in pursuit of a mutual goal.

Often friction exists in a variety of relationships besides among players, such as between coaches, parents, administration, faculty, officials, and fans. The *I* conflict resolution technique works well in all situations.

SUMMARY

Remember a few key points that will help you cope with conflicts successfully:

- Take care of the conflict as soon as you can control your emotions.
- Take responsibility for how you feel.
- Do not attack the other person. Your goal is to come up with a solution, not to blame.
- Talk to the person you have a conflict with privately and keep it that way.

Conflict isn't all bad. It creates communication and interaction. It is much better than apathy. If handled correctly, it improves working relationships and keeps everything in the open, with fewer grudges. Make conflict resolution work for you and your team.

CHAPTER 26

Parents

Parents of athletes can be your biggest headache or your biggest help. It all depends on how you approach them. However, no matter what you do, there will be a few with whom you never will get along. With some preliminary groundwork, you can develop functional, working relationships with most. How do you do this?

SUPPORTIVE PARENTAL INVOLVEMENT

One way is to incorporate them into your coaching staff (don't pay them, of course). Delegate their roles; let them know what you need them to do. If they know what is expected of them (and what is not), they are more likely to do their jobs willing and adequately.

So, what is naturally their job? They have their children's welfare in mind and can provide the best support for them. If you use that as the basis of their job description and define it, you have a win/win situation. You can't just ignore parents, they won't go away, and shouldn't. Coaches need to work with them. High school state championship coaches have lost their jobs because they couldn't work with parents. Parents can be powerful allies or enemies.

If you look at all the people involved with your sport as a team (on the same side, hopefully), you will realize it is like a triangle or a three-legged stool: you (the coaching staff), the athlete, and the athlete's parents/guardians (see Figure 26.1). All must work harmoniously in their roles to form a successful team. If one falters, you crash, or end up being not quite as successful as you could be.

You need parents to coach attitude. You need them to be supportive of their children, to encourage them, and to help enforce rules (which were put in place for their best interests). In the end everyone benefits, but especially (and this is important to them) their children.

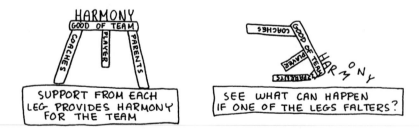

FIGURE 26.1 Parents, players, and coaches are like a three-legged stool—each part is critical for success.

Pat Summitt (1998b) gives an excellent example of this as she tells the story in her book, *Reach for the Summit*, of how a parent helped Pat's team win the NCAA championship in women's basketball for the University of Tennessee. Pat's practices were grueling, and she had warned this parent (Sheryl) that her daughter may want to come home, but she asked her if she would support the team by encouraging her to stay. The following is an excerpt from the book.

> One afternoon the mother called Pat Summitt and told her "I got that call you told me about." Kyra, her daughter, had called her mom crying. She had asked to come home.... She said it was the worst December of her entire life.
>
> Pat asked Sheryl, "Well, what did you tell her?"
>
> Sheryl said, "Pat, it was one of the hardest things I've ever had to do. But I told her she couldn't come."
>
> Sheryl, bless her heart, talked to Kyra for half the night. In doing so, she played her own role in our '97 championship. She explained to Kyra that four hard years was nothing compared to the thirty-five or fifty years of hard labor she'd be looking at if she quit school. She comforted her and encouraged her. But she didn't give in.
>
> When I say that without Kyra we wouldn't have won our fifth national championship, I'm not exaggerating.

And, in the end, it was all worth it. (pp. 168–169)

Supportive Parental Roles

Here are some keys to create a working relationship with the parents of your athletes.

■ **Communication.**   Let the parents know what is happening well before it happens. Be honest and forthright. Do not make promises you can't or don't intend to keep. Tell them their status in your organization and what you want them to do to help. Define their role.

■ Hold a mandatory parent meeting (at least one parent must attend) before the season starts but after your team has been chosen. Keep the meeting short, informative, and direct. (You might offer light refreshments served by the athletes.) Review the team rules. Ask if they have any questions. Have both parents sign the form indicating they understand the rules, because they are then both accountable for the information, and signing signifies that they comply with the rules (see the appendix).

■ Hand out season match schedules and practice times. If your school participates in a drug testing program, it is a good idea to provide that information and explain how it will work for their child. Many schools have an athletic trainer who needs a parent permission signature to work with their child and to take a child to the hospital if he or she is injured. On these signature cards the parent should indicate medical history, problems, or medication that pertains to their child.

■ Introduce your coaching staff to the parents and have the staff give a brief synopsis of their goals and expectations. Let the parents get to know the coaching staff. Their children are going to spend a great deal of time subjected to the coaches' leadership, and it is comforting to know something about the people that are in charge.

- Make sure the parents understand the proper procedure they need to follow if there is a problem they feel needs to be addressed. This is in the rules that they signed. Briefly:

    1. The first step is for the player to talk to the person on the team involved in the conflict (coach or teammate).
    2. The second step is for the parent(s) and the player to make an appointment to talk to the coach (but not on game day).
    3. The last step is for the parents and player to talk to the athletic director.

Explain that just as they would rather hear about a problem directly from their child than from the principal, you would like them to follow the same policy.

- One of the biggest problems that happens to coaches occurs when a parent confronts them on game day. The parent may approach them before, during, or after a match with comments designed to pressure them into playing their child more, or to let them know how unhappy they are with their coaching decisions, or to just plain tell them how to coach.

This creates more stress and distraction during a time that is already hectic. When this occurs, it usually causes a hindrance to your coaching abilities, whether your mind is preoccupied thinking about it, you are affected emotionally, or you start second-guessing yourself. It also causes a problem with the athletes, who may wonder how you are going to react to their parent's interference and how it will affect them. Everyone loses.

How do you prevent this parental interference? You must communicate well and follow through. You can't bluff and expect this to work. When you review the rules that state that problems cannot be discussed with you on game day (see rules in appendix), explain to them that you can't allow that interference for the previously mentioned reasons, and add that you are sure they will agree. You need them to follow the procedure they have signed. If they do not, you need to follow through with the penalty.

- Give the parents information defining the role of a supportive parent/coach. In the next section, the ten commandments for parents of athletic children are discussed. All parents with athletic children should follow them.

Ten Commandments for Parents of Athletic Children

1. Let your children know that win or lose, you love them unconditionally. You are proud of their efforts and are not disappointed with them. You are the people in their lives who always give positive reinforcement.

2. Show them you are pleased that they chose to play sports and accept all the challenges that come with trying to better themselves in practices and games. Let them know that you understand how hard it is to constantly put themselves on the line in front of peers and spectators.

3. Be completely honest about your child's athletic ability, attitude, and sportsmanship. Remember that you don't know what happens in practice; you can't second-guess the coach's decisions, because you don't have all the information.

4. Let your children live their own lives. Try not to relive your athletic life through your children. You had your time, now it is their turn. Don't pressure them to shine for your own ego. Remember, you made mistakes too.

5. Coach attitude, but don't coach skill. Leave that to the team coach. Refrain from the inclination to try to make your child just a little better by giving them tips on the way home from matches, or at dinner, or when they are trying to go to sleep.

6. Don't compete with the coach. You each have different roles to fill; leave them theirs and work on your own. "It takes a village to raise a child." Be glad you have an excellent adult role model contributing to the upbringing of your child. But remember they are human; they will make mistakes.

7. Never compare the skill, athletic ability, or attitudes of your child with other members of the team, at least not within their hearing. A team needs all kinds of different athletes to fulfill essential roles. Celebrate your child's special attributes.

8. Know your child's coach. Because of the special circumstances of a coach–player relationship, the coach has a tremendous potential to influence your child. Be aware of the coach's philosophy, attitudes, ethics, and knowledge.

9. Always remember that children tend to exaggerate both when praised and when criticized. Allow them time to cool off. Chances are, tomorrow they will have more appropriately evaluated a situation, while you may be just beginning to investigate. If the situation warrants following through, investigate quietly before overreacting.

10. Make a point of understanding courage and the fact that it is relative. Some are terrified of talking in public, whereas others are not. Some are afraid of a mouse but not of a bull. Everyone is frightened in certain circumstances. Explain that courage is not the absence of fear, but a means of doing something in spite of fear or discomfort. Be proud that your child has chosen to participate rather than spectate, to do and not only dream, to risk stumbling and rise to try again. Be supportive and encouraging; congratulate them when they succeed on their own.

Parents who follow the commandments will consider it high praise indeed when, later in life, their children say, "My parents were always there for me, and were my best support. I couldn't have done it without them. I want to be just like them."

A copy of the commandments is in the masters appendix. As the coach, you should watch for articles on sportsmanship and parents' roles in sports, and hand them out at your parents meeting.

SPORTSMANSHIP—A MATTER OF ATTITUDE

Try to impress on your athletes and their parents that sportsmanship is not only associated with sports, but that it is a part of daily life. The term is broad enough to include such qualities as fairness, honesty, acting with candor, integrity, sincerity, and freedom from malice or prejudice.

Sportsmanship is a matter of attitude. Some say attitude is everything, whereas others say that success in life is based 85 percent on attitude and 15 percent on knowledge. The right attitude helps motivate athletes toward attaining positive goals and relationships that will last the rest of their lives.

The best way to encourage athletes and instill good sportsmanship is to expose the athlete to great examples such as coaches, parents, or teachers who relate well to others and enjoy good relationships. Actions make the greatest impressions. Good sportsmanship is contagious and, likewise, so is poor sportsmanship.

Sportsmanship is the shared responsibility of parents and coaches. Together they instill a lasting impression.

TIPS FOR WORKING WITH PARENTS

Following are some specific suggestions that can help you work effectively with parents during your season:

■ Encourage "parent things," such as their wearing matching shirts, player number buttons, hats, pendants, and so on. Encourage them to act as a team in the stands, encouraging each other, understanding their situation, and so forth. Express gratitude for the great support they have provided in the past.

■ Remind them how devastating it is when their child makes a mistake and another parent comments negatively about it. It is only natural for them to hope that parent's child will make a mistake so they feel vindicated, which destroys the team atmosphere and may produce bad feelings.

■ It is a good idea to audibly let the parents know the very obvious fact that you know you aren't perfect: You make mistakes in coaching, just like they have done in parenting, but you are going to do the best you can with all the experience and knowledge you have gained, just as they are. You will learn and grow from each mistake, as they and their children will.

■ Let the parents know how much you appreciate their support. Some ways to accomplish this include the following. At the last home match of the season, it would be a magnanimous gesture to recognize generally all the parents of your teams by having them stand up and having your teams (frosh, JV, varsity) present them with something the athletes have prepared for their parents. Your senior players and their parents could come forward for special recognition.

If you have an award banquet, or some sort of celebration at the end of your season, make sure you thank the parents for their support and have some specific examples in mind. Just as your athletes love to be praised, so do their parents.

■ If all else fails, try the fear strategy: On asking one football coach if he had any parent problem, his answer was "No, they are too afraid of me. I lead them to think I am a homicidal maniac and they don't dare talk to me!" To each his own.

SUMMARY

In summary, it is important to use your own personality to create a partnership with your athletes' parents that works for all concerned. Include the parents as an essential and important part of the team. Keep them informed of the role you need them to fill in your team's journey to success. And after all is said, good luck!

CHAPTER 27

Administration and Support Personnel

There are more people who contribute to or detract from you team's success than coaches and parents. No man is an island, and the quicker coaches realize this and develop skills to work positively with all people, the better off their team will be.

There are people who are vital in running your program, and yet often coaches don't even recognize their contributions. According to the coaches, these people are expected to do their jobs. But, if they aren't there, it sure can throw a wrench in the works. So, who are the support personnel?

- The administration in a school setting includes the superintendent (dean), school board (trustees), principal, athletic director, and secretaries.
- Faculty, other sports coaches, student body, and cheerleaders.
- High school coaches, assistant coaches, junior high coaches, and club ball coaches.
- Trainers and team physicians.
- Statisticians, managers, scorekeepers, announcers, and ball shaggers.
- Bus drivers.
- The maintenance crew.
- Officials and line judges.

It takes the cooperation of all these people to run a team successfully. There are several things you can do to help make this conglomeration work together like a well-oiled machine. Some general suggestions include the following:

1. Good communication
2. Treating all with respect
3. Being honest
4. Being organized
5. Delegating, and then letting them do their jobs
6. Compromising (seeing the big picture)
7. Acknowledging their contributions with praise and reward

Who you work with and the role you are expected to play depends entirely on your coaching situation: whether you are a college, high school, junior high, club ball, head, or assistant coach. Even though your role might vary, it will take most of these people, in one capacity or another, to fill all the needs of your team. The following information, if implemented, can have a tremendous positive influence on your team.

ADMINISTRATION

Some coaches do not stay very long in their jobs, and the reason is very seldom because of lack of wins. They just can't get along with their administration. They have different concerns and objectives. To circumvent this problem, it is important that you find out what is expected of you, and then try to work within those parameters.

Don't go over your immediate superior's head. Follow the chain of command, just as you want your team to do when they have a problem. If you don't get what you want or feel you rightly deserve, present your case and then accept the answer. If you still feel strongly about your position, you could ask your superior's permission to go to a higher authority, but you should abide by his or her ultimate decision. You want to establish up-front and honest communication that engenders trust.

Learn to compromise. Try to understand other people's point of view, and be willing to meet them halfway on some issues. Be reasonable. Realize that if they compromise in your favor, they will be pressured to compromise with other staff members.

Live within your means. In other words, do not overspend your budget. Be honest about your expenditures and document everything. Try never to take money personally from players. If you don't have a secretary to deal with money matters, make sure you write receipts for all money that is given to you. If you handle this issue properly, no one will question your honesty. A few dollars are not worth losing your integrity over.

Be grateful for your administrator's support. Express this openly. Honey attracts more bees than vinegar. Just as using positive reenforcement in coaching brings out the best in your athletes, being upbeat with administrators creates generosity and feelings of *bonhomie* with them.

Handle your own team problems. Administrators do not appreciate being dragged into internal team disputes. Being a good communicator with your athletes and their parents will lessen the number of disgruntled individuals, especially if you have a complaint policy for them to follow.

Secretaries

Secretaries do a lot of work behind the scenes and often are neglected (see Figure 27.1). Simple courtesies, such as saying thank you and expressing your appreciation, go a long way. Do not expect them to do things, ask. People usually don't mind helping others if it is acknowledged and genuinely appreciated. Sometimes secretaries might have to run interference for you or take verbal abuse from irate patrons. Kind words are a small price to pay for all you receive from your secretaries.

Athletic Directors

Keep your athletic director (AD) in the loop. Let him or her know what you are doing in your organization (see Figure 27.2). Directors hate to be caught ignorant of subordinates' actions, especially actions for which they are responsible. ADs are trying to keep all programs running smoothly, within the guidelines of each organization's rules, not just yours. They have several coaches with whom to work, all of whom think their sport is the most important.

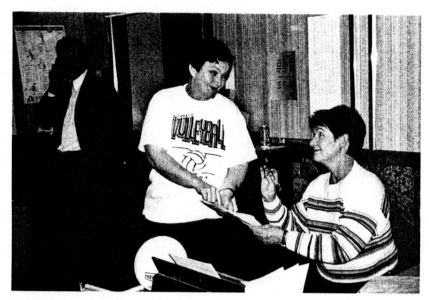

FIGURE 27.1   Secretaries

FIGURE 27.2   Athletic Director

FELLOW COACHES

Ideally, all coaches in the same system like and support each other, but this is not always the case. One of the best ways to get along with the coaches of other sports is by having a similar focus point: the well-being of the athlete. Many coaches share athletes, or pass them on. Again, if the top priority is what is best for the athlete (not your sport), the decisions made will be more compatible.

Be willing to compromise with the other coaches. Good coaches are usually intense and highly focused. It is hard for them to see the big, or complete, picture when they are honing in on their specialty. If you want their support, begin by supporting them. Ask how their games went. Cheer for them at their events, and encourage your players to be supportive too.

Loyalty to fellow coaches is essential. Do not get drawn into negative discussions about coaches by athletes, parents, or others. You would appreciate the same considerations from them if the situation were reversed.

The camaraderie that results from good relationships with fellow coaches extends to their athletes. Players will treat others in much the same manner as coaches treat each other. This can enhance your team's performance, because they feel respected by their peers, and it creates a lower stress atmosphere.

FACULTY

Teachers can influence your players' attitudes. Coaches like to think the world begins for athletes when the players walk through the gym doors. Obviously, this is not so. Again, if your focus is on the whole well-being of your athletes, their education beyond the volleyball court is important to you.

If teachers know your policy and where your priorities lie regarding education, they will be supportive and willing to work with you and your athletes. Coaches make teachers' job harder when they take students out of classes for matches, because teachers then must do more late work and give make-up tests. Many dedicated teachers will use their own time to help athletes catch up. The least coaches can do is support their efforts.

There are several things you can do to help your athlete's education along, and to work with, not against, your fellow teachers.

1. Let your team know that education is a high priority.
2. Take athletes out of school as little as possible. Arrange weekend matches or tournaments. And the team doesn't need a half hour to board the bus.
3. Prior to leaving for matches, encourage athletes to go to classes they will miss and get assignments.
4. Have study sessions on the bus or while other teams are playing.
5. Ask teachers to let you know if one of your athletes is struggling in their subject, and find out what you can do to help. Follow through with that athlete, then get back to the teacher and check on your player's progress.
6. Work privately with students that need help. Arrange for tutors.
7. Compromise. Because you take students out of their classes, you need to allow your players to be late to practice once in a while to make up a test if practice time is the most convenient time for the teacher.

Once your peers know your policy toward education, you will have one more support group rooting for your success and not throwing obstacles in your way.

STUDENT BODY AND CHEERLEADERS

Peers have a tremendous effect on your athletes' self-esteem. The student body's respect for your program and the efforts of your team is important to your players. The kudos and recognition they receive while striving for excellence drives them harder to achieve.

Because of this, you need to appreciate the impact peers have on your team and acknowledge it. If the fans know you recognize and need their support, they are much more enthusiastic with their efforts. Mentioning them in newspaper articles, thank you speeches, individually in the halls and classroom, and on announcements are simple, but effective, ways of encouraging greater support.

Teach your cheerleaders volleyball terms, such as *kills, aces,* and *side-outs,* to help personalize cheers for volleyball. Make sure they feel welcome and appreciated, because they can add support for your team. Remember to give them bus schedules if they are to ride with the team, and be sure there are enough seats for them. If you are overwhelmed with all these things, delegate an assistant coach, captain, or player to help communicate with them.

VOLLEYBALL COACHING STAFF

Far and away the most important ingredients in building a great coaching staff—assuming all things are equal in terms of knowledge—is that everybody has a passion for the game; a real love for the athlete himself; and genuine commitment and loyalty to each other, one coach to another. That's the way you build a staff and the rest you can work out. (Odom, 1997, p. 81)

Probably nothing will influence the success of your program greater than your coaching staff. This includes the coaches of your feeder programs as well. The way an athlete is introduced to a sport has a tremendous influence on how far he or she will be able to progress. If each coach simply has to build on an athlete's skill level, and not go back and fix problems or reteach a skill, he or she can achieve great heights. If all coaches are focused and pulling in the same direction, the odds are they'll not only reach their destination more often, but they will also enjoy the trip along the way. Problems will be fewer and smaller, and the athletes will have a better experience with less confusion. Knowing the role you are expected to play is essential.

The next section lists some ideas to help define the role of the head coach.

Head Coaches' Responsibilities

1. Choosing a coaching staff
2. Making final decisions on tryout cuts or choosing recruits
3. Ordering uniforms and equipment
4. Choosing the type of offense/defense
5. Scheduling matches
6. Arranging transportation, motels, and restaurant reservations
7. Scheduling practices
8. Handing out/collecting uniforms
9. Advising the school of times and dates your athletes will be absent for your sport
10. Setting general team atmosphere
11. Establishing team rules
12. Dealing with administration
13. Parent meeting responsibilities
14. Collecting parent permission papers and ensuring athletic fees are paid
15. Overseeing facilities (gym and net system) for practices and matches
16. Arranging public relations and team pictures
17. Setting up individual and team camps

18. Running spring programs and open gym times
19. Scouting opponents (or delegating it)
20. Educating players on nutrition, rest, and hydration
21. Encouraging year-round weight/conditioning programs
22. Dealing firsthand with injured players
23. Choosing year-end awards
24. Running awards night banquet
25. Handing out thank you cards and giving kudos

The First Coach

If you are the coach of a beginners program, find out what the division coach above you expects. You are both, after all, working ultimately for the success of the athlete. Attend coaching clinics together and establish a good working relationship. Ask the upper-level coach for suggestions and input pertaining to the skills of the athletes you have already sent them. Constant evaluation and change are the only ways to stay ahead of the game.

You are critical in establishing the correct basics these athletes will use for the rest of their careers. Push for exactness and discipline. Weed out the coachable from the noncoachable. It is under your tutelage that the desire to excel is developed. Plant the seed and, with the collective efforts of a unified coaching staff, bring to fruition each individual's potential. Here are some skills and attributes that you should establish.

1. Teaching players how to work
2. Correcting basic skills
3. Teamwork (how to get along with others)
4. Respect for the coach
5. Obedience (how quickly they mind)
6. Practice skills (or etiquette), such as shagging and chasing their own balls, following directions, tossing balls correctly, and taking water breaks
7. Following the chain of command
8. Dealing with problems
9. Substitutions
10. Winning and losing graciously
11. Containing anger and proper treatment of opponents
12. Dealing with mistakes (not letting them become overwhelming, and learning from them)

This is quite a demanding list to teach young adolescents. But just think of the caliber of athletes that will arise from a beginning like this.

Secondary Coaches

Take your lead from college programs. Always look forward. Go to local college matches, and establish relationships with their coaching staff. Be observant and attend to new skills being introduced (such as jump serving and setting).

You need to look back too at your feeder programs. They are invaluable to your success. Some suggestions to help improve these are

1. Offer junior high or elementary skills clinics.
2. Encourage administration to allow the coaches of programs for younger athletes to attend coaching clinics with you.

3. Set up volleyball demonstrations and miniclinics with the elementary physical education specialist. Use your varsity players to help with the younger grades. This generates interest and desire. Help the specialist with suggestions to lower the net and obtain good balls that cannot hurt. If they have difficulty obtaining good balls, as you get new balls each year, you could pass some of your older ones to them.

4. Allow the younger teams into your ball games free. (They will bring paying parents many times.)

5. Toward the end of your season, and theirs, recognize their efforts at a home match. Invite them and their coach to stand and be recognized.

6. Encourage club ball participation, or supervise an open gym in the off-season and run tournaments that include the preteens.

7. Talk to your administration. Try to get them to see the importance of a unified coaching effort on the success, not only of your sport, but of the individual player. If you accomplish this, they will be more apt to ask for your input in selecting replacement coaches, sending them to coaches' clinics, putting more money (thus emphasis) into the program, having adequate facilities, and supporting the athletic program at statewide administration meetings.

8. Praise and recognize the efforts of these coaches. When you are successful, share the glory. Spotlight their contributions in your quest for excellence; it won't lessen your success, but rather it will enhance it.

Your Immediate Coaching Staff

Coach Edwards of BYU shares an excellent perspective on selecting coaches, "Healthy diversity, one of me is plenty for any staff. If I met someone just like me, I wouldn't hire him. I've tried to always have a diverse coaching staff, with perspectives coming from a variety of directions" (Edwards & Benson, 1995, p. 94).

The coaches you select should be role models. Their actions will have more effect than any words on your players. They need a passion for the game and a love of teaching. Each must care deeply about their players and put them first in consideration. They must, above all, be fully committed to your program and the role they are asked to play in it.

They need to have an opinion and be willing to share it. Coach John Wooden sums it up, "I never want a yes-man for an assistant. In reality, I guess I wanted a rebel; someone who would stand up to me. A man who agrees with you merely inflates your ego and can't be of much help" (Wooden & Jamison, 1988, p. 117).

Once you have gathered your coaching staff, there are some keys to coordinating their activities:

1. Outline their responsibilities. They need to know the role you expect them to play.

2. Delegate and then get out of the way. Don't meddle. Let them do it their way. If you want it done your way, do it yourself.

3. Include them in most decision making.

4. Be organized.

5. Encourage open communication. Ask for and use their suggestions. Encourage them to offer constructive criticism. Have open dialogue. Pay attention to their body language. Give and take suggestions.

6. Take them to coaching clinics. See that they get perks, such as T-shirts. Buy matching coaching shirts if you can. Make sure they have the equipment and

supplies they need. Small perks go a long way in helping them feel part of something and important.

7. Praise them. Acknowledge their accomplishments, contributions, and strengths. Make them feel indispensable and they will be.

TRAINERS, TEAM PHYSICIANS

Communicate and don't take these people for granted. Develop personal relationships with these vital components of your team. Don't use your players as go-betweens. Talk to the trainers personally about each player with whom they are working. Listen to their suggestions for preventive measures regarding injuries.

Make sure they know when you practice and have a game schedule so they can have your players taped and ready. Share your philosophy about conditioning, stretching and injury prevention, and care with them. Listen to their ideas. They are the professionals in that area.

STATISTICIANS, MANAGERS, SCOREKEEPERS, ANNOUNCERS

Stats are crucial for individual and team evaluation. Good managers are hard to find and even harder to keep from year to year. They are usually volunteers and receive very little recognition for their efforts. However, there are some keys to working with them so they will return next year to help again.

1. Treat them like human beings, not slaves. Be polite and express appreciation. Do not allow your team to order them around. They are equals.
2. Include them in your team decisions. Invite them to team dinners or other gatherings.
3. If you hand out perks to your team (such as T-shirts), provide them for the statisticians and managers.
4. They are not beasts of burden. Have your team haul the balls and equipment in and out of matches. Determine who will do that with game consequences in practices. It makes for some very intense matches.
5. Make sure your athletes understand and appreciate the statisticians' and managers' roles on your team.

BUS DRIVERS

Many teams spend innumerable hours riding buses to matches. An incompetent driver can leave you and your team stressed out before the match even begins. Some suggestions to improve this include the following:

1. Try to have the same driver each time. Request (if you can) the person who is most congenial and competent.
2. Schedule the bus to arrive at least 15 minutes before departure time.
3. Keep your players in control. That is your job, not the bus driver's.
4. Observe bus etiquette and safety procedures.

5. When you get home and your team leaves the bus, make sure they pick up all their garbage. Have consequences if they leave even one piece of paper (one ladder for one object). After they are all off the bus, go back and inspect it. You will have all the drivers wanting to take your team.
6. Treat the driver respectfully, and so will your team
7. If you are staying overnight, exchange phone and room numbers with the driver in case he or she needs to get in touch with you. Provide a time schedule. Make sure the room is quiet.
8. Communicate. Let the driver know what you expect.

MAINTENANCE CREW

The facilities you play in, their condition, and appearance are important to your program. The people who care for the facilities have a vital role on your team but are usually the most overlooked. If they get the nets up late or forget to prepare for a match on game day, it wreaks havoc on your psyche.

Communication and appreciation are the keys to a good working relationship. The crew wants to do their job and needs your cooperation to do so. They get very frustrated if they are asked to produce a microphone or table at the last second.

If your team wants clean floors, ask the janitor to leave a dust mop in the gym. Use this as another opportunity for a game consequence. Losers can sweep the floor for a week before practice.

OFFICIALS/LINE JUDGES

Officials

After all the work coaches do to get the competitive edge, they often neglect the most obvious support staff of all, the officials. Not only do they neglect them, but they often antagonize them by behaving rudely.

Officials rule the match. They call the plays as they see them, making split-second decisions that affect the outcome. Why would you want to make them dislike you and your team? If you constantly question their decisions (or lack thereof) and berate them, they can't have very good feelings toward you. It is not their job to take abuse. You cannot make enemies of them and then expect them to officiate your match without bias. It isn't very smart to put the game-winning decision in the hands of someone whom you have antagonized.

Officials play a very important role in volleyball. They should be respected and treated accordingly.

1. Get to know their names.

2. Greet them when you arrive at the match.

3. At home matches have their paychecks ready and pay them at the beginning of the game. Make sure your facilities are in tip-top shape: Chairs or benches should be where they belong; towels should be available for water spills or sweat. Ensure that the correct balls (and precisely inflated) are being used, and that the net is the correct height and padding is in place. Provide a schedule detailing what

matches and nets they are assigned to. If they are officiating multiple matches, provide refreshments (drinks).

4. Genuinely compliment them on good calls or an excellent match.

5. Be generous. They will make mistakes, but then again, so will you. You aren't a perfect coach, and they aren't perfect referees. Give them some slack.

6. If you do have a suggestion that would improve their officiating, do not offer it on game day. Wait for a more opportune time. But be aware that you had better be willing to take constructive criticism as a coach too, if you think they should as officials. Turnabout is fair play.

Line Judges

Line judges are very important. They have to stay intense and focused throughout the whole match. They must know and understand the rules almost as well as the referees, especially the ones that pertain to them. They need to be decisive. Too often, coaches ask inexperienced people to do this job, which leads to embarrassment on their part, missed calls, and frustration for the team and coaches.

Line people make all the close calls. If they miss touches on the ball from a block or if part of the ball touches the line, fans, players, and coaches often erupt. How many of these people ever acknowledge the great calls? The coach should remember to compliment a line judge for an excellent job. Then the line judges tend to try hard to deserve those congratulations again. Words are easy to use and can either encourage or destroy a line judge. Which would benefit your team?

SUMMARY

None of what we have discussed in this chapter takes much time or effort to implement, but the dividends paid off by doing so can be substantial. The hardest part is recognizing the need. Now you have the resources to recognize the needs. Enjoy piloting your smooth-running machine.

CHAPTER 28

Public Relations and the Press

Good public relations are a much-needed part of any program, but one of the most neglected. Coaches are so busy with the pressing job of running their team that this aspect of the game gets overlooked. Public relations are important for two main reasons:

- It helps draw patrons to your matches so that your program's budget will be solvent.
- It gives recognition to the accomplishments of your players and teams. This is very important, because it raises the importance of your program in your community, and it is great for your players' self-esteem and growth.

Coaches are busy, and there are several ways of getting help with this issue. For example, ask for or assign an assistant coach, delegate certain aspects to your athletic director, or put a student assistant (manager) in charge of tabulating stats. Ultimately, though, it is the head coach's responsibility to follow through and make sure it gets done.

MEDIA PROMOTION

Here is a list of things that need to be taken care of in the area of media promotion:

- Match schedules need to be sent to each school on your season agenda, any nearby upper division schools, local newspapers and the school newspaper, local radio stations, and local television stations.

- Match results need to be distributed immediately following your match (day-old news in sports is no news). Call in your information to local newspapers and radio and television stations. Have a list of phone numbers and the name of each contact person handy. They appreciate it if you are consistent with your calls and if you contact them even if you lose. It is the responsibility of each home team to call in league scores (because the away team is traveling).

For each of the media, the information you should provide is as follows.

For radio and television stations, provide your name, your school, the opponent's name, and the score. For the newspapers, provide all of the above, plus your current win/loss record (league and overall). A copy of the win/loss chart is available in the masters appendix. Glue it in the front of your scorebook, and update it after every match. This is a quicker and more efficient method to use when reporting scores and the win/loss record to the press than hunting through the scorebook. You could also provide outstanding stats—individual and team (make sure these are tabulated correctly with the universal method). Include kills (number of kills minus misses divided by total attack attempts), assist kills (setter), serve-receive ratio, the most digs, the most aces or serve percentage, blocks, any outstanding team totals (for example, eight team aces, or a total team attack ratio of 32 percent), and a coach's quote about the match.

If any of these public relations outlets do not want to carry information on your team, have your team's parents or patrons help you out. If they read a certain newspaper or listen to a specific radio or television station and don't get any news about your matches, have them call or write in and tell that media source they want to know about your team. If enough do this, the media will be glad to follow the progress of your program.

Many newspapers, radio stations, and television stations have an athlete of the week or month. Make sure your sport is featured. Any kudos you can give your team will help. Positive information disseminated to the public helps increase the awareness and perception about your team. This in turn will raise the level of your program's importance with your patrons and administration. The positive results from that open many doors for you and your team.

What about putting information about your team on-line? Many schools (junior highs, high schools, and colleges) have home pages on the Internet. Your team could have its own Web page in the sports section. If you don't currently have one, get approval from the administration, then find a savvy computer student who needs a project for an advanced computer class. Furnish the student with team and individual action pictures, statistics, rosters, and a schedule. It would be good to have a coach's corner also, with your picture, win/loss record, volleyball history, and any personal data.

When the public attends your matches, what are you doing to help them enjoy being there or to entice them to come again? Here are some ideas.

- Post prices that are easily understandable (no surprises). If possible, provide discounted season tickets for your faithful following.

- Be sure seats are in good repair, easily accessible, dusted, and clean.

- Views should not be obstructed (basketball backboards should be out of the way; cheerleaders and students should stay in their own section so they aren't standing in front of patrons).

- Run matches efficiently (no overlong warm-ups). Use ball people (shaggers).

- The score should be visible: Use scoreboards, not only flip charts.

- Distribute programs with team pictures and roster and the visiting team's roster. This is also a place you can highlight a player, coach, last year's results, and so on.

- Provide simple and basic rules. Many fans get irate with officials over misunderstanding rules. You could have a rule information sheet inserted in the program that they can peruse during warm-ups.

- Give local junior high or high school volleyball teams free tickets to specified home matches.

■ Use local junior high or high school volleyball players as ball shaggers. Give them team T-shirts. Also recognize outstanding players (such as a leading server for the junior high).

■ Have contests in between matches: A favorite one is serving. While your team rests, stretches out, or talks to the coach, designate someone to get out a cart of balls, put prizes on the other side of the court, and have people line up who want to serve at the prizes. Whoever hits one wins the prize. This can be done in as few as five minutes if run efficiently. It really helps to bring out the students. You could also have a parent and adult line. How do you get prizes? Ask your athletic director, booster club, parent committee, or an assistant coach to round them up. If a prize is a coupon for food, you can make a poster of the coupon big enough to hit. You could have several different prizes, such as hats, mugs, T-shirts, Frisbees, or whatever your imagination can dream up.

■ Some schools students and patrons like wearing T-shirts, hats, or buttons that support their team. You could start out small with buttons or by ascertaining whether the parents would be interested in purchasing shirts or hats that support your team or an individual player. Minibanners are popular, too. You could talk to the booster club, parents, or cheering squad about sponsoring any of these.

SUMMARY

Whatever you choose to do, don't neglect your public relations. The benefit to your program is multifaceted. Word of mouth will spread news about your team. With a little work orchestrated by you, your team will develop a in a very positive environment. For many of your athletes, that newspaper clipping will be all they have for their memories. Don't let them down.

CHAPTER 29

Coaching Ethics

How far will you go to win? Are you always right? Is it okay to stretch the rules in your favor or to use any technique to get the most out of your athletes? Why not? It is in their best interest, isn't it? Can you quietly take money or personal perks from the budget or your players? Do you deserve more than you are getting now, anyway?

Before you start coaching, you need to make some ethical decisions. What is right or wrong, and how far will you go to succeed? Because of the intense and stressful atmosphere of the sports arena, coaching can bring out the worst or the best in people. Which will it be in your case?

SETTING AN EXAMPLE

Your example has a huge impact on your players; it is your responsibility to be a positive role model. If you lose your temper with an official or opponent or player, your example presents your athletes with a behavior that you seem to believe is acceptable. Notice that when coaches treat officials disrespectfully, so do their players. If a coach loses control and kicks the bench, the players will too.

Have you ever seen a little boy or girl doing something exactly like his or her mom or dad? Coaches have so much influence on and spend so much intense time with their players that they have a tremendous impact on the athletes. The relationship is very similar to that of a child and a parent. The time in a youth's life when coaches are working with them is usually the time parents' influence is fading. Because of this, it is imperative that schools emphasize hiring ethical coaches.

We hear terrible accounts of how some coaches have misused power by molesting, stealing money, or having their athletes use steroids. These are a few extreme examples about which the public does not often hear. Much more common and almost as insidious are the coaches who rob their players of self-esteem and confidence by sarcasm, punishment, and ridicule. Sometimes the opposing coach is the best player you've got by ruining his or her own players' self confidence. When one of their athletes makes a mistake, they attack the athlete verbally or remove him or her from the game, and that player subsequently has difficulty gaining confidence under pressure and maintaining focus on the game. What are coaches doing to their players that will have such a lifetime effect?

Consider the coaches who question every official's call. They disagree with the line people, are constantly pleading with refs to call it even, or complain about the other team. Where are they directing their own and their teams' attention?

Who's fault is it going to be in their minds if they lose the game? Of course, if it isn't their own fault, they can't control the outcome.

What are coaches teaching their players when they encourage illegal practices like screening (just don't get caught) or dishonesty? What about comments such as "let's go ahead and do it, just don't tell the administration; what they don't know won't hurt them"; or "if the official doesn't see you, it is okay"; or "Sally, your teammate isn't getting the job done, but don't tell her I said so."

You'll find it is hard to ask your athletes to

- Be on time if you aren't.
- Control their temper if you can't.
- Work hard if you don't.
- Stay focused when you aren't.
- Be honest if you aren't.
- Communicate if you don't.
- And so on.

You'll find while watching your team that they are a reflection of yourself. Make sure it is a picture of which you can be proud. Most important for you is to realize that the traits they pick up from you will often last a lifetime and be passed on to multitudes of other people. This thought should be held uppermost in your consciousness during your whole coaching career. What are your primary goals? To turn out great volleyball players or great people who can play volleyball?

Playing sports is a wonderful tool to ingrain excellent ethical characteristics in people. So what are the characteristics you want to instill in your players? Following are just a few that lend themselves to team sports:

- Self-control
- Self-confidence
- Enthusiasm
- Selflessness, kindness, consideration, thoughtfulness
- Focus
- Holding up under pressure
- Loyalty
- Communication
- Problem solving
- Appreciation of excellence
- Fairness and fair play
- Taking responsibility (no excuses)
- Better the ball (improve in all conditions)
- Patience
- Hard work and hustle
- Self-reliance
- Obedience
- Respect
- Goal setting
- Coachability
- Teamwork
- Intensity
- Learning and growing from mistakes

No one is perfect. Everyone makes mistakes, even coaches. Consider which is worse: insisting you haven't made a mistake or admitting it and getting on with life? Which approach will your players respect the most? And again, what are you teaching them?

SUMMARY

When speaking about ethics and sports, it is impossible to do so without including one of the most ethical coaches of all time. John Wooden once said, "Be more concerned with your character than with your reputation, because your character is what you really are, whereas your reputation is merely what others think you are" (Wooden & Jamison, 1997, p. 28).

CHAPTER 30

Information for the College-Bound Athlete

What can you do to assist an athlete who wants to continue playing volleyball in upper-division schools? Are you responsible for helping that athlete get a scholarship? There is a considerable amount of pertinent information athletes need to pursue their dreams, but where do they find that information?

You, their coach, will naturally be the first person they will turn to to find out what they need to know. The biggest problem coaches face in helping the recruiting process is staying current. The rules and regulations of recruiting are different for each division of higher learning, and they change almost every year. Yet, there is some information that is useful generally in helping all college-aspiring athletes.

Another problem coaches have is time (or lack of it). It takes a great deal of time and money (stamps, phone calls, and so on) to gather and disseminate each individual's information to all the schools to which it should go. Coaches have many athletes, and what they do for one needs to be done for all. The coach's primary obligation should be to concentrate on coaching a quality team that has a good reputation for producing talented athletes.

So, are you, the coach, responsible for obtaining a college athletic scholarship for your athlete? No. That is up to the parents and athletes themselves. No one should expect a coach to find him or her a scholarship. The coach should, however, assist with the individual's statistics (approach and block jump, reach, match statistics, and so on), personal award information (most valuable player, hustle award, offensive player of the year), match videos, and a recommendation letter or statement. If you personally know some college coaches, a phone call or a letter early in the year about an aspiring athlete would be appropriate.

Most parents and athletes have no clue where to start and need someone to point them in the right direction. The best time to disseminate college-recruiting information is at the beginning of your season, preferably at the parent meeting you hold. It is a good idea to provide some handouts with explicit directions on what type of letters to write, the information to include, phone numbers to call about current recruiting rules, and college or university addresses (or where to access them).

GUIDE FOR THE COLLEGE-BOUND STUDENT

Athletes and their parents need to be familiar with the rules and procedures that pertain to college-bound athletes, in addition to the financial aid that is available. They can call or write the following three agencies, which govern the three major divisions. The information is free of charge. You and the athletes' parents should order the information each year to keep current. Rules, scholarships, awards, evaluations, phone contacts, and signing dates change every year.

- NCAA Guide for the College-Bound Student-Athlete
  The National Collegiate Athletic Association
  6201 College Boulevard
  Overland Park, KS 66211-2422
  1-800-638-3731
- NAIA Guide for the College-Bound Student-Athlete
  National Association of Intercollegiate Athletics
  6120 South Yale Avenue, Suite 1450
  Tulsa, OK 74136
  (918) 494-8828
- NJCAA Guide for the College-Bound Student-Athlete
  National Junior College Athletic Association
  P.O. Box 7305
  Colorado Springs, CO 80933
  (719) 590-9788

NCAA INITIAL-ELIGIBILITY CLEARINGHOUSE

Any athlete who wishes to participate in intercollegiate athletics during his or her first year of college in Division I or II must be registered with the NCAA clearinghouse before becoming eligible to play. The forms are available from a high school counselor or from the NCAA Guide for the College-Bound Student-Athlete, which students can send away for and receive free (address above). There is a fee, and several academic documents are required. It is recommended that students apply for certification at the end of their junior year.

This clearinghouse gathers all the academic information from the student and the high school and certifies that the student is eligible to compete by the NCAA standards. The NCAA will send the athlete's eligibility status to any Division I or II college that requests it. (Note that the athlete cannot ask for it to be sent; rather, the college must make the request.)

Athletes are encouraged to register at the end of the junior year (as more of their high school term will be completed and their SAT/ACT scores should then be available).

DON'T WAIT TO BE DISCOVERED

There are many college-caliber athletes who go undiscovered every year. The number one reason is exposure, or lack of it. College coaches can't recruit athletes unless they know about them. College coaches don't have time to read several states' local newspaper articles about high school stars. Most high schools are playing volleyball while college coaches are immersed in their own season, which limits their time to scout prospects. So, how do they find out about possible recruits? Usually from scouting tournaments (where they can see lots of schools and players), recruiting services, word of mouth, newspapers, sending letters to high school coaches asking about any college-caliber athletes, and calling contacts (usually ex-players around the nation).

Knowing this, your athletes need to market their names to several (up to 200 is suggested) upper-division schools if they want to improve their scholarship opportunities. The major key in obtaining an athletic scholarship, besides ability, is exposure. High school coaches cannot be expected to write, address, and send out 200 profiles on each of their college-caliber athletes, let alone pay the cost of mailing them. Again, it is up to the athletes and their parents.

Now, when, how, what, and where to get started in the recruiting process.

When should high school students start sending out information?

Colleges prefer to start portfolios on possible recruits during the students' sophomore year. An earlier exception would be if athletes are playing varsity during their freshmen year. Information should not be sent any later than the beginning of the athlete's junior year in high school. If a college coach is serious about a recruit, he or she will want an opportunity to see the athlete play. A college's recruiting program creates the foundation for the team's success. That is why the top percentage of the recruits warrant intense personal scrutiny by the head coach (who has a limited amount of time). Thus, college coaches prefer earlier contact rather than late.

How do athletes choose the colleges in which they are interested?

The information is found in two primary sources: the school counselor and the Internet.

> **Counselors.** Many secondary schools have access to a career information system (CIS) or similar program in their counseling departments that is helpful. Counselors also have books with phone numbers and addresses for universities.
>
> **Internet.** Looking up specific colleges by name will generate specific in-depth information. There are also several sources for checking out the availability of scholarship opportunities. Either surf on the Web, or get the names of sites from school counselors. We hesitate to provide addresses, because it is difficult to stay current with all that are available.

Following are some suggestions on what prospective college athletes should look for:

- First in importance is the educational aspect. What colleges have the courses the athlete is interested in pursuing? What is the college's reputation for job placement? The primary reason an individual goes to college should be to get an education, not to play sports.

- Second is the level of play in which the athlete is interested in competing or has the talent to participate (Division I, II, or III).

- What financial scholarship opportunities are available? (athletic or otherwise).

- Third, how far away is the university? The athlete and his or her parents need to understand that because colleges try to represent a wide variety of states on their campus, they make many scholarship opportunities available to students who are farther away. Compare the cost of driving or flying home with the cost of a college education. If your athlete needs a scholarship, the probability that he or she will obtain one greatly increases if the student is willing to go to a school farther away from home.

■ Concerning enrollment, how many students are enrolled at a particular school? Does it have a religious affiliation? And what is the male-to-female ratio?

■ What are the entrance requirements?

Where should students send information?

■ Students should send letters and applications directly to the head coach of the school. They should never use generic titles (such as Southern University's Head Volleyball Coach). The athlete should do the homework and use the current coach's name.

■ The Internet has free recruiting services available. Students can search for and fill out the information requested (they should check volleyball recruiting services).

■ High school coaches receive many feelers (letters from college coaches asking for information on any players that are interested in playing college volleyball and have the talent). Students should let their coach know that they would like to be considered for these or given the information to fill out and send themselves.

■ Another option for students is to contact a professional recruiting service. This is by far the easiest choice but usually costs a considerable amount of money. Students should research each service and be aware of scams, such as guaranteeing an athlete a scholarship, money back if unsuccessful, or their claims to do all the work.

Following are some tips high school athletes can use to get noticed (besides marketing).

■ Play club ball. Upper-division schools lean heavily toward players who have played club ball. Those athletes show dedication, a great love for the game, and willingness to spend time and money to go the second mile. They come away from club ball participation polished and with an increased level of experience in the game. A good club ball program can take a high school athlete one step higher. It does take lots of time and money, but it can be perceived as a potential investment if they obtain a scholarship.

■ Attend college summer camps. If the college of their choice has a summer camp, which the head coach runs, encourage your athlete to attend. That way the college coach gets a first-hand look at the prospect for several days. The coach can ascertain the player's athletic ability and coachability, skill level, teamwork, attitude, and so on. The only restriction is that the student cannot participate after his or her senior year (check current recruiting restrictions).

Your athletes should find out about a camp or clinic that supplies profiles to college coaches. Be aware, however, that players' athletic ability usually will be evaluated by one person who will place them in the college division level they think they are capable of playing. If they attend a clinic and show college-caliber skills, they will be placed on a list that many college coaches purchase.

What do your students send?

- **Introductory (or Cover) Letter.** A sample letter is included in the masters appendix. Use the coach's name. Request information the athlete is looking for and a brief introduction. The athlete should make sure to include a return address and phone number.

- **Profile.** (A sample is included in the masters appendix.) The profile contains personal statistics (and a current picture), academic achievements, athletic statistics, and achievements. The athlete could add a few comments from his or her coach and the names of former high school alumni who played college ball (and where they played).

- **Videotapes.** Do not send a videotape unless a coach has requested to see one (students could ask if the coach would like to see one, though). Students should be mindful of the college coach's time restrictions; keep videos to a minimum length of 15 to 20 minutes. This should be an enticer film including name, address, uniform number and color, identifying features (such as hair color and style), scores, and statistics; samples of basic skill performance, such as setting, spiking, passing, serving, or blocking (2 to 5 minutes in length); some game footage, showing a variety of skills (students should identify their position, such as starting front-left corner, sliding to middle). Student should include what comprises their range of talents. If they are hitters, feature the different attacks in their repertoire; setters should show different sets they are capable of, attacks (dumps), and so on. They should showcase themselves (10 to 15 minutes).

The type of video sent says a lot about the student as a person. It should be done well, informational, and organized. Students should make several copies (at least five) and do not always expect them back. They should be available to send promptly when requested. On the match segment, it might be of interest to include the opposing team, the date, and the outcome of the match.

TIPS TO HELP ATHLETES BEING RECRUITED

How can your athletes tell if they are being seriously recruited? What is the parent's role in the recruitment process, and what do some of the terms mean, such as *redshirting* and *partial scholarships* or *walk-ons?* Read on.

1. First (and this is extremely important), your athletes should answer every inquiry letter they receive from colleges, *even if they are not interested in attending that college at the moment.* They may change their minds between the sophomore year and the end of the senior year and shouldn't limit their options.

2. Your athletes can tell if college recruiters are noticing them if they start receiving letters at the beginning of their junior year in September and October.

3. Athletes should know the dates the first phone contact can be made. If the head coach calls an athlete on that day, he or she is on top of the recruiting list.

4. Parents or guardians should screen calls. They should keep a record of who called and when. They should find out who is calling, whether the caller has seen their son or daughter play, whether he or she is planning a home visit, if an official campus visit for the child will be provided, and if an early signing is an option.

5. Parents and athletes should do their homework and get information about the colleges that are interested in the student.

6. Home visits can be extremely awkward, mostly because of the athlete's uncertainty about how to behave and what is expected. Here are some suggestions that can decrease the stress associated with a coach visiting an athlete's home. There are two evaluations taking place: the coach's evaluation of the athlete and the family, and the athlete and his or her family's evaluation of the coach.

- Candidates should supply light refreshments.
- They should find common interests they share.
- They should ask questions about the college (prepare these beforehand).

7. Athletes are only allowed five paid visits to colleges. Colleges also are limited in how many paid visits they can offer. Your players can tell how high they rank on the recruiting list if the college coach invites them on a paid, official visit, even if they are close to the school. Other helpful hints are

- As a general rule of thumb, students should wait to conclude all home visits before scheduling campus visits.
- Parents may accompany the athlete. Colleges cannot pay for the transportation of the parents unless they drive the athlete to the campus. They can pay for the parents' and athlete's accommodations and meals once they arrive. The coaching staff will have an agenda for the 48 hours the athlete is allowed on campus. Usually a team player or host will give them a tour. The recruit should get to know the other players on the team because he or she may be spending countless hours with them if that college is chosen. Candidates can talk to students not on the team and get a feel for the college and town.

8. Redshirting means the player will practice with the team but will not participate in their regular season matches. Thus, it isn't counted as one of their four eligible years of competition. Schools will do this for a number of reasons. Injury, pregnancy, or illness are some, and it may happen anytime in a person's career.

A freshman redshirt is different. Many athletes take five years to complete college. It usually takes that long because of their demanding athletic schedules. If they play the first four years, they still attend college in their fifth year but are ineligible to play. They are in their prime, at their best, unable to contribute to the program but still attending classes at the university. Coaches perceive the freshman year, when new college players are integrating into their systems, as a time when they are getting used to being away from home and the college atmosphere. First-year college athletes will probably sit on the bench a large part of the time. It is a necessary, but usually wasted, year as far as contributing to the success of the team is concerned. Unless they start or play a majority of the time, it is wiser to redshirt them the first year, thus giving them four active playing years. If this is an option the school is offering, the athlete definitely needs to find out if the school is going to pay for all five years, and not just the four playing years.

9. Sometimes a college coach will make an offer of only tuition (no housing, food, and so on) or guaranteed housing for one semester or year. Maybe your athlete will be encouraged to walk-on in the fall with the bait of a scholarship kept in reserve for one walk-on candidate. If there are no other options, the athlete may be forced to accept these offers. That is why it is important for athletes to be in a position to negotiate or bargain. Student athletes do that by having other schools interested in them (which started by contacting and answering lots of schools).

Most schools do not have the scholarships or money available that most of us think they do. Because recruiting is the backbone of the success of their programs, coaches will use any legal monetarily avenue available to them to help a recruit pay for his or her college education. Two factors that could help are the athlete's scholastic abilities and the distance he or she lives from the university. Either of these could be critical in obtaining a scholarship. It is, therefore, very important to encourage your athletes to work hard on the academic portion of their lives, as well as their athletic prowess.

SUMMARY

The responsibilities of the head high school coach toward their college prospects are being a good coach and supplying statistics, match information (such as videos and scores), and encouragement. Remind your athletes that after the fact of being a college-caliber athlete, the main key is exposure. Good luck!

CHAPTER 31

Summer Camps

There are a variety of summer camps available for your athletes, such as individual skills, setting, spiking, defense, or team camps. There are camps for pre–high school, high school, and elite players. Most colleges offer sessions on their campus or have traveling camps that will come out and put on a three- to five-day clinic at your school as long as a minimum amount of athletes is guaranteed.

How important is participation in summer clinics to the success of your program? The more you put in, the more you get out. It also depends on how good the camp is and the efforts of the athletes. For the most part, clinics have an excellent impact on improving your program for three main reasons:

1. The more touches on the ball, the more control of the ball, the better the player.
2. Many times, even though the clinician will teach the same skills you have taught, your athlete will finally grasp the concept, either because of different cues or simply because it is repeated in a different way by a different person. It helps to have another person validate your teachings.
3. If you attend the camp with your athletes, you can always learn something, whether it is new cues, drills, strategies, and so on.

There is another bonus if you have some players who are college material: It is a good time to get the college coach to look at them. The college coaches will have them for a week's session and will have ample time to observe their work ethics, attitude, coachability, teamwork, and skill. Many college coaches start portfolios on athletes during their freshman or sophomore years from the camps they host.

INDIVIDUAL CAMPS

Asking a clinician to run a camp at your school will allow more of your players access, because the costs are much less. So you will have more players participating. You will have to provide the courts, balls, and first aid for the clinic. It will also be up to you to advertise and collect the money. Depending on how you set it up, you may be compensated for your time, or, if you try to keep it as inexpensive for your athletes as possible, you may not. You might also have to provide sleeping arrangements for the clinicians if they come from very far away. If you don't have enough athletes, you could open up your camp to neighboring schools to participate. Some schools charge a fee for the use of their gyms, and that will have to be figured into the fee as well.

Post all the camp offers that come to you so your athletes can see what is available. You'll always have some enthusiastic kids looking for any way to improve. Encourage them to go to one of the college camps.

Your setter is the quarterback of your team, and if he or she can attend a good setter's camp, it will improve your whole team's performance. No other player touches the ball more than the setter, who takes every second ball. The choices they make in your offense, the improvement in their transition, and the speed with which they run your attacks can change your whole game.

TEAM CAMPS

Team camps can make a huge difference in a team's performance. They are great bonding experiences for a team, they help coaches get in touch with the new athletes coming into their program, and they give a great deal of game experience to players who may have sat on the bench a lot. You will find much more information about team camps in Chapter 32.

JUNIOR HIGH CAMP

One of the best things you can do for your program is to put on a junior high camp (see Figures 31.1. and 31.2). You can either bring in clinicians or run the camp yourself. If you choose to put on the camp yourself, it is a win/win situation. You are improving your feeder program while your high school athletes get a refresher

FIGURE 31.1   Junior high and high school coaches communicate.

FIGURE 31.2 Junior High Volleyball Player Feeder Programs

course, and if you choose to do so, your athletes will get money to help with their summer camps.

Many high school coaches put on their own junior high camp. Here are some suggestions to make it successful:

■ Send the information to the junior high coaches and have them distribute it. Put the information in the paper and on flyers. Ask your high school players to pass the word.

■ Have your high school players help coach. If you can have three campers to one high school player/coach, the junior high campers receive great individual attention. It will be a big draw for your camp. Each camper will get immediate feedback, which is excellent. It is also great for your athletes. In order to teach, they have to know the information. It is a good review and puts emphasis on the basics. Using your high school players to demonstrate puts pressure on them to do it right, and a correct demonstration is the best way to teach.

■ You could run two 3-hour sessions for three days. One could be for youth without any experience and the second for youth with experience.

■ It is a good idea to have frequent water breaks. Halfway through each session, stop and have a break with cold treats, like popsicles or snowcones.

■ Junior high students love rewards and prizes. Spend some of the camp money on T-shirts, mugs, balls, bags, and so forth. You could provide a reward for the camper who can name the most coaches. You could also provide little rewards for the groups who win in drills, such as socks, gum, or lip salve. Many companies will donate mugs or hats or coupons, too.

■ At the end of the camp, give free passes to each camper to attend your first home match. It is a perk for them and gets you a bigger crowd, and many of them will bring someone else, maybe a paying family member, who will increase your gate receipts.

- Run your camp similar to a practice, with little talk and lots of demonstrations and ball handling. Create successful situations, such as serving overhand from the three-meter line and stepping back with each successful serve.

- Change groups often and change the coaches (your players) at least three times a session. That way, if they don't have a good group or coach, it won't be for long.

- Talk to your high school athletes before the first session. Explain to them what you need and expect them to do. You want the campers to have a good experience, and most of that will depend on your high school players' rapport with them. Impress the need to be positive and to tell the campers what the high school players want to see, not what the campers are doing wrong. Tell them to be upbeat and call the campers by their names (have name tags for coaches and campers).

- Pay your high school players for helping. They will be able to use the money for their camps, and it will encourage positive attitudes in their parents toward your program.

- Have your assistant coach keep track of which of your athletes come and what sessions they work so you can pay them accordingly.

- It is a good idea to run all the camp money through the school, if the secretaries are willing. That way everything stays honest and each camper has a receipt.

SUMMARY

One of the very best ways to get a jump on the season and improve your team is by having your athletes participate in summer camps. Improving your feeder programs is another way of ensuring a top team. Both take time and commitment from you and your coaching staff. You have to decide how dedicated you are to your team's success in volleyball and how much time you are willing to spend.

Following is a sample junior high information sheet and entry form. Also included is Carl McGown's high school volleyball clinic outline. The clinic outline could be simplified and shortened for younger campers.

JUNIOR HIGH INFORMATION SHEET AND ENTRY FORM

Your High School Presents Future Volleyball Stars Individual Skills Camp

We would like to invite you to come to our Individual Fundamental Skills Volleyball Camp for [current year] fifth, sixth, seventh, eighth, and ninth grade students. It will be hosted by *[Fill in your school name]* High's varsity coach, _____. We feel that it will be an excellent opportunity to learn and improve on your skills, because we specialize in small groups, which means lots of participation! There will be one coach for no more than three players. Information is as follows:

Dates: _____ (Thursday through Saturday)
Place: Your High School gym

Time:	Eighth and ninth grades (those who have had one or more years' experience): 9:00–12:00 A.M.
	Fifth to seventh grades (of the coming school year): 1:00–4:00 P.M.
Cost:	$30.00
Deadline:	_____ (Friday before the camp)

We have limited gym space and want all campers to have room to participate, so we are only accepting the first 24 applicants in each division (12 per court).

Please make checks payable to: Your High Volleyball, and mail to the following:

Junior High Volleyball Camp
Your High School
Street Number
City, State, Zip Code
OR

Bring it in to Your High school or district office

Come dressed and ready to play! See you there. Any questions please call Varsity Coach _____.

Work Phone: _____ Home Phone: _____

Please detach and keep the top portion as a reminder of the details.

Parents: Please fill out and return with your $30.00 (made out to Your High Volleyball) by _____. Parent or guardian must sign each application before it will be accepted.

Name: _____ (Please print)

Home Address: _____

City: _____ State: _____ Zip: _____

Phone: _____ Age: _____ Next year in school: _____

Please note any medical conditions we should be aware of.

Signed   _____
(Parent or Legal Guardian)

SAMPLE SCHEDULE FOR HIGH SCHOOL CAMP

Monday Morning

Forearm Pass

Keys	Drills	In-a-Row
1. Wrists and hands together	1. Throw, hit, catch	10
2. Straight and simple	2a.	20
	2b.	10 (each middle)
3. Face the ball, angle the arms	3.	45 (right then left)
4. Shuffle (side to side, with partner toss)	4. Butterfly	12
5. See the server, see the ball	5. Go to 15 (two ways)	

Monday Afternoon

Serve (serving is like throwing)

Keys	Drills
1. Bow and arrow	1. Ball and a wall
■ Stand sideways	2. Serve and chase 10 in a row
■ Hold ball in one hand	3. Monarch of the court (lose a point if you miss a serve)
■ Keep hitting elbow up	
2. Toss, step, hit (on heel of hand)	
3. Swing to target	

We need to teach a jump serve to some of the best players. Teach one of two methods:

1. Step, toss with right hand, and take the rest of the four-step approach.
2. Step, step, toss with left hand, and take the rest of the four-step approach.

Spike

Keys	Drills
1. Four steps (right, left, right, left) ■ Right foot forward ■ Small, bigger, biggest ■ Slow, faster, fastest ■ Second step on three-meter line 2. Arms forward (not up), back, up 3. Bow and arrow arm swing 4. First step when ball is set	1. You go, I throw (second step toss) 2. I throw, you go 3. Spiking lines

Overhead Pass

Keys	Drills	In-a-Row
1. Shape early	1. Throw, hit, catch	10
2. Extend (like passing a basketball)	2a.	20
	2b.	10 (each middle)
3. Square to the target	3.	45 (right then left)
4. Butterfly with spikers		

Tuesday Morning

Individual Defense (forearm pass, run to, sprawl, pancake, fist, tomahawk)

Keys	Drills
1. Ball, setter, ball, hitter (B, S, B, H) 2. Feet apart, arms ready	1. Coach hits at one line 2. Coach hits at three lines 3. Six-hit partner pepper 4. First time

Block

Keys	Drills
1. Footwork 2. Handwork	1. Six trips (5-3-3, 5-2-2, 3-3-3, 3-2-2, Q3-3-3, Q3-2-2) 2. Six trips versus a table

Tuesday Afternoon

Block

| 1. Eye work | 1. Ball, setter, ball, hitter. Six on one side (defense). Other side, two lines of hitters and setter. Coach tosses to setter, setter underhand passes back to coach, who passes it back, setter sets to hitter. Watch blockers' eyes. Play for a certain period of time, then offense hits until they lose 15. Quick score. Wave through. |
| 2. Opposite volleyball (Chapter 15) | 2. Serve plus one in a row. |

Wednesday Morning

1. Three in a row S/R ladder (Chapter 14)
2. Fours, throw one (Chapter 14)
3. Two-way wash table (Chapter 15)

Wednesday Afternoon

1. Positional dig lines
2. Triples tourney. Use the standings from Wednesday morning's S/R ladder to organize the teams. Divide the court into two sides. Give each of the players a number.

1OH											
2CB											
3S/O											
4OH											
5CB											
6S/O											
7OH											
8CB											
9S/O											
10O											
11C											
12S/											

Play this schedule:

Round 1 (one side of the net)	(the other side of the net)
1, 2, 3 vs. 4, 5, 6	7, 8, 9 vs. 10, 11, 12
1, 2, 6 vs. 4, 5, 3	7, 8, 12 vs. 10, 11, 9
1, 5, 3 vs. 4, 2, 6	7, 11, 9 vs. 10, 8, 12
4, 2, 3 vs. 1, 5, 6	10, 8, 9 vs. 7, 11, 12

Round 2

1, 2, 3 vs. 7, 8, 9	4, 5, 6 vs. 10, 11, 12
1, 2, 9 vs. 7, 8, 3	4, 5, 12 vs. 10, 11, 6
1, 8, 3 vs. 7, 2, 9	4, 11, 6 vs. 10, 5, 12
7, 2, 3 vs. 1, 8, 9	10, 5, 6 vs. 4, 11, 12

Round 3

1, 2, 3 vs. 10, 11, 12	4, 5, 6 vs. 7, 8, 9
1, 2, 12 vs. 10, 11, 3	4, 5, 9 vs. 7, 8, 6
1, 11, 3 vs. 10, 2, 12	4, 8, 6 vs. 7, 5, 9
10, 2, 3 vs. 1, 11, 12	7, 5, 6 vs. 4, 8, 9

There are 12 different match ups to play, so it is probably best to play each of them for four minutes with quick scoring. Playing games to 15 total points also works very well.

3. Last ball (Chapter 15)
4. Six best passers. Take the six top passers from the S/R ladder and put three on each side. The object is for them to make 10 perfect passes (a missed serve counts as a perfect pass) in a row within 10 minutes. The other six players are divided up, three on each side, serving.

Thursday Morning

1. Spiking lines versus blockers. Organize the groups so that there are two spiking lines and a single blocker for each spiking line. Work with the blockers to help them watch ball, setter, ball, hitter.
2. Exchange, four in-a-row (Chapter 14)
3. Monarch (Queen/King) of the court, throw one (Chapter 14)
4. Neville's pepper (Chapter 14)
5. Serve-toss (Chapter 15)

Thursday Afternoon

1. Butterfly the servers (Chapter 14)
2. Spiking lines. Organize the groups so that there are two spiking lines. Have each hitter start at the net. Make a fake block and then use transition footwork to run off the net. While the spiker is running off the net, the coach throws a ball to the setter, who sets the ball to the transition hitter.
3. Exchange. Two of three for six trips. Exchange as before, but this time the object is to kill the ball. The coach throws the ball to the player who made the error. Quick score. Best two of three to 15 wins.
4. Plus three (Chapter 15)
5. Scramble (Chapter 15)

Friday Morning

1. The coach hits at waves. Play four groups of three. The coach hits at a group and they pass, set, spike. Use plus, zero, minus scoring. + = spike, 0 = just over, − = not over (hitting error).
2. Three-people pepper. Play for one-minute bouts. Trade partners. Repeat three times (Chapter 14).

3. Setting pressure. The coach tosses balls everywhere for setter to set. Allow five minutes per setter. Setters should set with their hands. Setters compete for the most perfect sets. They are setting to three spiking lines.
4. Exchange, for in-a-row. Use the same routine as on Thursday. Hopefully the score will be better this time.
5. Outside hitters' tournament (plus/minus) (Chapter 14)
6. Two-way wash table (see Wednesday morning). We want to determine if the camp has produced an increase in the ability to side-out, so we compare Wednesday to today. The best way to score this is with golf scoring with an opportunity to press. Depending on how much time you have, you will need to decide how many serves you want each server to have. It takes approximately 30 seconds per point-scoring attempt.

Carl McGown Camp Schedule

Monday	Tuesday	Wednesday	Thursday	Friday
T-shirts, handouts, intros	Review serve, spike, set	Ball warm-up (partners)	Ball warm-up	Ball warm-up (coach to hit at waves)
Objectives: 1. Work hard 2. Compete 3. Improve individually 4. Improve as a team 5. Have fun	1. Basic drills 2. You go, I throw 3. Butterfly with coach 4. Butterfly with spikers	Stretch	Stretch 1. Spiking lines versus blockers (work on ball, setter, ball, hitter) 2. Exchange, for in-a-row 3. Monarch of the court, throw 1 (toss to serving team, they get three hits); three rounds (games to 25 total points) 4. Use Monarch of the court scores to create four teams for Neville's pepper (3 minutes) 5. Serve, toss, (one or two ways depending on how much time you have); little point score is 11–11 (11–11 is 67% side-out)	Stretch 1. Partner pepper (one minute, four times) rotate partners 2. Setting pressure (5 minutes per setter?) 3. Exchange, for in-a-row (compare to Thursday) 4. Outside hitters tournament 5. Wash table—two way (compare to Wednesday)
Rules: 1. Hustle: during drills, when shagging, and between drills when getting drinks 2. Try for every ball 3. Don't catch the ball 4. Be on time (10 minutes early)	Defense: forearm pass, run to, sprawl, pancake, tomahawk	Three in a row S/R ladder—three for 10 minutes (does 3 × 3 work?)		
	Keys: 1. Ball, setter, ball, hitter 2. Feet apart, knees bent, arms ready	Use three in a row S/R scores to group for fours, throw one; games to five little points for a big point, game to 15 big points.		Home
Forearm pass 1. Keys 2. Basic drills 3. Butterfly with coach 4. Go to 15—two ways	Drills: 1. One line 2. Three lines 3. Partners 4. First time	Wash table—two way (it takes approximately 30 seconds per serve and toss)		
Review forearm pass 1. Keys 2. Basic drills 3. Butterfly	Blocking (eye work, footwork, and handwork) 1. Six trips 2. Six trips versus a table	Ball warm-up in threes		
Serving (jumpers for top kids) 1. Keys 2. Ball and a wall 3. Serve and chase 4. Monarch of the court (start with a serve)	Teach transition footwork to left-, middle-, and right-side hitters	Stretch 1. Positional dig lines 2. Triples tourney 3. Last ball (play rotations 3, 6, 4, 1, 5, 2); first team to 4 wins 4. Six best passers (from S/R ladder) 10 in a row or ten minutes	Ball warm-up (butterfly the servers) 1. Spiking lines (start at net, work on transition footwork) 2. Exchange; games to 15, rally score; best two out of three for six lines 3. Plus three; first the middles, then the middles and the left-side hitter, then the middles and the right-side hitter.	
Spiking 1. Keys 2. You go, I throw 3. I throw, you go	Discuss offense—five to one (if it fits the players on the team) 1. Three passers 2. Specialize positions 3. Stack hitters	Night off		
		Camp barbecue		
		Recreational activities for coaches?		

Carl McGown Camp Schedule

Monday	Tuesday	Wednesday	Thursday	Friday
				(continued)

(continued)

Monday	Tuesday	Wednesday	Thursday	Friday
Overhead pass 1. Keys 2. Basic drills 3. Butterfly with spikers Work on player weaknesses Then Monarch of the court, work up, throw one to defense (to hit it over)	Discuss defense 1. Middle back in middle/middle 2. First two-thirds of the court 3. Tips down the line 4. Off blocker—one-third, two-thirds Warm-up in threes with ball Stretch and drills 1. Ball, setter, ball, hitter 2. Opposite volleyball (serve plus one in a row) Doubles ladder		4. Transition block 5. Scramble (3, 6, 4, 1, 5, 2) Alpha numeric tourney (end with entire gym as one court)	

CHAPTER 32

Hosting and Participating in Tournaments

Participation in tournaments is one of the fastest and best ways to improve a team. Playing one match right after another gives your players more opportunities in similar game situations to correct and improve their skills and thought processes. Playing against opposing teams with a wide variety of attacks, defenses, serves, and serve receives extends an athlete's perspective and repertoire.

There are several different tournament opportunities available for your teams. You can host one during the season or run a tournament in the summer as a fundraiser to benefit your team. Summer camps are one of the best ways of raising your team's skill level. And, as a finale, most leagues have a district, league, regional, or state championship tournament for the varsity level. With a little organization you can extend that to a final tournament for your junior varsity, sophomore, or younger teams too (not at a state organizational level, but with your school as a host, for the experience).

HOSTING A TOURNAMENT

Some factors to be considered when hosting a tournament are

- The number of teams to invite
- Varsity, JV, or junior high or middle school skill level
- The number of courts available
- The level of competition (larger school, smaller, top teams, and so on)
- Referees
- Cost to you and fee to charge other teams
- Line judges
- Scorekeepers
- Charge at the gate
- Format of tournament (round robin, pool play, double elimination)
- Type of scoring (quick or regular), scoring caps (stop score at a certain number regardless of whether a team has reached a two-point advantage)
- Number of guaranteed matches (most teams would like three to five a day of regular scoring, or six to eight of quick scoring)

The basic formats you have to choose from to run a tournament are round robin, pool play, or elimination. You can use a combination of all three if you want.

ROUND ROBIN

In round robin all teams play each other. They can play one match, one game, or two games. You could go to 11 or 15 points for each with regular scoring, put caps on them, or use a quick-scoring format. A simple way to set this up with six teams is shown in the accompanying diagram. You could increase or decrease the number of teams using the same format.

Keep one team in the same place and rotate the rest clockwise. If you have an odd number of teams, use the left-top position as a bye (a rest—the team does not play in that round) and have all the teams rotate around it.

(1)	(2)	(3)	(4)	(5)
1 vs. 2	1 vs. 6	1 vs. 5	1 vs. 4	1 vs. 3
6 vs. 3	5 vs. 2	4 vs. 6	3 vs. 5	2 vs. 4
5 vs. 4	4 vs. 3	3 vs. 2	2 vs. 6	6 vs. 5

If this is the only format you use, you will invariably have to use tiebreakers, and there are several available:

- Head to head competition.
- Win/loss record with either matches or games.
- Total points for and total points against.
- Toss the coin.

POOL PLAY

In pool play, you seed (place according to skill level) teams into groups. They play a round robin format; when they finish, they can either play off in a double- or single-elimination tournament (where their placings in the pool would seed them into the tournament) or simply go head-to-head with each pool playing first to first, second to second, and so on. An example follows:

Pool A

First set
    1 vs. 2
    4 vs. 3

Second set
    1 vs. 4
    3 vs. 2

Third set
    1 vs. 3
    2 vs. 4

Pool B would have the same format as Pool A. Teams play each other in a round robin. Then the winner of pool A could play the winner of pool B for first and second place; second place could play second for third and fourth place, and so on. That would guarantee each team four matches.

SINGLE- OR DOUBLE-ELIMINATION TOURNAMENT

These are very simple tournaments to run, but if this is the only format you use, some teams will be out within only one or two matches. These are usually used in conjunction with round robin or pool play. You have to be careful and place, or seed, teams according to their skill levels—your goal is to have the two best teams playing in the last match of the day and not be eliminated by each other on the way.

REGULAR VERSES QUICK SCORING

Regular scoring allows teams to take risks, to try new things, and to make mistakes without penalties (points). Matches take longer, and players will have fewer matches with this type of scoring. To make these matches shorter, yet allow teams to risk, you can put a cap on the points, such as to 11, or cap at 15, or to win by one.

Quick scoring speeds up matches so more matches can be played, but a team is penalized for risking. The team that is careful and plays sure, smart, and safe will win. Many tournaments use a combination of these two types of scoring, with the first two games regular, and if it goes to a third, quick, with a cap of 17. You could put caps of 15 on the first two

PUTTING A TOURNAMENT TOGETHER

Once you have decided what type of tournament you want to run, you need to contact the teams you would like to enter. Send out invitations. Provide the following information:

- The date
- Location
- The teams that are being invited
- The format you plan to run
- The cost

Ask invitees to respond by a certain date. You could contact them by e-mail if you have all their addresses.

Once you have your teams, seed them in the format you have chosen, and send back the information to them. Make sure you have a firm commitment. Many leagues have contracts to sign. This should all take place after your season is finished but well in advance of the next season. Approximately one month before your tournament is to be held, send out another information letter with

- Date
- Time
- Format
- Cost

You also need to notify teams if they need to furnish line and scorebook people, the cost at the gate for spectators, locker room arrangements, shower facilities, and towels.

Include your phone number, return address, and information about when they can reach you with any questions.

SUMMER TEAM CAMP TOURNAMENTS

Going to a team camp in the summer and playing 20 matches in one week is a compressed version of many teams' whole season. There they have the opportunity to focus with intensity and bring cohesiveness to their team. The more chances to contact, or touch, the ball during a real match increases the athlete's confidence and repertoire. There are certain things to look for when choosing a team camp.

1. Cost: What you get for your money.

2. Number of matches.

3. Good referees.

4. Safe, roomy courts.

5. Format: Players shouldn't compete all day; the camp should offer a morning and an afternoon schedule. Do they have freshmen or junior varsity teams playing varsity teams? Is the competition good? Athletes attend to get beat. Tough competition makes a better team, because they find your weaknesses.

6. Clinic session: One of our favorite and most productive parts of team camp is a one-hour coaching session each day for an individual team with a clinician, on what part of the game the team wants to work on (for example, defense, passing, offense, or serving).

7. Camps should not be too far from home, though it is good if the team has to stay over, because it serves as a bonding process. You could camp at KOAs or stay at motels or friends' homes. A coach can also get a lot of problems resolved before the season, as you find out who gets along with whom and uncover any attitude problems you may have when your team stays together for a week. It is nice if you are only a few hours away in case some players need to be sent home because of sickness or discipline problems. If you are too close, though, it is easy for them to let other things in their life distract them from the tournament (such as work or friends). They don't have to rely on each other.

8. Perks might include T-shirts for your team and coaches and awards for the top teams.

FUNDING FOR SUMMER TEAM CAMP TOURNAMENTS

Money is always a big issue. Make sure your team knows well in advance the cost of the camp to which they are going. There are lots of fundraisers available if you choose to go that route. One idea that benefits all concerned is a junior high individual skills camp. If you coach a high school team, you can run this camp with all your players helping you as coaches. Each of the girls or boys that help coach will get money from the camp to be used toward their summer camp. Parents appreciate this help, the junior high program benefits, and your players' skills improve from teaching volleyball. It is a win/win situation.

TOURNAMENT IDEAS

- Host a tournament in the off season or during the summer as a fundraiser. Offer doubles, triples, co-ed, women's, men's, junior high, and high school tournaments.

- Host a tournament during your season according to what your state rules allow. You could host a freshman, sophomore, junior varsity, or varsity tournament. You could hold it during the season or as a season finale for the younger teams (as a sort of district or league championship for them).

- Contact club ball directors in your area and ask if they need more tournaments in their region. Volunteer to host one.

- When you host a tournament, make it a first-class one. Send out the information early, with the bracket. Have your team call lines and keep score. Put towels and ice water on each court. Have a hospitality room for coaches and referees. Sweep floors in between matches. Get eating establishments to give free drink coupons, and so on.

- Give awards such as T-shirts, new balls, or trophies.

- When hosting a tournament, you can charge admission at the gate to earn more money.

- Your players and their parents could run a concession stand to accommodate the visiting teams and make extra money.

SUMMARY

Tournament participation can be an excellent way to improve your team. If you take advantage of tournaments and allow your players to risk and fail or risk and succeed, your team will rise to a higher level of play. It is an intense way to gain experience playing volleyball, which is something all teams need.

Masters for Coaches

MENTAL CHECKLIST FOR SETTERS

1. Memorize terminology, symbols, and signals of the offense.

2. Rank each hitter by position.

3. Identify any special considerations for each hitter. (Do they have trouble lining up off-hand, need more time transitioning, hit better when set tighter on the net, and so on?). Include cues that will improve their hitting.

4. Rank each hitter by his or her ability to hit the following sets:

    (a) High sets

    (b) Combination sets

    (c) Quicks or slides

    (d) Back-row sets

5. Which attackers can be set after they've made an error (blocked or unforced)? Which cannot be set?

6. Who would you set in each of the following situations and why?

    (a) We need a side-out.

    (b) We need a point.

    (c) We need the ball kept in play (they may not have as many kills, but they have fewer errors).

7. List your starting lineup, including key subs.

First rotation

For each rotation, rank at least three plays beginning with what you feel is the most effective and why.

1. _____

2. _____

3. _____

4. _____

5. _____

6. _____

PREMATCH PREPARATION

1. What are my options in each rotation?

    1. _____

    2. _____

    3. _____

    4. _____

    5. _____

    6. _____

2. What are the positive points and negative points for each rotation?

    1. _____

    2. _____

    3. _____

    4. _____

    5. _____

    6. _____

3. Who are the best hitters in each rotation?

    1. _____

    2. _____

    3. _____

    4. _____

    5. _____

    6. _____

4. Where is the opponent's weakest/strongest blocker?

SERVE-RECEIVE CHART

1

2

3

4

5

6

TRYOUT LETTER

[School Letterhead]

Dear _____,

We would like to thank you for taking your time and energy to try out for the _____ High volleyball team. You have made a definite contribution by participating and making it possible to hold a try out.

It is a difficult time, the most difficult in all aspects of our coaching, we feel, to make the decision to keep some and to let others go. We always try to make our decision unbiased and based on fact. Be assured, whether you make the team or not, our main consideration was whether you could someday be a contributor to the varsity program. This is difficult to measure and is something over which we agonize. We do not want to waste your time or have you sit on the bench and feel as if you are not helping our program.

This year, you have / have not been chosen to be on the team. If you would like to review the reasons for this decision, please feel free to fill out the enclosed form for an appointment and give it to the office or one of the coaches.

Thank you for contributing to the quality of _____High's volleyball program. Your participation has pushed all to higher excellence.

Sincerely,

_____ High School Volleyball Coaching Staff

PRACTICE SCHEDULE

Date _____

Time	Purpose	Drill	Consequences
	Prepractice		
	Pass/Serve		
	Hitting/Blocking		
	Defense		
	Game		
	Cool-Down		

Notes:

PRACTICE CHART

Date _____

Name

Name

Volleyball Match Stats Chart

Date _____

Game _____

#	Attack			Serving				Passing			Opponent			
	Ks	Os	E/Bs	Back row	Totals	Points	X	A/E	3s	2s	1s	Os	X/%P	Stuffs	Cts
Totals															

SCOUTING CHART

Team   Date

Starters   Subs

1

2

3

4

5

6

STATS CHART

Opponents _____   Date _____   V, JV, F _____

Name	Serve Receive (3, 2, 1, 0)	%	Attacks (K, 0, –)	%	Digs (+, –)	#
Team totals						

STATS CHART

Opponents _____   Date _____   V, JV, F _____

Name	Serve (4, 3, 2, 1, 0)	%	MA	Sets (1, K, –)	%	Blocks (S, O, –)	#
Team totals							

STATISTICS INSTRUCTIONS

1. Serves

4 = Ace (not a playable up)

3 = Up, but not settable by setter (could bump it, or others could set it)

2 = Setter can set to two places, but be unable to run a quick attack

1 = Perfect pass, the setter could run a quick attack or all options

0 = Missed serve

*Total score and divided by number of attempts = difficulty of serves (should be better than 2.5)

Subtract the number of misses from the number of attempts and divide by the number of attempts = percent of good serves (should be 90% or better). M/A = Individual miss and ace totals.

2. Serve Receive

0 = Opponent's ace

1 = Up, but not settable by setter (could bump, others could set)

2 = Setter can set, but cannot run a quick attack

3 = Perfect pass, setter can run quick attack or all options

*Total score divided by number of attempts = % of serve-receive reception (should be >2.25)

3. Attacks

K = Kill, not dug into a playable ball (not a free ball pass—includes spikes, down balls, tips, oversets that are stuff-blocked)

O = Hit is in but opponents are able to dig up for a play

– = Hit is out of bounds, in the net, or blocked for a stuff; attacker is in net (if blocked but dug up = O)

*Subtract – from K and divide by total number attacks = kill % (should be 25% or better from your outside hitters)

4. Blocks

S = Stuff block (no return)

O = Blocked but opponent is able to play it up

– = Blocker in net, block out of bounds, or ball caught in between net and player and opponent is unable to keep it in play

*Two ways of totaling: (1) total all blocks (S and O); (2) subtract minus blocks only from O blocks, keep a total of stuffs per game and O blocks per game.

5. Sets

1 = Good set

K = Set hit for a kill (termed an assist)

– = Overset, setter in net or over center line, illegal set, miss set, out of bounds, etc.

*Subtract minus sets from kills and divide by total attempts = kill assist %

6. Digs

1 = Playable dig off of attack (not free ball pass)

*Total number of digs (very important stat—must have digs to convert and make points)

HYDRATION AND NUTRITION TIPS

Fluids

- 72% of the body's muscle mass is made up of water.
- *Dehydration* causes fatigue, lack of coordination, cramps, headaches, and increased risk of illness.
- 2% loss of body weight affects performance (equivalent to a 150-pound person losing 3 pounds).
- *How much:* Weigh yourself and start exercising. For every pound lost, you should drink 2 cups of water.
  - Do not rely on thirst; it puts back less than half the water you need.
  - Water cannot hydrate the body in one hour before a workout. This will overload the kidneys, and you will have to urinate.
  - Drink whether thirsty or not every time you pass a fountain (all day long) and at every opportunity during practices and games.
  - A minimum of eight 8-ounce glasses a day is recommended.
- *Check to see if you are hydrated.* Urine should be pale yellow or clear. If it is dark yellow, you are becoming dehydrated.
  - Caffeine increases dehydration. It is a diuretic, and if it is taken in a carbonated drink form, extra water from your system is needed to dilute the 12% glucose to 6%.
  - Alcohol increases dehydration even more than caffeine. The color of urine will be pale, even though the muscle is being dehydrated.
- *Sports drinks are beneficial.*
  - Do not drink sports drinks only during competition, but during practice also; otherwise stomachaches are possible.
  - Juice is about 10% glucose solution. It will stay in the system until more fluid becomes available to dilute it to a 6% solution that can be used in the muscles. It dehydrates the muscles. So, if an activity will take place within one hour, athletes should stick with sports drinks.
- *Some fluid guidelines:*
  - Before exercise: Drink 8 to 24 ounces of fluid more than one hour before and 4 to 8 ounces of fluid immediately before exercise.
  - During exercise: Drink at least 4 to 8 ounces of fluid every 15 to 20 minutes.
  - After exercise: Drink 16 ounces of fluid for every pound of body weight lost.

Foods

- Consume calories at three main meals and two smaller snacks. The following foods are recommended for athletes:
  1. Grains: cereals, popcorn, breads, rice, some crackers, pasta.
  2. Legumes: beans, peas, lentils.
  3. Vegetables: carrots, potatoes, spinach, corn, dark green leafy varieties, tomatoes, squash, cabbage, turnips, and so on.
  4. Fruits: bananas, apples, oranges, peaches, grapes, tangerines, melon, prunes, and so on.
  5. Tuna fish (in water), most filets, cod, halibut, catfish. Most fish is great if not battered and fried.
  6. Poultry (not fried), with skin removed, in small portions (3–6 oz.).
  7. Beef and pork are usually so high in fat that they should be consumed in moderation only.
  8. Milk products: skimmed or 2% milk, yogurt, and so on.

Recommendations to complement these foods include the following:

- Eat before becoming hungry.
- Drink generous amounts of fluids with each meal.
- Eat with as much variety as possible.
- Follow the *sports nutrition motto:* All foods in moderation.
- Be smart about when to choose which foods.

Because there is no refrigeration on buses or vans, consider the following suggestions:

1. Try packing a cooler with fruits (strawberries, bananas, apples, oranges, peaches, plums, and so on) and vegetables (carrots, celery, tomato juice).
2. Try dried fruits, such as apricots, banana chips, raisins, dates, dried apple, or pineapple (remember to drink lots of water).
3. Try canned fruit, such as peaches, pears, applesauce, pineapple, or V-8 juice.
4. Try grains, such as bagels, pretzels, popcorn (no butter), crackers (saltines, Ritz, graham), vanilla wafers, rice cakes, animal crackers, granola bars, taco chips, muffins, breads, Pop-tarts, dried cereal (Frosted Mini-Wheats).
5. Other suggestions include cheese sticks, yogurt, chocolate milk, cans of tuna, chicken, peanut butter sandwiches, Fig Newtons, peanuts or other nuts, packets of cheese and crackers.

- Avoid gastrointestinal stress; eat familiar foods, especially when on the road.
- Avoid fried or high-fat foods on game day (they digest too slowly).
- Three days before a game the most important meal is eaten.
- If you want to perform well, eat well seven days a week.

Precompetition Meal

Two to three hours prior to the game, have a light (between 400 and 1,000 calories), high–complex carbohydrate meal with moderate protein, low fat, and very low fiber, accompanied by 24 ounces of fluids. Larger meals interfere with respiration and place excessive stress on the circulatory system.

Some athletes feel better if they have something light in their stomachs for a match. If so, from 30 minutes to 2 hours before game time, choose light snacks, such as yogurt, a banana, toast, a bagel, fruit, juice, a power or energy bar, chocolate milk, a bowl of oatmeal, and lots of fluids. Stay away from carbonated drinks.

If eating a meal before exercise doesn't fit in with your schedule or you lack the appetite, have 8 to 16 ounces of a sports drink 30 minutes to an hour before exercise for an energizing dose of carbohydrate.

After Exercise

Immediately after exercise (within two hours), eat carbohydrates (the body will absorb them quickly into the muscle).

Tournaments

There is a 30-minute window when the body will load up to 100 grams of carbohydrates back into the muscle. Good sources of carbohydrates include bagels, bananas, yogurt, chocolate milk, power bars, Gatorade, and fat-free Fig Newtons. These will provide you energy for the next day. If games are scheduled within 30 minutes of each other, drink sports drinks.

BRIGHAM YOUNG UNIVERSITY MEN'S VOLLEYBALL

- Warm-up

(5 minutes on the exercise bike and stretching)

- Max's should be recorded on the back
- Week sequence = L-M-H-L-(Max + L)-L-M-H-L

Name_____

Light (L) week = 3 × 12
Medium (M) week = 4 × 8
Heavy (H) week = 5 × 5

Cycles last for 1 week

L week

Exercise	R	W	R	W	R	W	R	W
Cleans (3 × 5—75%)								
Bench press—65%								
Squats—60%								
Straight leg deadlift								
Pullovers—65%								
Oblique-torso (15 each way)	30		30		30			
Ab crunches	30		30		30			
Back hyperextension	25		25		25			

M week

Exercise	R	W	R	W	R	W	R	W
Cleans (3 × 3—85%)								
Bench press—75%								
Squats—70%								
Straight leg deadlift								
Pullovers—75%								
Oblique-torso (15 each way)	30		30		30			
Ab crunches	30		30		30			
Back Hyperextension	25		25		25			

H week

Exercise	R	W	R	W	R	W	R	W
Cleans (3 × 2—95%)								
Bench press—85%								
Squats—80%								
Straight leg deadlift								
Pullovers—85%								
Oblique-torso (15 each way)	30		30		30			
Ab crunches	30		30		30			
Back hyperextension	25		25		25			

WIN–LOSS CHART

Predistrict

Won _____ Season Record _____ Lost _____

Your score	Opponent	Opponent score

MATCH LINEUP

Team Roster

Team _____

Check one: Home ☐   Visitor ☐

Player number	Player name

Game 1

4	3	2
5	6	1

Game 4

4	3	2
5	6	1

Game 2

4	3	2
5	6	1

Game 5

4	3	2
5	6	1

Game 3

4	3	2
5	6	1

GOALS CHART

Team

1._____

2._____

3._____

4._____

5._____

Individual

1._____

2._____

3._____

4._____

5._____

VOLLEYBALL TEAM RULES

1. Practice

A. No missed practices unless prior approval is received from the coach. (Do not tell a teammate; they can't give you approval.) Consequences may include the following:

- For one unexcused practice, you do not play in the next match.
- For two unexcused practices, you're off the team.

B. No tardiness. This means you are dressed, taped, and ready to play at your coach's designated starting time. If not, there are immediate consequences.

2. Conduct

A. No swearing or verbal abuse of opponents, teammates, coaches, or family.

B. While sitting on the bench, there will be a supportive atmosphere for your fellow teammates.

C. We are a classy team and we expect your conduct to reflect that. Enough said.

D. All team members will ride to and from games on the bus unless prior approval is given to ride with parent. Infractions will result in same penalty as missed practices.

3. Curfew

A. Practice nights: 10:30 P.M.

B. Game nights: 10:00 P.M.

C. Weekends: 12:30 P.M.

- If you have special circumstances that need addressing, you need to speak with your coach before the event.
- Same penalty as 1 & 2.

4. Grades

All students must have and maintain a 2.0 grade point average and are allowed only one failing grade to be able to play. If you are struggling in a subject, please notify your coach, and appropriate tutoring will be made available.

5. Game day

A player must be in attendance at school or they will not be allowed to participate in the match that day.

6. Problems

If a problem arises, the following procedure should be followed:

- First step: Player should talk to the coach. (If that does not resolve the situation satisfactorily, go to the second step.)
- Second step: Parents *and* player should make an appointment to talk to the coach, but not on game day. (If that does not resolve the situation, go to the third step.)
- Third step: Player and parents should talk to the athletic director.

Just as parents would rather have coaches talk to a child first about a problem coaches have with players, coaches would rather players talk to them, rather than hear about a situation through the grapevine.

The penalty for not following the procedure will be the removal of the player from the team.

Remember, it is a privilege, not a right, to play sports.

Players' and *both* parents' or guardians' signatures are required, signifying that they understand and agree to abide by the rules.

Athlete: _____

Parents/Guardians: _____, _____

TEN COMMANDMENTS FOR PARENTS OF ATHLETIC CHILDREN

1. Let your children know that win or lose, you love them, unconditionally. You are proud of their efforts and are not disappointed with them. You are the people in their lives who always give positive reinforcement.

2. Show them you are pleased that they chose to play sports and accept all the challenges that come with trying to better themselves in practices and games. Let them know that you understand how hard it is to constantly put themselves on the line in front of peers and spectators.

3. Be completely honest about your child's athletic ability, attitude, and sportsmanship. Remember that you don't know what happens in practice; you can't second-guess the coach's decisions, because you don't have all the information.

4. Let your children live their own lives. Try not to relive your athletic life through your children. You had your time, now it is their turn. Don't pressure them to shine for your own ego. Remember that you made mistakes too.

5. Coach attitude, but don't coach skill. Leave that to the team coach. Refrain from the inclination to try to make your child just a little better by giving them tips on the way home from matches, or at dinner, or when they are trying to go to sleep.

6. Don't compete with the coach. You each have different roles to fill; leave them theirs and work on your own. "It takes a village to raise a child." Be glad you have an excellent adult role model contributing to the upbringing of your child. But remember, they are human; they will make mistakes.

7. Never compare the skill, athletic ability, or attitudes of your child with other members of the team, at least not within their hearing. A team needs all kinds of different athletes to fulfill essential roles. Celebrate your child's special attributes.

8. Know your child's coach. Because of the special circumstances of a coach–player relationship, the coach has a tremendous potential to influence your child. Be aware of the coach's philosophy, attitudes, ethics, and knowledge.

9. Always remember that children tend to exaggerate both when praised and when criticized. Allow them time to cool off. Chances are, tomorrow they will have more appropriately evaluated a situation, while you may be just beginning to investigate. If the situation warrants following through, investigate quietly before overreacting.

10. Make a point of understanding courage and the fact that it is relative. Some are terrified of talking in public, whereas others are not. Some are afraid of a mouse but not of a bull. Everyone is frightened in certain circumstances. Explain that courage is not the absence of fear but a means of doing something in spite of fear or discomfort. Be proud that your child has chosen to participate rather than spectate, to do and not only dream, to risk stumbling and rise to try again. Be supportive and encouraging; congratulate them when they succeed on their own.

Parents who follow this mantra will consider it high praise indeed when, later in life, their children say, "My parents were always there for me, and were my best support. I couldn't have done it without them. I want to be just like them."

SAMPLE PROFILE

Student name:

Student address:

Student statistics:

Parents' names:

DOB: Age:

Present status: (Junior)

Height: Weight:

Standing reach:

Approach jump:

Blocking jump:

Positions played:

Uniform number(s):

High school

    Address, phone, fax, and e-mail:

    Projected graduation date:

    High school coach's name, address, and phone number:

Club team

    Club coach's name, address, and phone number:

Student's photo goes here

Academic achievements

    GPA:

    SAT/ACT scores:

    Academic awards:

    Planned course of study:

High school volleyball alumni college participants

    Name and college:

    Coach's comments:

(or include a letter of recommendation from your coach)

Athletic achievements and awards:

    (high school/club achievements)

    (personal awards, all-star team)

    Statistics:

    Other athletic awards:

SAMPLE COVER/INTRODUCTORY LETTER FOR STUDENT-ATHLETE PROSPECT

Date
Your name and address
College coach's name and address

Dear Coach:

I am researching schools for my future education. I am very interested in learning more about your school, team, and academic program and would like to be considered as a candidate for future recruitment.

I am currently in my junior year in high school, playing outside hitter at the varsity level since my sophomore year. I am 6'1" and have participated three years in the Davis competition. Scholastically, my cumulative GPA is a 3.65, and my main interest is in English literature. I am attaching a profile for you to peruse.

I would appreciate any information you could send me in relation to your academic and athletic programs. If you are interested in any further data, please feel free to contact me (phone number) or my coach (phone number).

Thank you for your time, and I look forward to hearing from you.

Sincerely,

Player's name
Enclosure

MATCH-SPECIFIC CHECKPOINTS FOR SETTERS

(These are best reviewed using a video.)

1. Am I predictable?

2. Am I accurate? If not, which sets are inaccurate and why?

3. Am I neglecting anyone, and if so, why?

4. Are any hitters struggling? Why?

5. Who's hot?

6. Were there any patterns in the last four sets?

7. Do I own the middle blocker? (Does the middle blocker move with any motion?)

8. Review hitting, setting, and side-out charts.

JUNIOR HIGH INFORMATION SHEET AND ENTRY FORM

Your High School Presents Future Volleyball Stars Individual Skills Camp

We would like to invite you to come to our Individual Fundamental Skills Volleyball camp for [current year] fifth, sixth, seventh, eighth, and ninth grade students. It will be hosted by *[Fill in your name school]* High's varsity coach, _____. We feel that it will be an excellent opportunity to learn and improve on your skills, because we specialize in small groups, which means lots of participation! There will be one coach for no more than three players. Information is as follows:

Dates:	_____ (Thursday through Saturday)
Place:	Your High school gym
Time:	Eighth and ninth grades (those who have had one or more years' experience): 9:00–12:00 A.M.
	Fifth to seventh grades (of the coming school year): 1:00–4:00 P.M.
Cost:	$30.00
Deadline:	_____ (Friday before the camp)

We have limited gym space and want all campers to have room to participate, so we are only accepting the first 24 applicants in each division (12 per court).

<u>***Please make checks payable to:***</u> Your High Volleyball, and mail to the following:

Junior High Volleyball Camp
Your High School
Street Number
City, State, Zip Code
OR

Bring it in to Your High school or district office

Come dressed and ready to play! See you there. Any questions please call Varsity Coach _____.

Work Phone: _____ Home Phone: _____

Please detach and keep the top portion as a reminder of the details.

Parents: Please fill out and return with your $30.00 (made out to Your High Volleyball) by _____. Parent or guardian must sign each application before it will be accepted.

Name: _____ (Please print)

Home Address: _____

City: _____ State: _____ Zip: _____

Phone: _____ Age: _____ Next Year in School: _____

Please note any medical conditions we should be aware of:

Signed _____
(Parent or Legal Guardian)

Albom, M. (1997). *Tuesdays with Morrie*. New York: Doubleday.

Bradley, B. (1998). *Values of the Game*. New York: Artisan.

Canfield, J., and Hansen, M. V. (1994). *Dare to Win*. New York: Berkley.

Danforth, W. H. (1991). *I Dare You*. St. Louis, MO: American Youth Foundation.

Edwards, L., and Benson, L. (1995). *LaVell: Airing It Out*. Salt Lake City, UT: Shadow Mountain.

Engerbretson, D. (1979). "Parents, Kids and Fly Rods." *Fly Fishing* (late season), 22–27.

Forbes, M. (1998, November). "Quotable Quotes." *Reader's Digest*, 73.

Fronske, H. (1997). *Teaching Cues for Sport Skills*. Boston: Allyn & Bacon.

Fronske, H., and McGown, C. (1996). *Complete Volleyball for Coaches*. Dubuque, IA: Kendall Hunt.

Gallwey, W. T. (1982). *The Inner Game of Tennis*. New York: Random House.

Giovanni, N. (2000). Quotation. Retrieved from the World Wide Web: http://www.quoteworld.org

Henry, F. M. (1968). "Specificity vs. Generality in Learning Skills." In *Classical Studies on Physical Activity*, edited by R. C. Brown & G. S. Kenyon. Englewood Cliffs, NJ: Prentice-Hall (Originally published 1958).

Holtz, L. (1998). *Winning Every Day*. New York: HarperCollins.

Jackson, P. (1995). *Sacred Hoops*. New York: Hyperion.

Jordan, M. (1998). *For the Love of the Game*. New York: Crown.

Lee, T., and Genovese, E. (1988). "Distribution of Practice in Motor Skill Acquisition: Learning and Performance Effects Reconsidered. *Research Quarterly for Exercise and Sport, 59*, 277–287.

Maine Secondary School Principals Association. (November, 1990). "Ten Commandments for Parents with Athletic Children." *Maine Principal Newsletter*.

Majerus, R. (1999). *My Life on a Napkin*. New York: Hyperion.

Marteniuk, R. (1976). *Information Processing in Motor Skills*. New York: Holt, Rinehart and Winston.

McGown, C. (1998). *Canyon Volleyball*. Provo, UT: Canyon Inc.

McIntyre, P. T. (2000). Quotation. Retrieved from the World Wide Web: http://open-mind.org/SP/Quotes.htm.

Merki, M. B., and Merki, D. (1989). *Health: A Guide to Wellness*. Mission Hill, CA: Glenco.

National Federation of State High School Associations. (1999). *High School Volleyball Rules Book*. Kansas City, MO: Robert F. Kanaby.

National Strength and Conditioning Association. (1996). *A Position Paper and Literature Review of Youth Resistance Training*. Colorado Springs, CO: National Strength and Conditioning Association.

Neville W. J. (1990). *Coaching Volleyball Successfully*. Champaign, IL: Human Kinetics.

Nixon, J., and Locke, L. (1973). "Research on Teaching Physical Education." In *Second Handbook of Research on Teaching*, edited by R. Travers, 1210–1240. Chicago: Rand-McNally.

Odom, G. D. (1997). *The End Is Not the Trophy*. Durham, NC: Carolina Academic.

Pavlou, K., and Blackburn, G. L. (1984). "Eating to Win." *Science of Food and Agriculture, 2*, 10–15.

Peters, L. (1996, May). "Quotable Quotes." *Reader's Digest*.

Physical Fitness in Children and Youth. (1988). *Physical Fitness in Children and Youth. The American College of Sports Medicine (MSSE), 20:4*, 422–423.

Pitino, R. (1997). *Success Is a Choice*. New York: Broadway.

Powell, C. (1998, November). "Quotable Quotes." *Reader's Digest*, 73.

Rushall, B., and Pike, F. (n.d). *Training for Sports and Fitness*. Melbourne, Australia: Macmillan.

Sale, D., and MacDougall, D. (1981). "Specificity in Strength Training: A Review for the Coach and Athlete." *Canadian Journal of Applied Sport Sciences, 6*, 87–92.

Schlappi, M. (1998). *Bulletproof Principles for Striking Gold*. Salt Lake City, UT: Publishers Press.

Schmidt, R. A. (1975). *Motor Skills*. New York: Harper & Row.

Schmidt, R. A. (1982). *Motor Control and Motor Learning. A Behavioral Emphasis*. Champaign, IL: Human Kinetics.

Summitt, P. (1998a). *Raise the Roof*. New York: Broadway.

Summitt, P. (1998b). *Reach for the Summit*. New York: Broadway.

Swindoll, C. (2000). Quotation. Retrieved from the World Wide Web: http://www.cybernation.com/victory/quotations/authors/quotes_swindoll_charles.html

USOC Sports Medicine Division. (n.d.). *Precompetition Eating*. Omaha, NE: International Center for Sports Nutrition.

Vande Zoude, E. (n.d.). *Winning Attitudes*. Colorado Springs, CO: U.S. Olympic Training Center.

Weisskopf, V. (1990). *The Privilege of Being a Physicist*. New York: W. H. Freeman.

Wolf, R., and Attner, P. (1998). *The Packer Way*. New York: St. Martins.

Wooden, J., and Jamison, S. (1997). *Wooden. A Lifetime of Observations and Reflections on and off the Court*. Chicago: Contemporary.

Wooden, J., and Tobin, J. (1988). *They Call Me Coach*. Chicago: Contemporary.